Annie's Favorite Crochet Dolls

Editorial Director
Andy Ashley

Production & Photography Director
Ange Van Arman

Editorial
Senior Editor
Jennifer Simcik McClain

Editor
Liz Field

Editorial Staff
Shirley Brown, Alva Lea Edwards, Donna Jones,
Nina Marsh, Donna Scott, Diane Simpson, Ann White

Photography
Scott Campbell, Tammy Coquat-Payne

Book Design & Production
Greg Smith, Minette Collins Smith

Production Assistants
Joanne Gonzalez, Betty Radla

Product Presentation
Design Coordinator
Sandy Kennebeck

Inhouse Designer
Mickie Akins

Design Copy
Linda Moll Smith

Sincerest thanks to all the designers and other professionals
whose dedication has made this book possible.
Special thanks to David Norris and Kaye Stafford
of Quebecor Printing Book Group, Kingsport, Tennessee.

Library of Congress Cataloging-in-Publication Data
ISBN: 0-9655269-1-7
First Printing: 1997
Library of Congress Catalog Card Number: 96-79701
Published and Distributed by
Annie's Attic, LLC, Big Sandy, Texas 75755
Printed in the United States of America.

Cover: *Lisa Diane*, pattern instructions begin on page 108.

Contents

Dear Friends,

I don't remember when I didn't love dolls!

When I was a young girl growing up in Kansas, dolls were my constant companions. Together we sailed away on the tawny seas of the wheat fields surrounding us to lacy pink lands of make-believe.

Whether it was a humble figurine fashioned tenderly from cornhusks by my grandmother, or the giant-sized panda bear won at the county fair, or the exquisite baby doll I received for my sixth birthday, I treasured all my dolls as friends and confidantes.

Dolls are still close to my heart. Even as my love for crochet grew into the needlecraft business now known as Annie's Attic, I have continued to collect, and design dresses for, dolls of all styles and sizes.

Now, for the first time after almost two decades of crochet pattern publishing, I've compiled over 50 perennial and personal favorites into this book, an exclusive collection for doll lovers and crocheters alike to cherish.

In the seven chapters of Annie's Favorite Crochet Dolls, *you'll find dozens of ways to celebrate the charming versatility of dolls and their meanings in our lives.*

In "Around the Home," you'll discover both whimsical and practical domestic helpers as dolls disguise tissues and display potpourri. "Animal Attractions" spotlights our affinity for furry friends like bunnies, puppies and teddy bears.

"Cultural Creations" imparts an exotic glimpse of other lands and peoples, while "Darling Doll Clothes" provides patterns aplenty for that irresistible urge to update dolly's wardrobe.

"Childhood Treasures" recalls the carefree days when dolls were the playmates of our youthful imaginations, while "Fashion Doll Fun" is a more grown-up, but no less exuberant, foray into style-making for 11½" dolls.

Our book wouldn't be complete without "Special Occasion Dolls" for treating ourselves and our loved ones with crocheted commemorations of festive moments.

This very special volume pays homage to our universal fondness for dolls and recognizes that they are not mere trifles or childish playthings. Dolls are symbols of our fondest dreams, extensions of our crochet creativity and petite personifications of those we hold dear.

When it comes to collecting and creating dolls, we don't ever want to grow up!

Happy Crocheting,

Annie

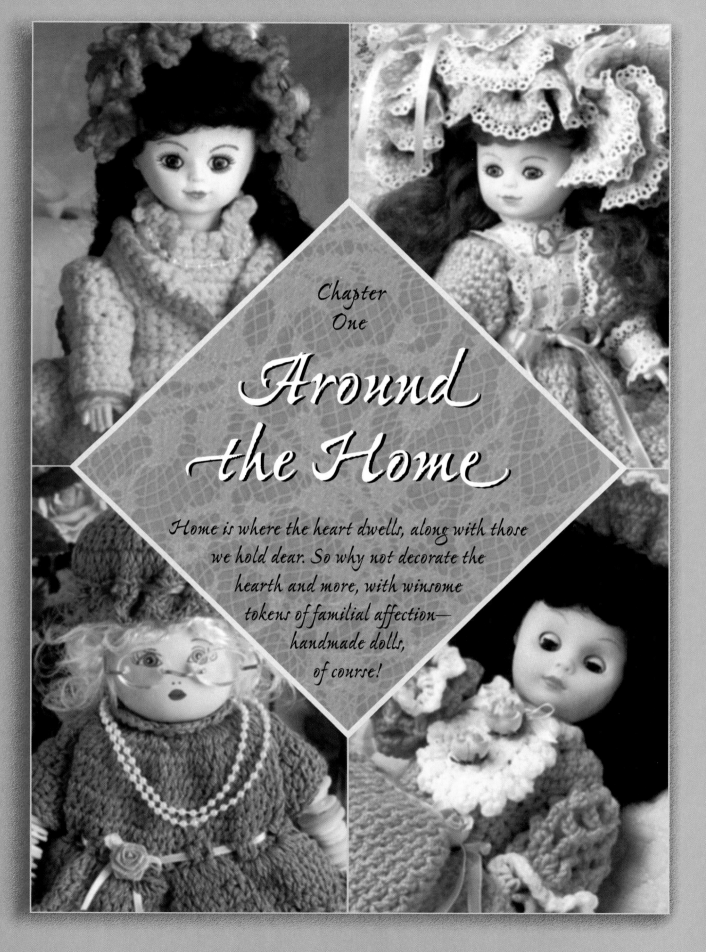

Chapter
One

Around the Home

Home is where the heart dwells, along with those
we hold dear. So why not decorate the
hearth and more, with winsome
tokens of familial affection—
handmade dolls,
of course!

Sweetheart Doll Wreath

Design by Carol Alexander

Finished Size: Wreath is approximately 21" across × 22" high.

Materials for Doll:
- 7¾ oz. lt. blue worsted yarn
- 11½" porcelain-type doll
- 1½ yds. of 1¼" white double-edged beading lace
- 10 yds. of ½" white gathered lace
- 2 yds. lt. blue ⅜" satin ribbon
- 1 yd. lt. blue ¼" satin ribbon
- ⅜" lt. blue craft cameo
- Pair of small pearl pierced earrings
- Three size 4/0 snaps
- Hot glue gun and glue
- White sewing thread
- Sewing and tapestry needles
- F hook or hook needed to obtain gauge

Additional Materials for Wreath:
- 16" white heart-shaped plastic foam wreath with 12" opening
- 1 yd. of lt. blue lace fabric
- 1½ yds. of 2¾" lt. blue gathered lace
- 1½ yds. of 1¼" white gathered lace
- 2⅔ yds. of ¾" white double-edged lace ribbon
- 1½ yds. lt. blue 8-mm. strung pearl beads
- Nine lt. blue 1" artificial rosebuds
- Three berry picks with green leaves and several large off-white pearl beads
- Ecru gypsophila floral filler
- Two 1" plastic rings

Gauge: 9 sts = 2"; 9 sc rows = 2"; 5 dc rows = 2¼".

Basic Stitches: Ch, sl st, sc, hdc, dc, tr.

Special Stitches: For **hdc decrease (hdc dec),** yo, insert hook in next st, yo, pull lp through st, insert hook in next st, yo, pull lp through st, yo, pull through all 4 lps on hook.

For **5-dc cluster (cl),** yo, insert hook in next st, yo, pull through st, yo, pull through 2 lps on hook, (yo, insert hook in same st, yo, pull through st, yo, pull through 2 lps on hook) 4 times, yo, pull through all 6 lps on hook.

DRESS
Bodice
NOTE: *Front of row 1 is right side of work.*

Row 1: Starting at neck, ch 20, sc in second ch from hook, sc in next ch, 2 sc in next ch, (sc in each of next 2 chs, 2 sc in next ch) 2 times, sc in next ch, (2 sc in next ch, sc in each of next 2 chs) 3 times, turn. *(25 sc made)*

Row 2: Ch 1, sc in each st across, turn.

Row 3: Ch 1, sc in each of first 2 sts, 2 sc in next st, (sc in each of next 2 sts, 2 sc in next st) 3 times, sc in next st, (2 sc in next st, sc in each of next 2 sts) 4 times, turn. *(33)*

Row 4: Ch 1, sc in each of first 2 sts, 2 sc in next st, sc in each of next 2 sts; for **armhole,** ch 6 loosely, skip next 5 sts; sc in next 4 sts, 2 sc in next st, sc in each of next 3 sts, 2 sc in next st, sc in next 4 sts; for **armhole,** ch 6 loosely, skip next 5 sts; sc in each of next 2 sts, 2 sc in next st, sc in each of last 2 sts, turn. *(39 sts and chs)*

Row 5: Ch 2 *(counts as first hdc),* hdc in next st, **hdc dec** *(see Special Stitches),* hdc in each of next 2 sts, sc in next 6 chs, (sc in each of next 2 sts, sc next 2 sts tog) 3 times, sc in next 9 sts and chs, hdc in each of next 2 sts, hdc dec, hdc in each of last 2 sts, turn. *(34 sts)*

Row 6: Ch 1, sc in first 4 sts, (sc next 2 sts tog, sc in each of next 3 sts) across, turn. *(28)*

Row 7: Ch 1, sc in first 4 sts, (sc next 2 sts tog, sc in next 4 sts) across, turn. *(24)*

Row 8: Ch 1, sc in each st across, turn.

Row 9: Ch 1, sc in first 6 sts, sc next 2 sts tog, sc in next 8 sts, sc next 2 sts tog, sc in last 6 sts, turn. *(22)*

Row 10: Ch 1, sc in each st across, turn.

Rnd 11: Working in rnds, ch 1, sc in first 10 sts, sc next 2 sts tog, sc in last 10 sts; skip first sc of this rnd, join with sl st in **back lp** *(see Stitch Guide)* of second sc; **do not turn or fasten off.** Mark skipped st. *(20)*

Skirt
Rnd 1: Working this rnd in **front lps,** ch 3 *(counts as first dc),* 2 dc in same st as ch-3, 3 dc in each st around, skip marked st, join with sl st in top of ch-3. *(60 dc made)*

Rnds 2–3: Ch 3, dc in each st around, join.

Rnd 4: Ch 3, dc in next st, 2 dc in next st, (dc in each of next 2 sts, 2 dc in next st) around, join. *(80)*

Rnds 5–6: Ch 3, dc in each st around, join.

Rnd 7: Ch 3, dc in each of next 2 sts, 2 dc in next st, (dc in each of next 3 sts, 2 dc in next st) around, join. *(100)*

Continued on page 8

Continued from page 7

Rnd 8: Ch 3, dc in each st around, join.

Rnd 9: Ch 3, dc in each of next 2 sts, dc next 2 sts tog, (dc in each of next 3 sts, dc next 2 sts tog) around, join with sl st in **front lp** at top of ch-3. *(80)*

Rnd 10: To form **ruffle**, working this rnd in **front lps**, ch 4 *(counts as first hdc and ch-2)*, (hdc, ch 2) in each st around, join with sl st in second ch of ch-4. *(80 ch sps)*

Rnd 11: Ch 1, (sc, ch 3) 2 times in first ch sp, (sc, ch 3) 2 times in each ch sp around, join with sl st in first sc. *(160 ch sps)*

Rnds 12–13: Ch 1, (sc, ch 3) in each ch sp around, join.

Rnd 14: (Ch 3, 2 dc, ch 3, 3 dc) in first ch sp, sc in next ch sp, *(3 dc, ch 3, 3 dc) in next ch sp, sc in next ch sp; repeat from * around, join with sl st in top of first ch-3. *(80 ch sps)*

Rnd 15: Sl st in each of next 2 dc, (sl st, ch 6, dc, ch 4, dc, ch 3, dc) in next ch sp, (dc, ch 3, dc, ch 4, dc, ch 3, dc) in each ch sp around, join with sl st in third ch of ch-6. *(320 dc)*

Rnd 16: (Sl st, ch 1, sc) in next ch sp, ch 3, sc in next dc, (ch 3, sc) 2 times in next ch sp, ch 3, sc in next dc, ch 3, sc in next ch sp, *sc in next ch sp, ch 3, sc in next dc, (ch 3, sc) 2 times in next ch sp, ch 3, sc in next dc, ch 3, sc in next ch sp; repeat from * around, join with sl st in first sc. Fasten off.

Sleeves

NOTE: *Do not join or turn unless otherwise stated. Mark first st of each rnd.*

Rnd 1: Working around one armhole, join with sc in fourth ch at underarm, sc in next ch, 2 sc in next ch, 2 hdc in side of sc, hdc in last worked st on row 3, 2 hdc in each of next 5 sts, hdc in next worked st, 2 hdc in side of sc, 2 sc in next ch, sc in each of last 2 chs. *(24 sts made)*

Rnd 2: Sc in each sc and hdc in each hdc around.

Rnds 3–6: Sc in each st around.

Rnd 7: (Sc next 2 sts tog) around. *(12)*

Rnd 8: (Sc in next 4 sts, sc next 2 sts tog) around. *(10)*

Rnds 9–13: Sc in each st around. At end of last rnd, join with sl st in next st. Fasten off.
Repeat on other armhole.

HAT

NOTE: *Do not join or turn unless otherwise stated. Mark first st of each rnd.*

Rnd 1: Ch 2, 6 sc in second ch from hook. *(6 sc made)*

Rnd 2: 2 sc in each st around. *(12)*

Rnd 3: (Sc in next st, 2 sc in next st) around. *(18)*

Rnd 4: (Sc in each of next 2 sts, 2 sc in next st) around. *(24)*

Rnd 5: (Sc in each of next 3 sts, 2 sc in next st) around. *(30)*

Rnd 6: (Sc in next 4 sts, 2 sc in next st) around. *(36)*

Rnd 7: Working this rnd in **back lps**, (sc in next 4 sts, sc next 2 sts tog) around. *(30)*

Rnds 8–10: Sc in each st around. At end of last rnd, join with sl st in **front lp** of next st.

Rnd 11: To form **ruffle**, working this rnd in **front lps**, ch 4 *(counts as first hdc and ch-2)*, (hdc, ch 2) in each st around, join with sl st in second ch of ch-4. *(30 ch sps)*

Rnd 12: Ch 1, (sc, ch 3) 2 times in first ch sp, (sc, ch 3) 2 times in each ch sp around, join with sl st in first sc. *(60 ch sps)*

Rnd 13: Ch 1, (sc, ch 3) in each ch sp around, join.

Rnd 14: (Sl st, ch 6, dc, ch 4, dc, ch 3, dc) in next ch sp, (dc, ch 3, dc, ch 4, dc, ch 3, dc) in each ch sp around, join with sl st in third ch of ch-6. *(240 dc)*

Rnd 15: (Sl st, ch 1, sc) in first ch sp, ch 3, sc in next dc, (ch 3, sc) 2 times in next ch sp, ch 3, sc in next dc, ch 3, sc in next ch sp, *sc in next ch sp, ch 3, sc in next dc, (ch 3, sc) 2 times in next ch sp, ch 3, sc in next dc, ch 3, sc in next ch sp; repeat from * around, skip last dc, join with sl st in first sc. Fasten off.

FINISHING

Working across back and neck edges, with right side of work facing you, join with sc in end of row 11 on left back side of Bodice, sc in end of each row across to row 1, ch 1; working in remaining lps on opposite side of starting ch on row 1, sc in first ch, ch 3, sc in next ch, ch 3, skip next ch, sc in next ch, (skip next ch, sc in next ch, ch 2, sc in next ch, ch 3, skip next ch, sc in next ch) across to other end of row 1. Fasten off.

Lapping edge of left back over right back of Bodice, sew snaps evenly spaced down back opening.

From beading lace, cut two 6" pieces, two 4" pieces, one 24" piece and one 8" piece. Weave ³⁄₈" ribbon through each piece of beading lace and cut ½" longer on each end.

Placing edge of beading section at center front, glue one 6" piece of beading lace on right side of Bodice from waist to neck edge, around right side of neck edge and down right side of back. Cut off any extra lace. In same manner, glue second 6" piece of beading lace on left side of Bodice from waist to neck edge *(overlapping first piece with edges of beading sections touching)*, around left side of neck edge and down left side of back.

Turn ribbon end under ½" and sew in place. Glue cameo to center front neck edge.

Overlapping ends ½" and cutting off any extra lace on each piece, sew one 4" piece beading lace around last rnds on each Sleeve; sew 24" piece around rnd 9 on Skirt; sew 8" piece

Continued on page 18

Annie Air Freshener

Design by Beverly Study

Instructions begin on page 10

Annie Air Freshener

Finished Size: Approximately 14½" tall.

Materials:
- Worsted yarn:
    - 5 oz. white
    - 1 oz. fleshtone
    - 1 oz. gold
    - Small amounts of pink and green
- Small amount red sport yarn
- Two tiny black shank buttons
- Polyester fiberfill
- Powdered blush
- Tapestry needle
- F hook or hook needed to obtain gauge

Gauge: 5 sc = 1"; 5 sc rows = 1".

Basic Stitches: Ch, sl st, sc, dc.

Note: Work in continuous rnds; do not join rnds unless otherwise specified. Mark first st of each rnd.

HEAD
Rnd 1: With fleshtone, ch 2, 6 sc in second ch from hook. *(6 sc made)*

Rnd 2: 2 sc in each st around. *(12)*

Rnd 3: (Sc in next st, 2 sc in next st) 6 times. *(18)*

Rnd 4: Sc in next st, 2 sc in next st, (sc in each of next 2 sts, 2 sc in next st) 5 times, sc in next st. *(24)*

Rnd 5: 2 sc in next st, (sc in each of next 3 sts, 2 sc in next st) 5 times, sc in each of next 3 sts. *(30)*

Rnds 6–13: Sc in each st around.

Rnd 14: (Sc next 2 sts tog, sc in each of next 3 sts) 6 times. *(24)*

Rnd 15: Sc in each of next 2 sts, (sc next 2 sts tog, sc in each of next 2 sts) 5 times, sc next 2 sts tog. *(18)*

Rnd 16: (Sc next 2 sts tog, sc in next st) 6 times *(12)*. Stuff Head.

Rnd 17: (Sc next 2 sts tog) 6 times. *(6)*

Rnds 18–19: Sc in each st around.

Rnd 20: 2 sc in each st around. *(12)*

Rnd 21: Sc in each of next 3 sts, ch 4, sc in second ch from hook and in each of next 2 chs, sc in next 6 sts, ch 4, sc in second ch from hook and in each of next 2 chs, sc in each of next 3 sts. *(18)*

NOTE: *In next rnd, you will be working on both sides of ch-4.*

Rnd 22: Sc in next 6 sts, 3 sc in next st, sc in next 11 sts, 3 sc in next st, sc in next 5 sts, join with sl st in first st. Fasten off. *(28)*

DRESS
Rnd 1: Beginning Bodice and working in **back lps** *(see Stitch Guide)* of rnd 22 on Head, join white with sc in first st, sc in each st around.

Rnds 2–3: Sc in each st around.

Rnd 4: Sc in next 11 sts, 2 sc in next st, sc in next 5 sts, 2 sc in next st, sc in next 10 sts. *(30)*

Rnd 5: Sc in each st around.

Rnd 6: Sc in next 11 sts, sc next 2 sts tog, sc in next 5 sts, sc next 2 sts tog, sc in next 10 sts. *(28)*

Rnd 7: Sc in each st around.

Rnd 8: Sc in next 11 sts, sc next 2 sts tog, sc in each of next 3 sts, sc next 2 sts tog, sc in next 10 sts. *(26)*

Rnd 9: Sc in each st around.

Rnd 10: Sc in next 10 sts, sc next 2 sts tog, sc in each of next 3 sts, sc next 2 sts tog, sc in next 9 sts. *(24)*

Rnd 11: (Sc in each of next 2 sts, sc next 2 sts tog) 6 times, join with sl st in first st. *(18)*

Rnd 12: Beginning Skirt and working in **front lps**, ch 1, 2 sc in each st around, join with sl st in first sc. *(36)*

Rnd 13: Ch 3, 2 dc in next st, (dc in next st, 2 dc in next st) around, join with sl st in top of ch-3. *(54)*

Rnds 14–18: Ch 3, dc in each st around, join.

Rnd 19: Ch 4, (dc in next st, ch 1) around, join with sl st in third ch of ch-4.

Rnd 20: Ch 3, dc in next ch-1 sp, (dc in next st, dc in next ch-1 sp) around, join. *(108)*

Rnds 21–28: Ch 3, dc in each st around, join. At end of last rnd, fasten off.

Skirt Edging
Join pink with sc at back of Skirt on rnd 28, *[skip next st, (dc, ch 1, dc, ch 1, dc) in next st, skip next st], sc in next st; repeat from * around to last 3 sts; repeat between [ ], join with sl st in first sc. Fasten off.

BODICE CLOSURE
Rnd 1: With white, ch 2, 6 sc in second ch from hook. *(6 sc made)*

Rnd 2: 2 sc in each st around. *(12)*

Rnd 3: (Sc in next st, 2 sc in next st) 6 times. *(18)*

Rnd 4: Working in **back lps**, sc in each st around.

Rnds 5–12: Sc in each st around. At end of last rnd, fasten off. Stuff and shape Bodice to rnd 11. Sew **front lps** of rnd 3 on Closure to **back lps** of rnd 11 on inside of Bodice *(this holds stuffing in place and forms a cap that fits over top of can)*.

ARM (make 2)
Rnd 1: With fleshtone, ch 2, 6 sc in second ch from hook. *(6 sc made)*

Rnd 2: Working in **back lps**, (sc in next st, 2 sc in next st) 3 times. *(9)*

Rnds 3–5: Sc in each st around.

Rnd 6: Sc next 2 sts tog, sc in next 7 sts. Stuff

Arm as you work. *(8)*

Rnd 7: Sc next 2 sts tog, sc in next 6 sts. *(7)*

Rnd 8: Sc in each st around.

Rnd 9: Sc next 2 sts tog, sc in next 5 sts. *(6)*

Rnds 10–16: Sc in each st around.

Rnd 17: Sc next 2 sts tog, sc in next 4 sts. *(5)*

Rnd 18: Sc in each st around.

Rnd 19: Ch 3, sc in next 5 sts.

Rnd 20: Keeping ch-3 on outside of work for **thumb,** sc in each sc around.

Rnd 21: Sc in each st around, join with sl st in first sc. Leaving about 8" end for sewing, fasten off. Finish stuffing Arm. Weave 8" end through **front lps** of each st on rnd 21 and pull up tightly to shape hand. Fasten off.

Making sure thumbs are in correct position, sew Arms to shoulders by stitching two remaining **front lps** of rnd 1 on Arm to two remaining **front lps** of rnd 22 on Head at each shoulder.

COLLAR

Rnd 1: Holding Head toward you and working in remaining **front lps,** join white with sc at center back of rnd 22 on Head, sc in each st across back to Arm, 2 sc in each of next 4 sts around Arm, sc in each st across front to other Arm, 2 sc in each of next 4 sts around Arm, sc in each st across back, join with sl st in first sc. *(40 sc made)*

Rnd 2: Ch 1, sc in same st, sc in each st across back to Arm, *sc in each of first 3 sts around Arm, 2 sc in each of next 2 sts, sc in each of next 3 sts around Arm*, sc in each st across front to other Arm; repeat between first and second *, sc in each st across back, join with sl st in first sc. *(44)*

Rnds 3–5: Ch 1, sc in each st around, join with sl st in first sc.

Rnd 6: Ch 5, (skip next st, sc in next st, ch 5) 21 times, skip last st, join with sl st in first ch of ch-5. Fasten off.

Rnd 7: Join pink with sc in ch-5 sp at center back, (ch 5, sc in next ch-5 sp) 21 times, ch 5,

join with sl st in first sc. Fasten off.

FLOWER

With pink, ch 5; for **petal,** yo 2 times, insert hook in fifth ch from hook, yo, pull through, (yo, pull through 2 lps on hook) 2 times, *yo 2 times, insert hook in same ch, yo, pull through, (yo, pull through 2 lps on hook) 2 times; repeat from * 2 more times, yo and pull through all 5 lps on hook, ch 4, sl st in same beginning ch—*petal made,* ch 4; working in same beginning st, (petal, ch 4) 2 times. Leaving 6" for sewing, fasten off. *(3 petals)*

With tapestry needle and two strands gold, make one stitch in center of Flower. Leaving loose ends on right side of Flower, tie knot to secure. Trim ends. Sew Flower to left front side of Collar. With green, stitch three or four loops around Flower to resemble leaves.

HAIR

Fold 10-yard length of gold yarn in half two times, tie a knot at each end. Sew one end to side of Head. Holding yarn about 6" from sewn end, twist until tight; fold twist in half, sew end of twist beside first end. Continue across back of Head in a curve to make neckline with ten curls.

Wrap gold yarn around 4½" cardboard 40 times. With two 12" pieces of gold yarn, tie all loops together at each side of cardboard. Slide loops off cardboard. Using end of 12" pieces of yarn, sew one end to forehead at center front and other end to back of neck. Spread strands to cover back of Head and ends of curls.

With pink, ch 50. Fasten off. Tie in bow and sew to Hair at neckline.

FACE

Sew buttons on Head for eyes, pulling yarn tightly through Head to form dents and shape cheeks *(see photo).* Using red and fly stitch *(see Stitch Guide),* embroider mouth three rnds below eyes. Apply blush to cheeks. ❖

Tissue Cover Girls

Designs by Mary Layfield

Peach & Coral Outfit

Instructions begin on page 16

White & Turquoise Outfit

Doll Pick

Materials:
- 11½" fashion doll
- 14 × 61-hole piece 7-mesh plastic canvas
- Small amount white worsted yarn
- Tapestry needle

PICK
(Graphs are at right)
1: Cut all pieces according to graphs.
2: Remove legs from doll; insert one end of Pick Top through leg openings.
3: With white yarn, whipstitch *(see Stitch Guide)* one long edge of one Pick Side to one half of Pick Top matching dots on graphs; whipstitch other long edge to other half according to X's on graphs. Repeat with second Pick Side on opposite long edges of Pick Top. ❖

PICK SIDE
(6 × 27-hole piece)
Cut 2.

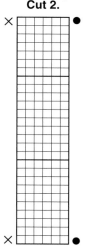

PICK TOP
(7 × 61-hole piece)
Cut 1.

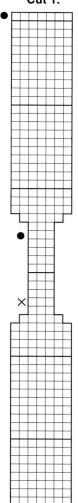

White & Turquoise Outfit

Finished Size: Fits over a standard-size tissue roll.

Materials:
- Worsted yarn:
    - 6 oz. white
    - 3 oz. turquoise
- Small amount white sport yarn
- 36" turquoise ⅜" satin ribbon
- 46" turquoise ⅛" satin ribbon
- 56" lt. green ¼" satin ribbon
- ½" ribbon roses:
    - Nine turquoise
    - Eight dk. pink
    - One lt. pink
- ¾" ribbon roses:
    - Two lt. pink
    - Two peach
    - Two lavender
- 6" of 4-mm. strung pearl beads
- Three size 2/0 snaps
- Doll Pick *(see instructions above)*
- Craft glue
- B and F hooks or hooks needed to obtain gauge

Gauge: F hook and worsted yarn, 9 sts = 2"; 9 sc rows = 2"; 5 dc rows = 2".

Basic Stitches: Ch, sl st, sc, dc, tr.

Special Stitches: For **beginning shell (beg shell),** (sl st, ch 3, dc, ch 1, 2 dc) in first st or ch sp.
For **shell,** (2 dc, ch 1, 2 dc) in next st or ch sp.
For **beginning V st (beg V st),** (ch 5, dc) in first st or ch sp.
For **V st,** (dc, ch 1, dc) in next st or ch sp.

Note: Use F hook throughout unless otherwise stated.

DRESS
Bodice
Row 1: Starting at waist, with white worsted

Continued on page 14

Continued from page 13

yarn, ch 25, sc in second ch from hook, sc in each ch across, turn. *(24 sc made)*

Row 2: Working this row in **front lps** *(see Stitch Guide)*, ch 1, sc in first 5 sts, 2 sc in next st, sc in next 12 sts, 2 sc in next st, sc in last 5 sts, turn. *(26 sc—front of row 2 is right side of work)*

Row 3: Ch 1, sc in first 6 sts, 2 sc in next st, sc in next 12 sts, 2 sc in next st, sc in last 6 sts, turn. *(28)*

Row 4: For **first back,** ch 1, sc in first 6 sts leaving remaining sts unworked, turn. *(6)*

Rows 5–8: Ch 1, sc in each st across, turn.

Row 9: Ch 1, sc in first 3 sts leaving remaining sts unworked, turn. *(3)*

Row 10: Ch 1, sc in each st across, turn.

Row 11: Ch 1, sc in each of first 2 sts, dc in last st, turn. Fasten off.

Row 4: For **front,** skip next 2 unworked sts on row 3, join white worsted yarn with sc in next st, sc in next 11 sts leaving remaining sts unworked, turn. *(12)*

Row 5: Ch 1, sc in each st across, turn.

Row 6: Ch 1, skip first st, sc in next 10 sts leaving last st unworked, turn. *(10)*

Rows 7–8: Ch 1, sc in each st across, turn.

Row 9: For **first shoulder,** ch 1, sc in each of first 3 sts leaving remaining sts unworked, turn. *(3)*

Row 10: Ch 1, sc in each st across, turn.

Row 11: Ch 1, sc in each of first 2 sts, dc in last st, **do not turn.** Fasten off.

Row 9: For **second shoulder,** skip next 4 unworked sts on row 8, join white worsted yarn with sc in next st, sc in each of last 2 sts, turn. *(3)*

Row 10: Ch 1, sc in each st across, turn.

Row 11: Ch 3 *(counts as dc)*, sc in each of last 2 sts, turn. Fasten off.

Row 4: For **second back,** skip next 2 unworked sts on row 3, join white worsted yarn with sc in next st, sc in last 5 sts, turn. *(6)*

Rows 5–8: Ch 1, sc in each st across, turn.

Row 9: Sl st in each of first 3 sts, ch 1, sc in each of last 3 sts, turn. *(3)*

Row 10: Ch 1, sc in each st across, turn.

Row 11: Ch 3, sc in each of last 2 sts. Fasten off. Sew shoulder seams.

Neck Trim

Row 1: With right side of work facing you, join white worsted yarn with sc in first st at center back edge, sc in each st, sc in end of each sc row and 2 sc in end of each dc row around neck to center back edge on opposite side, **do not turn.** Fasten off.

Row 2: Working in **back lps,** with B hook, join white sport yarn with sc in first st, *(ch 3, sc) 2 times in next st, ch 3, sc in next st; repeat from * across. Fasten off.

Glue one turquoise ribbon rose to center front on row 1 of Neck Trim.

Place strung pearl beads around front of Bodice below rose and tack ends to Bodice Backs at neck edge.

Sleeve (make 2)

Row 1: With white worsted yarn, ch 17, sc in second ch from hook, sc in each ch across, turn. *(16 sc made)*

Rows 2–4: Ch 3 *(counts as first dc)*, dc in each st across, turn.

Row 5: Sl st in each of first 3 sts, sc in next st, dc in next 9 sts, sc in next st leaving remaining sts unworked, turn.

Row 6: Sl st in each of first 3 sts, ch 3, dc in next 6 sts leaving remaining sts unworked, turn.

Row 7: Ch 3, (dc next 2 sts tog) 3 times. Fasten off.

Sew ends of rows 1–4 together.

For **Trim,** working in remaining lps on opposite side of starting ch on row 1, join white worsted yarn with sl st in first ch, (ch 3, sc in next ch) around, ch 3, join with sl st in first sc. Fasten off.

Cut an 8" piece of ⅛" turquoise ribbon; weave through sts of row 1, tie in bow at center top and glue in place to secure.

Sew Sleeves in armholes.

Underskirt

Row 1: With wrong side of Bodice facing you, working in unworked **back lps** of row 1 on Bodice, join white worsted yarn with sl st in first st, ch 3, sl st in same st, (ch 3, skip next st, sl st in next st) 5 times, (ch 3, sl st) 2 times in next st, (ch 3, skip next st, sl st in next st) 5 times, ch 3, skip next st, (sl st, ch 3, sl st) in last st. Fasten off. *(15 ch sps)*

Row 2: Join turquoise with sl st in first ch sp, ch 3 *(counts as first dc)*, 2 dc in same ch sp, 2 dc in each ch sp across, turn. *(31 dc)*

Row 3: Ch 4 *(counts as first tr)*, (2 tr in next st, tr in next st) across, turn. *(46 tr)*

Row 4: Ch 4, tr in each st across, turn.

Rnd 5: Working in rnds, ch 4, 2 tr in next st, (tr in next st, 2 tr in next st) around, join with sl st in top of ch-4. *(69)*

Rnd 6: Ch 4, tr in each st around, join.

Rnd 7: Ch 4, (2 tr in next st, tr in next st) around, join. *(103)*

Rnds 8–11: Ch 4, tr in each st around, join. At end of last rnd, fasten off.

Overskirt

Row 1: With right side of Bodice facing you, working in remaining lps on opposite side of starting ch on Bodice, join white worsted yarn with sl st in first ch, ch 4 *(counts as first dc and ch-1)*, dc in next st, (ch 1, dc in next st) across, turn. *(23 ch-1 sps)*

Row 2: Ch 3, (dc in next ch-1 sp, ch 1, dc in next

ch-1 sp, ch 2) across to last ch-1 sp, dc in last ch-1 sp, turn. *(24 dc)*

Row 3: Ch 5 *(counts as first dc and ch-2)*, dc in next st, (ch 2, dc in next st) across, turn.

Rnd 4: Working in rnds, ch 5, dc in next st, (ch 2, dc in next st) around, join with sl st in third ch of ch-5, **turn.**

Rnd 5: Beg V st *(see Special Stitches)* in first st, ch 1; ***V st** *(see Special Stitches)* in next st, ch 1; repeat from * around, join with sl st in third ch of ch-5. *(23 V sts)*

Rnd 6: (Sl st, beg V st) in ch sp of first V st, ch 1, (V st in ch sp of next V st, ch 1) around, join.

Rnd 7: (Sl st, beg V st) in ch sp of first V st, ch 2, (V st in ch sp of next V st, ch 2) around, join.

Rnds 8–9: (Sl st, beg V st) in ch sp of first V st, ch 3, (V st in ch sp of next V st, ch 3) around, join.

Rnd 10: Beg shell *(see Special Stitches)* in ch sp of first V st, ch 1; *shell, *(see Special Stitches)* in ch sp of next V st, ch 1; repeat from * around, join with sl st in top of ch-3.

Rnds 11–13: Beg shell in ch sp of first shell, ch 2, (shell in ch sp of next shell, ch 2) around, join.

Rnd 14: Beg shell in ch sp of first shell, ch 3, (shell in ch sp of next shell, ch 3) around, join.

Rnd 15: Beg shell in ch sp of first shell, ch 4, (shell in ch sp of next shell, ch 4) around, join. Fasten off.

Sew snaps evenly spaced down back opening of Bodice.

Motif (make 8)

Rnd 1: With white worsted yarn, ch 5, sl st in first ch to form ring, ch 6 *(counts as first tr and ch-2)*, (dc in ring, ch 2) 3 times; for **Tip,** (2 tr, ch 3, 2 tr, ch 2) in ring, (dc in ring, ch 2) 3 times; for **Tip,** (2 tr, ch 3, tr) in ring, join with sl st in fourth ch of ch-6. *(10 ch sps)*

Rnd 2: (Sl st, ch 3, dc, ch 1, 2 dc) in first ch sp, *3 dc in each of next 2 ch sps, (2 dc, ch 2, 2 dc) in next ch sp, ch 1, (2 tr, ch 3, 2 tr) in next ch sp, ch 1*, (2 dc, ch 2, 2 dc) in next ch sp; repeat between first and second *, join with sl st in top of ch-3. Fasten off.

With white worsted yarn, tack Motifs together at ch sp of each Tip to form Ring.

Motif Ring Edging

Rnd 1: Working around top edge of Ring, join turquoise with sc in any st on any Motif, sc in each st and in each ch around, join with sl st in first sc. Fasten off.

Rnd 2: Join white worsted yarn with sl st in first st, ch 4, (sc in next st, ch 4) around, join with sl st in first ch of first ch-4. Fasten off.

Rnds 3–4: Repeat rnds 1 and 2 around bottom edge of Ring.

For **each Motif,** cut a 7" piece of ¼" lt. green ribbon; tie in bow, trim ends even and sew centered on front of Motif.

Alternating turquoise and dk. pink ribbon roses, glue one to center of each lt. green bow.

Place ring around Skirt with Tips of Motifs at bottom edge; tack top half of each Motif to Skirt leaving bottom half extending below bottom edge *(see photo).*

Waist Trim

Rnd 1: With white worsted yarn, ch 16, 2 sc in second ch from hook, sc in each ch across with 3 sc in last ch; working in remaining lps on opposite side of starting ch, sc in each ch across, join with sl st in first sc.

Rnd 2: Ch 4, (sc in next st, ch 4) around, join with sl st in first sc. Fasten off.

Glue Waist Trim centered across front of Dress at waist.

Glue ⅜" turquoise ribbon centered across Waist Trim leaving long ends for ties; glue one each of lt. pink, turquoise and dk. pink ribbon roses centered on right side of Waist Trim *(see photo).*

Place Dress on Doll Pick and tie ribbon ties at back.

TIARA

With white worsted yarn, ch 35, sl st in first ch to form ring, ch 1, sc in each ch around, join with sl st in first sc. Fasten off.

Wrap ⅛" turquoise ribbon ten times around Tiara; cut off remaining ribbon. Glue ends on inside to secure.

Glue remaining ribbon roses evenly spaced around outside of Tiara.

Tie remaining ⅛" turquoise ribbon in a 1¼" bow leaving long ends for streamers; glue to back of Tiara. ❖

Peach & Coral Outfit

Finished Size: Fits over a standard-size tissue roll.

Materials:
- Worsted yarn:
  - 8 oz. peach
  - 3 oz. coral
- Six peach ¾" ribbon roses
- Three peach ½" ribbon roses
- 4" of 4-mm. strung pearl beads
- 5" of green 22-gauge floral wire
- Four size 2/0 snaps
- Doll Pick *(see instructions on page 13)*
- Craft glue
- Peach sewing thread
- Sewing and tapestry needles
- F hook or hook needed to obtain gauge

Gauge: 9 sts = 2"; 9 sc rows = 2"; 5 dc rows = 2".

Basic Stitches: Ch, sl st, sc, dc, tr.

DRESS
Bodice
Row 1: Starting at waist, with peach, ch 25, sc in second ch from hook, sc in each ch across, turn. *(24 sc made)*

Row 2: Ch 1, sc in first 5 sts, 2 sc in next st, sc in next 12 sts, 2 sc in next st, sc in last 5 sts, turn. *(26 sc—front of row 2 is right side of work)*

Row 3: Ch 1, sc in first 6 sts, 2 sc in next st, sc in next 12 sts, 2 sc in next st, sc in last 6 sts, turn. *(28)*

Row 4: For **first back,** ch 1, sc in first 6 sts leaving remaining sts unworked, turn. *(6)*

Rows 5–8: Ch 1, sc in each st across, turn.

Row 9: Ch 1, sc in each of first 3 sts leaving remaining sts unworked, turn. *(3)*

Row 10: Ch 1, sc in each st across, turn.

Row 11: Ch 1, sc in each of first 2 sts, dc in last st, turn. Fasten off.

Row 4: For **front,** skip next 2 unworked sts on row 3, join peach with sc in next st, sc in next 11 sts leaving remaining sts unworked, turn. *(12)*

Row 5: Ch 1, sc in each st across, turn.

Row 6: Ch 1, skip first st, sc in next 10 sts leaving last st unworked, turn. *(10)*

Rows 7–8: Ch 1, sc in each st across, turn.

Row 9: For **first shoulder,** ch 1, sc in each of first 3 sts leaving remaining sts unworked, turn. *(3)*

Row 10: Ch 1, sc in each st across, turn.

Row 11: Ch 1, sc in each of first 2 sts, dc in last st, **do not turn.** Fasten off.

Row 9: For **second shoulder,** skip next 4 unworked sts on row 8, join peach with sc in next st, sc in each of last 2 sts, turn. *(3)*

Row 10: Ch 1, sc in each st across, turn.

Row 11: Ch 3 *(counts as dc)*, sc in each of last 2 sts, turn. Fasten off.

Row 4: For **second back,** skip next 2 unworked sts on row 3, join peach with sc in next st, sc in last 5 sts, turn. *(6)*

Rows 5–8: Ch 1, sc in each st across, turn.

Row 9: Sl st in each of first 3 sts, ch 1, sc in each of last 3 sts, turn. *(3)*

Row 10: Ch 1, sc in each st across, turn.

Row 11: Ch 3, sc in each of last 2 sts. Fasten off. Sew Shoulder seams.

Neck Trim
With right side of work facing you, working in sts and in ends of rows, join peach with sc in first st at center back edge, (ch 4, sc in next st or end of next row) around neck to center back edge on opposite side. Fasten off.

For **necklace,** place strung pearl beads around front neck edge of Bodice just below neck trim; insert ends in shoulders and sew to inside of Bodice to secure.

Skirt
Row 1: With right side of Bodice facing you, working in remaining lps on opposite side of starting ch on row 1, join peach with sl st in first ch, (ch 3, dc) in same ch, dc in next ch, (2 dc in next ch, dc in next ch) across, turn. *(36 dc made)*

Row 2: (Ch 3, dc) in first st, dc in next st, (2 dc in next st, dc in next st) across, turn. *(54)*

Rows 3–4: Ch 3, dc in each st across, turn.

Rnd 5: Working in rnds, (ch 3, dc) in first st, dc in next st, (2 dc in next st, dc in next st) around, join with sl st in top of ch-3. *(81)*

Rnds 6–9: Ch 3, dc in each st around, join.

Rnd 10: (Ch 3, 2 dc) in first st, (dc in next st, 2 dc in next st) around, join. *(123)*

Rnds 11–13: Ch 3, dc in each st around, join.

Rnd 14: For **first ruffle,** (ch 6, skip next st, sc in next st) around, ch 3, join with dc in first ch of first ch-6.

Rnd 15: Ch 4 *(counts as first dc and ch-1)*, dc in same ch sp, ch 1, (dc, ch 1) 4 times in each ch sp around, (dc, ch 1) 2 times in same ch sp as first ch-4, join with sl st in third ch of ch-4.

Rnd 16: Sl st in first ch-1 sp, ch 4, (dc in next ch-1 sp, ch 1) around, join.

Rnd 17: Sl st in first ch-1 sp, (ch 4, sc in next ch-1 sp) around, ch 4, join with sl st in first sc. Fasten off.

Rnd 18: For **second ruffle,** working behind first ruffle in skipped sts on rnd 13, join peach with sl st in any st, (ch 6, sc in next skipped st) around, ch 3, join with dc in first ch of first ch-6. Fasten off.

Rnd 19: Join coral with sl st in first ch sp, ch 4

(counts as first dc and ch-1), dc in same ch sp, ch 1, (dc, ch 1) 4 times in each ch sp around, (dc, ch 1) 2 times in same ch sp as first ch-4, join with sl st in third ch of ch-4.

Rnds 20–21: Repeat rnds 16–17 of first ruffle.

Sew three snaps evenly spaced down back opening of Bodice.

JACKET
Bodice
Rows 1–3: Repeat rows 1–3 of Dress Bodice on page 16.

Row 4: For **first front,** ch 1, sc in first 6 sts leaving remaining sts unworked, turn. *(6)*

Rows 5–11: Repeat rows 5–11 of Dress Bodice first back.

Row 4: For **back,** skip next 2 unworked sts on row 3, join peach with sc in next st, sc in next 11 sts leaving remaining sts unworked, turn. *(12)*

Rows 5–8: Ch 1, sc in each st across, turn.

Rows 9–11: For **first shoulder,** repeat rows 9–11 of Dress Bodice first shoulder.

Row 9: For **second shoulder,** skip next 6 unworked sts on row 8, join peach with sc in next st, sc in each of last 2 sts, turn. *(3)*

Rows 10–11: Repeat rows 10–11 of Dress Bodice second shoulder.

Row 4: For **second front,** skip next 2 unworked sts on row 3, join peach with sc in next st, sc in last 5 sts, turn. *(6)*

Rows 5–8: Ch 1, sc in each st across, turn.

Rows 9–11: Repeat rows 9–11 of Dress Bodice second back.

Sew shoulder seams.

Peplum
Row 1: With right side of Jacket Bodice facing you, working in remaining lps on opposite side of starting ch on row 1, join peach with sc in first ch, sc in each ch across, turn. *(24 sc made)*

Row 2: Ch 1, sc in each of first 2 sts, (2 dc in next st, dc in next st) across to last 2 sts, sc in each of last 2 sts, turn. *(34 sts)*

Row 3: Ch 1, skip first st, sc in next st, dc in each of next 3 sts, (2 dc in next st, dc in next st) across to last 5 sts, dc in each of next 3 sts, sc in next st leaving last st unworked, turn. *(44)*

Row 4: Ch 1, sc in each of first 2 sts, (dc in next st, 2 dc in next st) across to last 2 sts, sc in each of last 2 sts, turn. *(64)*

Row 5: Ch 1, sl st in first st, (dc in next st, 2 dc in next st) 2 times, (tr in next st, 2 tr in next st) across to last 5 sts, (dc in next st, 2 dc in next st) 2 times, sl st in last st, turn. Fasten off. *(95 sts)*

Rnd 6: Working in rnds around outer edge of Bodice and Peplum, with right side of work facing you, join peach with sc in st at center back neck edge, sc in each st and in end of each row around with 2 sc in each corner at front neck edges, join with sl st in first sc. Fasten off.

Rnd 7: Join coral with sc in first st, sc in each st around with 2 sc in each corner at front neck edge, join. Fasten off.

Sew one snap on inside at center front waist edge.

Glue one ¾" ribbon rose centered on each front side of Peplum ½" from bottom edge.

For **Lapel,** turn neck edge of each front Bodice back ½"; tack in place.

Sleeve (make 2)
Row 1: With peach, ch 13, sc in second ch from hook, sc in each ch across, turn. *(12 sc made—front of row 1 is right side of work.)*

Rows 2–8: Ch 1, sc in each st across, turn.

Row 9: Ch 1, sc in each of first 3 sts, 2 dc in each st across to last 3 sts, sc in each of last 3 sts, turn. *(18 sts)*

Row 10: Sl st in each of first 3 sts, sc in next st, dc in each st across to last 4 sts, sc in next st leaving last 3 sts unworked. *(12 sts—sl sts are not counted as sts.)*

Row 11: Ch 1, sc in first st, dc in each st across to last st, sc in last st, turn.

Row 12: Ch 1, sc first 3 sts tog, (sc next 3 sts tog) 3 times, turn. Fasten off. *(4)*

Sew ends of rows 1–9 together, forming underarm seam.

Cut a 3" strand of coral yarn, wrap around wrist edge on row 1 of Sleeve and pull ends to inside at seam; glue in place.

Sew Sleeves in armholes.

Place Dress and Jacket on Doll Pick.

HAT
Rnd 1: With peach, ch 25, sc in second ch from hook, sc in each of next 2 chs, dc in next 18 chs, sc in each of next 2 chs, 3 sc in last ch;

Continued on page 18

Continued from page 17

working in remaining lps on opposite side of starting ch, sc in each of next 2 chs, dc in next 18 chs, sc in each of last 3 chs, join with sl st in first sc. Fasten off. *(49 sts)*

Rnd 2: Join coral with sc in first st, (ch 5, sc in next st) around, ch 5, join. Fasten off.

With wrong side of work facing you, weave floral wire through center of rnd 1; bend each end of wire under ¼" on inside of Hat to secure.

Glue four ¾" ribbon roses evenly spaced across center on right side of Hat; glue three ½" ribbon roses evenly spaced between ¾" roses.

Bend wire in Hat to fit shape of Head. ❧

Sweetheart Doll Wreath

Continued from page 8

around rnds 8–10 on Hat. Turn ribbon ends under ½" and sew in place. *(Cut all remaining lace pieces to fit as they are attached.)*

Sew ½" gathered lace under last rnds on Skirt and on Hat.

Position ruffles at front of Hat as desired and tack or glue in place. Cut a 16" piece of ¼" ribbon and tie in bow with two 1¼" loops, sew to last rnd of Hat at front.

Place Dress on doll. Tie remaining ⅜" ribbon around waist with bow at front.

Cut a 14" piece of ¼" ribbon, loop through last rnd at front of Skirt below right hand; raising edge of ruffle to doll's right wrist, tie ribbon in bow around wrist. Arrange ruffle and tack on underside to hold in place. Trim all ribbon ends.

With needle or straight pin, pierce holes in doll's earlobes. Dip posts of earrings lightly in glue and insert fully into holes.

Spread glue lightly around inside of rnd 13 on Hat and press on Head.

WREATH

With right side of both pieces facing you, place 1¼" white lace over 2¾" lt. blue lace, sew gathered edges together to form one 2¾"-wide double-layer lace.

Cut lace fabric into 2½"-wide strips. Beginning at bottom point of heart wreath form, wrap form with strips to cover completely, securing beginning and end of each strip to back side of form with glue. Wrap strips tightly around form for a smooth finish, and overlap all strips just enough to cover form completely and evenly.

Glue or tack the 2¾"-wide lace around outside edge of the wrapped wreath.

Glue the strung beads to the wreath in front of the 2¾"-wide lace.

Glue three rosebuds to center of each berry pick over leaves and beads.

Cut three 18" pieces of lace ribbon, shape *(do not tie)* each into a bow with three 2" loops *(see illustration).* Glue one to back of each berry pick.

Glue layers together at center.

Tack or glue doll to the left side of the wreath at all contact points and glue gypsophila to the right side as shown in photo; glue assembled berry picks over gypsophila.

For **Hangers,** tack the plastic rings to the back of the Wreath 4" on each side of the center point. ❧

Dolly Dreams Pajama Bag

Design by Virginia Zartman

Finished Size: Fits an 8" pillow doll.

Materials:
- Worsted yarn:
    - 20 oz. lavender
    - 9 oz. white
- 36" lavender $\frac{1}{4}$" ribbon
- 30" white $\frac{5}{8}$" ribbon
- Three lavender rosebuds
- 8" pillow doll
- Craft glue
- Tapestry needle
- G hook or hook needed to obtain gauge

Gauge: 7 sts = 2"; 3 dc rows = $1\frac{3}{4}$".

Basic Stitches: Ch, sl st, sc, hdc, dc, tr.

Continued on page 20

Dolly Dreams Pajama Bag

Continued from page 19

DRESS

Bodice

Row 1: Starting at waist, with lavender, ch 28, sc in second ch from hook and in each ch across, turn. *(27 sc made)*

Row 2: (Ch 2, hdc) in first st, hdc in each st across to last st, 2 hdc in last st, turn. *(29)*

Rows 3–4: Ch 2, hdc in each st across, turn.

Row 5: Ch 2, hdc in next 5 sts; for **armhole**, ch 6, skip next 3 sts; hdc in next 11 sts; for **armhole**, ch 6, skip next 3 sts; hdc in last 6 sts, turn. *(23 hdc, 12 chs)*

Row 6: Ch 1, sc in each st and in each ch across, turn. *(35 sc)*

Row 7: Ch 1, sc in each st across, turn.

Row 8: Ch 1, sc in first st, (sc next 2 sts tog) across, turn. *(18)*

Row 9: Ch 1, sc in each st across, turn. Fasten off.

Row 10: Join white with sl st in first st, (ch 2, sl st) in each st across. Fasten off.

Sleeve

Rnd 1: Join lavender with sl st in second skipped st on one armhole, ch 3, sl st in next st, ch 3, sl st in side of st on row 5, ch 3, sl st in next ch, ch 3, (skip next ch, sl st in next ch, ch 3) 2 times, skip next ch, sl st in side of st on row 5, ch 3, sl st in next skipped st, ch 1, join with hdc in first sl st. *(8 ch sps made)*

Rnds 2–6: Ch 3, (sl st in next ch sp, ch 3) around ending with ch 1, hdc in first ch of first ch-3.

Rnd 7: Ch 1, sc in first ch sp, sc in each ch sp around, join with sl st in first sc.

Rnd 8: Ch 3, (sl st in next st, ch 3) around, join with sl st in first ch of first ch-3. Fasten off.

Rnd 9: Join white with sc in any ch sp, (ch 2, sc, ch 2, sc, ch 2) in same ch sp, (sc, ch 2, sc, ch 2, sc, ch 2) in each ch sp around, join with sl st in first sc. Fasten off.

Repeat on other armhole.

Lace Front

Row 1: With white, ch 7, sc in second ch from hook and in each ch across with 3 sc in last ch; working in remaining lps on opposite side of starting ch, sc in next 5 chs, turn. *(13 sc made)*

Row 2: Ch 1, sc in next 5 sts, 2 sc in each of next 3 sts, sc in next 5 sts, turn. *(16)*

Rnd 3: Working in rnds, (ch 5, sl st) in **front lp** *(see Stitch Guide)* of each st around; work 3 sc evenly spaced across ends of rows at top edge, join with sl st in first ch of first ch-5. Fasten off.

Sew to front of Bodice with top edge below row 10.

Skirt

Row 1: With right side facing you, working in remaining lps on opposite side of starting ch on Bodice, join lavender with sl st in first ch, sl st in each ch across, turn. *(27 sl sts made)*

Row 2: Working in **back lps**, (ch 3, dc) in first st, (3 dc in next st, 2 dc in next st) across, turn. *(67 dc made)*

Row 3: Ch 3, dc in each st across, turn.

Row 4: Ch 3, dc in each of next 2 sts, (2 dc in next st, dc in next st) across to last 2 sts, dc in each of last 2 sts, turn. *(98)*

Rnd 5: Working in rnds, ch 3, dc in each st around, join with sl st in top of ch-3.

Rnd 6: Ch 3, dc in next 8 sts, 2 dc in next st, (dc in next 9 sts, 2 dc in next st) 8 times, dc in next 7 sts, 2 dc in last st, join. *(108)*

Rnds 7–12: Ch 3, dc in each st around, join.

Rnd 13: Working this rnd in **back lps**, ch 3, dc in each st around, join.

Rnds 14–17: Ch 3, dc in each st around, join.

Rnd 18: Working this rnd in **back lps**, ch 3, dc in each st around, join.

Rnds 19–23: Ch 3, dc in each st around, join. At end of last rnd, fasten off.

First Ruffle

Rnd 1: Working in **front lps** of rnd 12 on Skirt, join lavender with sl st in first st, ch 5, skip next st, (sl st in next st, ch 5, skip next st) around, ch 2, join with dc in first sl st. *(54 ch sps made)*

Rnds 2–5: (Ch 5, sl st in next ch sp) around, ch 2, join with dc in first ch of first ch-5. At end of last rnd, fasten off.

Rnd 6: Join white with sc in any ch sp, (ch 2, sc, ch 2, sc, ch 2) in same ch sp, (sc, ch 2, sc, ch 2, sc, ch 2) in each ch sp around, join with sl st in first sc. Fasten off.

For **Second Ruffle**, repeat First Ruffle in **front lps** of rnd 17 on Skirt.

HAT

Rnd 1: With lavender, ch 3, 14 dc in third ch from hook, join with sl st in top of ch-3. *(15 dc made)*

Rnds 2–3: (Ch 3, dc) in first st, 2 dc in each st around, join. *(30, 60)*

Rnd 4: Working in **back lps**, ch 3, dc in each st around, join.

Rnd 5: (Ch 4, tr) in first st, tr in next st, (2 tr in next st, tr in next st) around, join with sl st in top of ch-4. *(90 tr)*

Rnd 6: Ch 4, tr in each st around, join. Fasten off.

Rnd 7: Join white with sl st in first st, ch 3, skip

Continued on page 26

Sweet Scents

**Design by
Carol Alexander**

Finished Size: Fits approximately 9¾" tall doll.

Materials:
- Sport yarn:
    2½ oz. med. purple
    2½ oz. lt. purple
- 9¾" tall doll
- 1¾ yds. of ⅜" satin ribbon
- Ribbon roses:
    Two medium
    One small
- 4½" of ¾" gathered lace
- 2½" × 4" tulle
- Seven size 4/0 snaps
- Small amount dried potpourri
- Craft glue
- Sewing needle and thread
- C hook or hook needed to obtain gauge

Gauge: 5 sts = 1"; 2 dc rows = 1".

Basic Stitches: Ch, sl st, sc, hdc, dc.
Continued on page 22

Sweet Scents

Continued from page 21

DRESS

Row 1: Starting at neck, with lt. purple, ch 17, sc in each of second ch from hook, sc in each of next 2 chs, 2 sc in next ch, sc in each of next 3 chs, 2 sc in each of next 2 chs, sc in each of next 3 chs, 2 sc in next ch, sc in each of last 3 chs, turn. *(20 sc made)*

Row 2: Ch 1, sc in each st across, turn.

Row 3: Ch 1, sc in each of first 2 sts, (2 sc in next st, sc in next st) 4 times, (sc in next st, 2 sc in next st) 4 times, sc in each of last 2 sts, turn. *(28)*

Row 4: Ch 1, sc in each of first 2 sts, 2 sc in next st, sc in next st; for **armhole opening,** ch 5, skip next 5 sts; (sc in each of next 3 sts, 2 sc in next st) 2 times, sc in each of next 2 sts; for **armhole opening,** ch 5, skip next 5 sts; sc in next st, 2 sc in next st, sc in each of last 2 sts, turn. *(22 sc, 10 chs)*

Row 5: Ch 2 *(counts as first hdc),* hdc in next st, hdc next 2 sts tog, hdc in next st, sc in next 5 chs, (sc in each of next 3 sts, sc next 2 sts tog) 2 times, sc in each of next 2 sts, sc in next 5 chs, hdc in next st, hdc next 2 sts tog, hdc in each of last 2 sts, turn. *(28 sts)*

Row 6: Ch 1, sc in each of first 2 sts, (sc next 2 sts tog, sc in next st) 8 times, sc in each of last 2 sts, turn. *(20)*

Row 7: Ch 1, sc in each of first 3 sts, (sc next 2 sts tog, sc in each of next 2 sts) 4 times, sc in last st, turn. *(16)*

Rows 8–9: Ch 1, sc in each st across, turn.

Rnd 10: Working in rnds, ch 1, sc in each st around, join with sl st in first sc.

Rnd 11: For **underskirt,** working this rnd in **back lps** *(see Stitch Guide),* ch 3 *(counts as first dc),* dc in next st, 2 dc in each of next 12 sts, dc in each of last 2 sts, join with sl st in top of ch-3. *(28 dc)*

Rnd 12: Ch 3, dc in each st around, join.

Rnd 13: Ch 3, 2 dc in next st, (dc in next st, 2 dc in next st) around, join. *(42)*

Rnd 14: Ch 3, dc in each st around, join.

Rnd 15: Ch 3, dc in each st around, join with sl st in **back lp** at top of ch-3.

Rnd 16: Working this rnd in **back lps,** ch 3, dc in next st, 2 dc in next st, (dc in each of next 2 sts, 2 dc in next st) around, join with sl st in top of ch-3. *(56)*

Rnds 17–18: Ch 3, dc in each st around, join.

Rnd 19: Ch 3, dc in each of next 2 sts, 2 dc in next st, (dc in each of next 3 sts, 2 dc in next st) around, join. *(70)*

Rnds 20–21: Ch 3, dc in each st around, join. At end of last rnd, fasten off.

Top Ruffle

Rnd 1: Working in **front lps,** join lt. purple with sc in first st on rnd 10 of Dress, 3 sc in same st, 3 sc in next st, (4 sc in next st, 3 sc in next st) 7 times, join with sl st in first sc. *(56 sc made)*

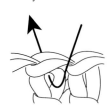

Rnd 2: Ch 5, skip next st, (sc in next st, ch 3, skip next st) around, join with sl st in second ch of ch-5. *(First 2 chs of ch-5 count as first sc—28 sts, 28 ch sps.)*

Rnd 3: Ch 5, sc in center ch of first ch sp, ch 2, (dc in center of next sc—*see illustration,* ch 2, sc in center ch of next ch sp, ch 2) around, join with sl st in third ch of ch-5. *(First 3 chs of ch-5 count as first dc—56 sts, 56 ch sps.)*

Rnd 4: Working in **dc sts only,** ch 6, (dc in center of next st, ch 3) around, join with sl st in third ch of ch-6. *(First 3 chs of ch-6 count as first dc—28 dc, 28 ch sps.)*

Rnd 5: Ch 5, sc in center ch of first ch sp, ch 2, (dc in center of next st, ch 2, sc in center ch of next ch sp) around, join with sl st in third ch of ch-5. *(56 sts, 56 ch sps)*

Rnd 6: Working in **dc sts only,** ch 6, (dc in center of next st, ch 3) around, join with sl st in third ch of ch-6. Fasten off. *(28 dc, 28 ch sps)*

Rnd 7: Working in **ch sps only,** join med. purple with sc in first ch sp, (ch 2, sc in same ch sp) 4 times, (ch 2, sc) 5 times in each ch sp around, ch 2, join with sl st in first sc.

Rnd 8: (Sl st, ch 4) in first ch sp, (sc in next ch sp, ch 3) around, join with sl st in first ch of ch-4.

Rnd 9: Ch 4, sc in first ch sp, ch 3, *(sc, ch 3, sc) in next ch sp, ch 3; repeat from * around, join with sl st in first ch of ch-4. Fasten off.

Bottom Ruffle

Rnd 1: Working in **front lps** of rnd 15 on Dress, join lt. purple with sc in first st, 4 sc in same st, 3 sc in each st around, join with sl st in first sc. *(128 sc made)*

Rnd 2: Ch 5, skip next st, (sc in next st, ch 3, skip next st) around, join with sl st in second ch of ch-5. *(64 sc, 64 ch sps)*

Rnd 3: Ch 5, sc in center ch of first ch sp, ch 2, (dc in center of next st, ch 2, sc in center ch of next ch sp, ch 2) around, join with sl st in third ch of ch-5. *(128 sts, 128 ch sps)*

Rnd 4: Working in **dc sts only,** ch 6, (dc in center of next st, ch 3) around, join with sl st in third ch of ch-6. *(64 dc, 64 ch sps)*

Rnd 5: Ch 5, sc in center ch of first ch sp, ch 2, (dc in center of next st, ch 2, sc in center ch of next ch sp) around, join with sl st in third ch of ch-5. *(128 sts, 128 ch sps)*

Rnd 6: Working in **dc sts only,** ch 6, (dc in center of next st, ch 3) around, join with sl st in third ch of ch-6. Fasten off.

Rnd 7: Working in **ch sps only,** join med. purple with sc in first ch sp, (ch 2, sc in same ch sp) 4 times, (ch 2, sc) 5 times in each ch sp around, ch 2, join with sl st in first sc.

Rnd 8: (Sl st, ch 4) in first ch sp, (sc in next ch sp, ch 3) around, join with sl st in first ch of ch-4.

Rnd 9: (Ch 4, sc) in first ch sp, ch 3, *(sc, ch 3, sc) in next ch sp, ch 3; repeat from * around, join with sl st in first ch of ch-4. Fasten off.

Sleeve

Rnd 1: Working around one armhole opening in remaining lps of ch-5 on row 4 and in sts and in ends of rows, join med. purple with sc in first ch, (ch 2, sc) in same ch, ch 2, (sc, ch 2, sc, ch 2) in each of next 4 chs, (sc, ch 2, sc, ch 2) in each of next 2 rows, (sc, ch 2, sc, ch 2) in each of next 5 unworked sts on row 3, (sc, ch 2, sc, ch 2) in each of last 2 rows, join with sl st in first sc. *(28 sc, 28 ch sps made)*

Rnds 2–3: (Sl st, ch 4) in first ch sp, (sc in next ch sp, ch 3) around, join with sl st in first ch of ch-4. At end of last rnd, fasten off.

Repeat on other armhole opening.

Finishing

For **back placket,** with left side of Dress facing you, join lt. purple with sc in end of row 10, sc in end of each row. Fasten off.

With sewing needle and thread, sew three snaps evenly spaced down back opening of Dress.

For **potpourri cover,** cut tulle according to cutting illustration. Glue gathered lace ribbon across bottom of tulle.

Sew or glue top of tulle over rnd 16 centered on front of Dress, sew or glue sides to Dress. Sew four snaps evenly spaced across bottom of tulle and on bottom of Dress. Place potpourri inside cover.

With sewing needle and thread, tack last rnds on top and bottom ruffles together at center front of Dress at potpourri cover, forming a "V" shape *(see photo).*

Cut 12" from ribbon, tie in bow.

Glue one med. ribbon rose to center of bow, glue bow to bottom ruffle where ruffles are tacked together.

Glue small ribbon rose to center front of Dress over rows 1 and 2. Place Dress on doll.

For **sleeve cap,** cut two pieces from ribbon each 8" long; tie one 8" piece through two ch sps on rnd 3 of one Sleeve above one arm *(see Sleeve Illustration).* Repeat on other Sleeve.

HAT

NOTE: *Work in continuous rnds, do not join or turn unless otherwise stated. Mark first st of each rnd.*

Rnd 1: Starting at crown, with lt. purple, ch 2, 6 sc in second ch from hook. *(6 sc made)*

Rnd 2: 2 sc in each st around. *(12)*

Rnd 3: (Sc in next st, 2 sc in next st) around. *(18)*

Rnd 4: (Sc in each of next 2 sts, 2 sc in next st) around. *(24)*

Rnd 5: (Sc in each of next 3 sts, 2 sc in next st) around. *(30)*

Rnds 6–7: Sc in each st around.

Rnd 8: (Sc in next 8 sts, sc next 2 sts tog) around, join with sl st in first sc. Fasten off. *(27)*

Rnd 9: Working this rnd in **front lps,** join med. purple with sl st in first st, (ch 3, sc, ch 2) in same st, (sc, ch 2, sc, ch 2) in each st around, join with sl st in first ch of ch-3.

Rnds 10–11: (Sl st, ch 4) in first ch sp, (sc in next ch sp, ch 3) around, join with sl st in first ch of ch-4. At end of last rnd, fasten off.

Cut 13" from ribbon, tie in bow. Glue med. ribbon rose to center of bow. Glue bow to center top of crown on Hat.

Tie remaining ribbon in bow around waist. ❧

SLEEVE ILLUSTRATION

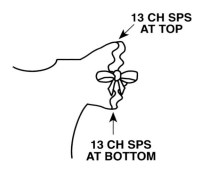

13 CH SPS AT TOP

13 CH SPS AT BOTTOM

TULLE CUTTING ILLUSTRATION

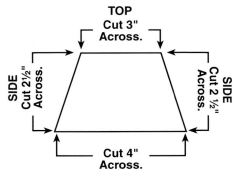

TOP
Cut 3" Across.

SIDE Cut 2½" Across.

SIDE Cut 2½" Across.

Cut 4" Across.

Trinket Box Debutante

Design by Virginia Zartman

Finished Size
Approximately 14" tall.

Materials:
- Worsted yarn:
    12 oz. yellow
    2 oz. blue
- 28" blue ¼" ribbon
- 10" square piece heavy cardboard
- One gallon plastic bleach jug
- Felt-tip marker
- 11½" fashion doll (*remove legs*)
- Craft glue
- Yellow sewing thread
- Sewing and tapestry needles
- Polyester fiberfill
- E and G hooks or hooks needed to obtain gauge

Gauges: G hook, 4 sc = 1"; 4 sc rows = 1".

Basic Stitches: Sl st, ch, sc, hdc, dc, tr.

LID

Lid Top

Row 1: Starting at bodice, with E hook and yellow, ch 15, sc in second ch from hook, sc in last 13 chs, turn. *(14 sc made—front of row 1 is right side of work.)*

Row 2: Ch 1, 2 sc in first st, sc in next 12 sts, 2 sc in last st, turn. *(16)*

Row 3: Ch 1, sc in first 4 sts, 2 sc in next st, sc in next 6 sts, 2 sc in next st, sc in last 4 sts, turn. *(18)*

Row 4: Ch 1, sc in first 6 sts, 2 sc in next st, sc in next 4 sts, 2 sc in next st, sc in last 6 sts, turn. *(20)*

Row 5: Ch 1, sc in first 6 sts, (2 sc in next st, sc in next 6 sts) 2 times, turn. *(22)*

Row 6: Ch 1, sc in first 6 sts, hdc in next st, 2 dc in each of next 8 sts, hdc in next st, sc in last 6 sts, turn. *(30 sts)*

Row 7: Working in **front lps** *(see Stitch Guide)*, ch 1, sc in first 7 sts, (sc next 2 sts tog) 8 times, sc in last 7 sts, turn. *(22)*

Row 8: Ch 1, sc in first 5 sts; for **armhole**, ch 8, skip next 2 sts; sc in next 8 sts; for **armhole**, ch 8, skip next 2 sts; sc in last 5 sts, turn. Fasten off. *(34 sts and chs)*

Row 9: Working in **back lps**, join blue with sl st in first st, (ch 3, dc) in same st, 2 dc in each st and in each ch across, turn. *(68 dc)*

Row 10: (Ch 3, skip next 2 sts, sl st in next st) across leaving last st unworked. Fasten off. *(22 ch sps)*

Rnd 11: For **skirt**, working in rnds, with G hook and right side facing you, working in remaining lps on opposite side of starting ch on row 1 of Bodice, join yellow with sl st in first st, sl st in each st around, join with sl st in first sl st. *(14 sl sts)*

Rnd 12: (Ch 3, 2 dc) in first st, 3 dc in each st around, join with sl st in top of ch-3. *(42 dc)*

Rnd 13: Ch 3, dc in each st around, join.

Rnd 14: Ch 3, 2 dc in next st, (dc in next st, 2 dc in next st) around, join. *(63)*

Rnd 15: (Ch 3, dc) in first st, dc in each of next 2 sts, (2 dc in next st, dc in each of next 2 sts) around, join. *(84)*

Rnd 16: Working in **front lps**, (ch 4, tr) in first st, 2 tr in each st around, join with sl st in top of ch-4. *(168)*

Rnd 17: Working in **back lps**, ch 4, tr in each st around, join. Fasten off.

Rnd 18: With E hook, join blue with sl st in first st, ch 3, skip next st, (sl st in next st, ch 3, skip next st) around, join with sl st in first ch of ch-3. Fasten off. *(84 ch sps)*

Rnd 19: Working in remaining **front lps** of rnd 16, with E hook, join blue with sl st in any st, ch 3, skip next st, (sl st in next st, ch 3, skip next st) around, join. Fasten off.

Lid Bottom

Rnd 1: With G hook and yellow, ch 3, 13 dc in third ch from hook, join with sl st in top of ch-3. *(14 dc made)*

Rnd 2: (Ch 2, hdc) in first st, 2 hdc in each st around, join with sl st in top of ch-2. *(28 hdc)*

Rnd 3: Ch 2, 2 hdc in next st, (hdc in next st, 2 hdc in next st) around, join. *(42)*

Rnd 4: Ch 2, hdc in next st, 2 hdc in next st, (hdc in each of next 2 sts, 2 hdc in next st) around, join. *(56)*

Rnd 5: Ch 2, hdc in each of next 2 sts, 2 hdc in next st, (hdc in each of next 3 sts, 2 hdc in next st) around, join. *(70)*

Rnd 6: Ch 3, dc in each of next 3 sts, 2 dc in next st, (dc in next 4 sts, 2 dc in next st) around, join. Fasten off. *(84 dc)*

Lid Assembly

Using Lid Bottom as pattern piece, cut circle from cardboard. Place doll in dress. Stuff skirt around doll; cover stuffing with cardboard circle and cover circle with crocheted Lid Bottom piece. Working through both thicknesses of Lid Top and Bottom in **back lps** only, with G hook, sl st in each st around, join with sl st in first sl st. Fasten off.

With tapestry needle and yarn, sew back opening of dress closed.

HAT

Rnd 1: With E hook and yellow, ch 3, 11 dc in third ch from hook, join with sl st in top of ch-3. *(12 dc made)*

Rnd 2: (Ch 3, dc) in first st, 2 dc in each st around, join. *(24)*

Continued on page 26

Continued from page 25

Rnd 3: Working in **back lps,** (ch 4, 2 tr) in first st, 3 tr in each st around, join with sl st in top of ch-4. Fasten off. *(72 tr)*

Rnd 4: Join blue with sl st in first st, ch 3, skip next st, (sl st in next st, ch 3, skip next st) around, join with sl st in first ch of ch-3. Fasten off. *(36 ch sps)*

Cut 8" piece ribbon, tie in small bow. With sewing thread and needle, sew bow to center of Hat.

Glue Hat at an angle to top of doll's head.

Tie remaining ribbon around waist with bow in front.

BOTTOM

Thoroughly clean bleach jug to avoid discoloring yarn. Measuring 5½" up from bottom of bleach jug, mark around jug with felt-tip marker. Cut jug around marked line. Set aside.

Outside

Rnd 1: With G hook and yellow, ch 3, 12 dc in third ch from hook, join with sl st in top of ch-3. *(13 dc made)*

Rnd 2: (Ch 3, dc) in first st, 2 dc in each st around, join. *(26)*

Rnd 3: Ch 3, 2 dc in next st, (dc in next st, 2 dc in next st) around, join. *(39)*

Rnd 4: Ch 3, (dc in next st, 2 dc in next st) around, join. *(58)*

Rnd 5: Ch 1, sc in each of first 2 sts, (2 sc in next st, sc in each of next 3 sts) around, join with sl st in first sc. *(72 sc)*

Rnds 6–14: Working these rnds in **back lps,** ch 3, dc in each st around, join. At end of last rnd, fasten off.

Inside

Rnds 1–5: Repeat rnds 1–5 of Outside.

Rnds 6–14: Ch 3, dc in each st around, join.

Rnd 15: Holding Outside and Inside pieces with wrong sides together and cut jug bottom between, working through **back lps** of both thicknesses, sl st in each st around, join with sl st in first sl st. Fasten off.

Ruffle

Rnd 1: Working in remaining **front lps** of rnd 13 on Outside, with G hook and Inside facing you, join yellow with sl st in any st, (ch 3, sl st in next st) around, ch 1, join with hdc in first ch of first ch-3. *(72 ch sps)*

Rnds 2–9: Ch 1, sc around joining hdc, (ch 3, sl st in next ch sp) around, ch 1, join with hdc in first sc.

Rnd 10: Ch 1, 2 sc around joining hdc, 2 sc in each ch sp around, join with sl st in first sc. *(144 sc)*

Rnd 11: (Ch 4, tr) in first st, 2 tr in each st around, join with sl st in top of ch-4. *(288 tr)*

Rnd 12: Working in **back lps,** ch 4, tr in each st around, join. Fasten off.

Rnd 13: With E hook, join blue with sl st in first st, ch 3, skip next st, (sl st in next st, ch 3, skip next st) around, join with sl st in first ch of first ch-3. Fasten off. *(144 ch sps)*

Rnd 14: Working in remaining **front lps** of rnd 11, with E hook, join blue with sl st in any st, ch 3, skip next st, (sl st in next st, ch 3, skip next st) around, join. Fasten off.

Place Lid on Bottom. ❖

Dolly Dreams Pajama Bag

Continued from page 20

next st, (sl st in next st, ch 3, skip next st) around, join with sl st in first sl st. Fasten off.

Weave 30" piece of ⅝" ribbon through sts of rnd 4. Tie in bow, trim ends.

BAG

Row 1: Working in **front lps** of row 1 on Skirt, join white with sl st in first st, ch 3, dc in next st, 2 dc in next st, (2 dc in next st, 3 dc in next st) across, turn. *(64 dc made)*

Row 2: Ch 3, dc in each st across, turn.

Rnd 3: Working in rnds, ch 3, 2 dc in next st, (dc in next st, 2 dc in next st) around, join with sl st in top of ch-3. *(96)*

Rnds 4–20: Ch 3, dc in each st around, join.

Rnd 21: Ch 1, sc in first st, ch 1, skip next st, (sc in next st, ch 1, skip next st) around, join with sl st in first sc. Fasten off.

Drawstring

With white, ch 130. Fasten off. Weave through stitches on rnd 21 of Bag. Pull tight, tie ends in bow.

FINISHING

Place Dress on doll. With matching yarn, sew back opening closed.

Tie 30" piece of lavender ribbon in bow around waist.

Tie remaining lavender ribbon in bow; tack or glue bow to top of Lace Front.

Glue one rosebud to center of Lace Front below bow. Glue second rosbud ½" below first rosebud. Glue remaining rosebud to bow at waist.

Place Hat on head. ❖

Granny Buttons

Design by Vicki Owen

Finished Size:
Approximately 7" tall in a sitting position.

Materials:
- 500 yds. mauve size 10 crochet cotton thread
- 80—100 various size white buttons *(old or new)*
- Wooden 2" doll head with painted face
- Wooden 2½" × 3" × 1½" block
- Drill and ¼" drill bit
- White curly hair
- Mini doll glasses
- Four 15"-long pieces of beading wire
- 1 yd. of ⅛" satin ribbon
- Two ribbon roses with leaves
- 8" and 8¼" lengths white strung beads
- Small decorative button or earring
- Polyester fiberfill
- No. 3 steel hook or hook needed to obtain gauge

Gauge: With two strands held together, 8 dc = 1"; 3 dc rows = 1".

Basic Stitches: Ch, sl st, sc, dc.

Continued on page 28

Granny Buttons

Continued from page 27

DRESS

NOTE: Use two strands of thread held together as one throughout.

Rnd 1: Starting at neck edge, ch 26, sl st in first ch to form ring; working in **back lps** *(see Stitch Guide),* ch 3 *(counts as dc),* 2 dc in each of next 24 chs, dc in last ch, join with sl st in top of ch-3. *(50 dc made)*

Rnd 2: Ch 3, (2 dc in next st, dc in next st) around to last st, dc in last st, join. *(74)*

Rnd 3: Ch 3, dc in each st around, join.

Rnd 4: Ch 3, dc in next 14 sts; for **armhole,** ch 5, skip next 6 sts; dc in next 33 sts; for **armhole,** ch 5, skip next 6 sts; dc in last 14 sts, join. *(62 dc, 10 chs)*

Rnd 5: Ch 3, dc in each dc and in each ch around, join. *(72 dc)*

Rnd 6: Ch 3, dc in next 4 sts, skip next st, (dc in next 5 sts, skip next st) around, join. *(60)*

Rnd 7: (Ch 3, 2 dc) in first st, 3 dc in each st around, join. *(180)*

Rnds 8–10: Ch 3, dc in each st around, join.

Rnd 11: (Ch 3, 4 dc) in first st, skip next st, sc in next st, skip next st, *5 dc in next st, skip next st, sc in next st, skip next st; repeat from * around, join. Fasten off.

Neck Trim

With neck edge facing you, working in remaining lps on opposite side of starting ch on rnd 1 of Dress, join with sl st in any st at center back, (ch 3, 4 dc) in same st as sl st, skip next st, *sc in next st, skip next st, 5 dc in next st, skip next st; repeat from * around, join with sl st in top of ch-3. Fasten off.

Sleeve

Rnd 1: Working in chs, in sts and in ends of rows around armhole, join with sl st in center ch of ch-5 at underarm, ch 3; evenly space 17 dc

around armhole, join with sl st in top of ch-3. *(18 dc made)*

Rnd 2: Ch 3, dc in each st around, join.

Rnd 3: Ch 1, sc in each st around, join with sl st in first sc. Fasten off.

Repeat on other armhole.

HAT

Rnd 1: Ch 4, 15 dc in fourth ch from hook, join with sl st in top of ch-4. *(16 dc made)*

Rnd 2: Ch 3, dc in each st around, join with sl st in top of ch-3.

Rnds 3–6: Ch 3, 2 dc in next st, (dc in next st, 2 dc in next st) around, join. *(24, 36, 54, 81)*

Rnd 7: Ch 3, dc in next st, skip next st, (dc in each of next 2 sts, skip next st) around, join. *(54)*

Rnd 8: (Ch 3, 4 dc) in first st, skip next st, *sc in next st, skip next st, 5 dc in next st, skip next st; repeat from * around, join. Fasten off.

FINISHING

Cut ribbon in half. Weave one ribbon piece through sts on rnd 7 of Hat; tighten slightly and stuff Hat with fiberfill. Tighten rnd to fit on top of Head and tie ends in bow at back of Hat. Glue one ribbon rose to center of bow.

Using drill and drill bit, drill holes through wooden block according to illustration for Legs and Arms.

With beading wire, thread 20–25 various size buttons on each wire to equal a 3" strand for each Arm and Leg.

Attach Arms and Legs to block through drilled holes by running wire through holes and twisting tightly to secure. Set block aside.

Place Dress on wooden Body. Weave remaining ribbon through sts on row 6 of Dress starting at right front; tighten slightly and tie ends in bow. Glue ribbon rose to center of bow.

Place strung beads around neck and dab a small amount of glue at back to hold in place.

Glue remaining parts in the following order: Decorative button or earring to center front on rnd 1 of Dress; head onto wooden doll Body; glasses on face; several small sections of white curly hair onto head; Hat on top of hair. ❣

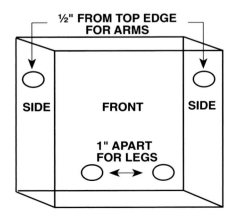

½" FROM TOP EDGE FOR ARMS

SIDE FRONT SIDE

1" APART FOR LEGS

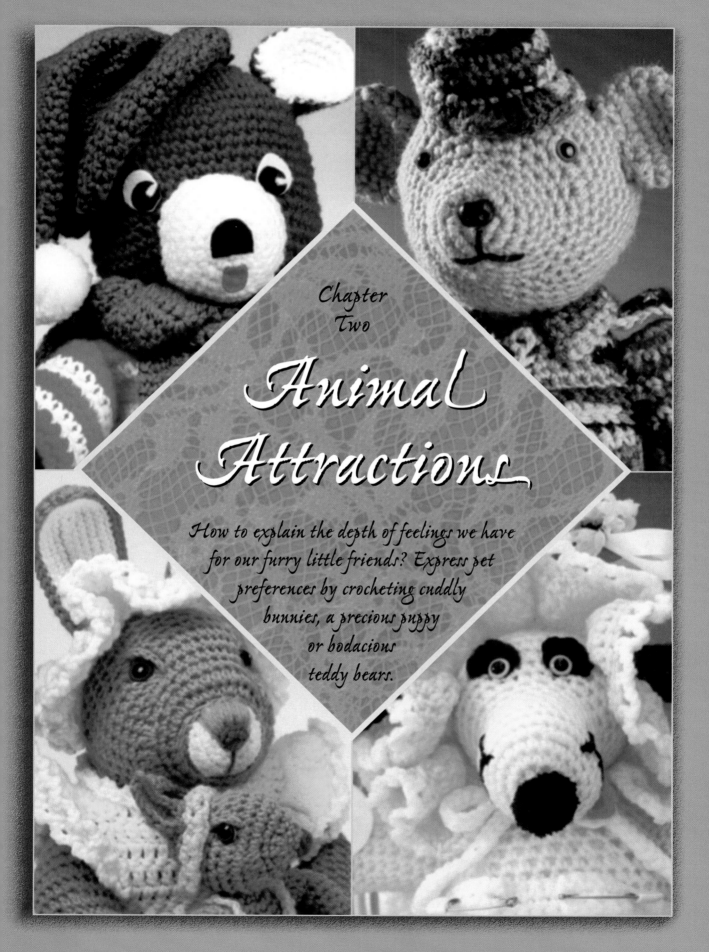

Chapter
Two

Animal
Attractions

How to explain the depth of feelings we have
for our furry little friends? Express pet
preferences by crocheting cuddly
bunnies, a precious puppy
or bodacious
teddy bears.

Little Orphan Arf Arf

Design by Mae Meats

Finished Size: Orphan is 7½" tall sitting without Bonnet. Basket holds six 2-oz. bottles of baby toiletries or 4"-tall toys.

Materials:
- Worsted yarn:
  - 10 oz. white
  - 7 oz. pink
  - 4 oz. off-white
  - 2 oz. brown
  - small amount each black and red
- Basket 6" diameter on bottom × 14" tall × 4" deep
- 2½" × 3" music box
- 9 yds. pink ¼" satin ribbon
- 4 yds. white ½" satin ribbon
- 24" of ¼" elastic
- Small bunch of silk flowers
- 6" square of white and scrap of pink felt
- Two 12-mm. animal eyes with washers
- Two ⅜" buttons
- Pacifier
- Five diaper pins
- Pink and white sewing thread
- Polyester fiberfill
- Craft glue
- 1" × 6" cardboard
- Sewing and tapestry needles
- H hook or hook needed to obtain gauge

Gauge: 7 sc = 2"; 7 sc rows = 2". 7 dc = 2"; 3 dc rows = 2".

Basic Stitches: Ch, sl st, sc, hdc, dc, tr.

ORPHAN

Eye Patch (make 2)
With brown, ch 2, (sc, 2 dc, sc) in second ch from hook. Leaving 6" for sewing, fasten off.

Body
NOTE: *Do not join rnds unless otherwise stated. Mark first st of each rnd.*

Rnd 1: Starting at bottom, with off-white, ch 2, 10 sc in second ch from hook. *(10 sc made)*
Rnd 2: 2 sc in each st around. *(20)*
Rnd 3: Sc in each st around.
Rnd 4: 2 sc in each st around. *(40)*
Rnds 5–10: Sc in each st around.
Rnd 11: (Sc next 2 sts tog, sc in next 8 sts) around. *(36)*
Rnd 12: (Sc next 2 sts tog, sc in next 4 sts) around. *(30)*
Rnds 13–14: Sc in each st around.
Rnd 15: Repeat rnd 11. *(27)*
Rnd 16: (Sc next 2 sts tog, sc in next 7 sts) around. *(24)*
Rnd 17: (Sc next 2 sts tog, sc in next st) around. *(16)* Stuff.
Rnds 18–19: (Sc next 2 sts tog) around. At end of last rnd, join with sl st in first sc. Fasten off. *(4)* Sew opening closed.

Head
Rnds 1–3: Starting at nose, repeat rnds 1–3 of Body.
Rnd 4: (2 sc in next st, sc in next st) around. *(30)*
Rnds 5–7: Sc in each st around.
Rnd 8: (Sc next 2 sts tog, sc in next st) around. *(20)*
Rnds 9–11: Sc in each st around.
Rnds 12–15: Repeat rnds 4 and 5 alternately. *(At end of last rnd, 45.)*
Rnd 16: (Sc next 2 sts tog, sc in next 7 sts) around. *(40)*
Rnds 17–18: Sc in each st around.
Rnd 19: (Sc next 2 sts tog, sc in next 8 sts) around. *(36)*
For **each eye,** place stem through second ch of Eye Patch; attach eyes with washers to rnd 13 with four sts between. Sew Eye Patches to Head as shown in photo.
For **nose,** wrap brown around 1" cardboard 60 times; slide loops off cardboard, tie separate 6" strand brown around center of all loops; cut loops. Trim ends. Sew to rnd 1.
Rnd 20: (Sc next 2 sts tog, sc in next 4 sts) around. *(30)* Stuff.
Rnd 21: (Sc next 2 sts tog) around. *(15)*
Rnd 22: Sc in first st, (sc next 2 sts tog) around. *(8)*
Rnd 23: (Sc in each of next 2 sts, sc next 2 sts tog) around, join with sl st in first sc. *(6)* Leaving 6" for sewing, fasten off. Stuff. Sew opening closed.

Sew rnds 13–17 to rnds 18–19 of Body.

With black, using outline stitch *(see Stitch Guide)*, embroider 5"-wide mouth over rnd 6 of Head. Embroider end of mouth over rnds

Continued on page 32

Continued from page 31

5–7 on each side.

For **tongue,** with red, ch 2, (sc, 2 dc, sc) in second ch from hook. Leaving 6" for sewing, fasten off. Sew to one side of mouth.

Ear (make 2)

Rnd 1: With brown, ch 11, sc in second ch from hook, sc in next 5 chs, hdc in next ch, dc in each of next 2 chs, 6 dc in last ch; working in remaining lps on opposite side of starting ch, dc in each of next 2 chs, hdc in next ch, sc in next 5 chs, 2 sc in last ch, join with sl st in first sc. *(25 sts made)*

Rnd 2: Ch 1, sc in first 10 sts, 2 sc in each of next 4 sts, sc in next 10 sts, 2 sc in last st, join. Fasten off. *(30)*

Sew Ears ¼" below eyes over rnds 15–18 on each side of Head.

Arm (make 2)

Rnd 1: With off-white, ch 2, 6 sc in second ch from hook. *(6 sc made)*

Rnd 2: 2 sc in each st around. *(12)*

Rnds 3–4: Sc in each st around.

Rnd 5: For **thumb,** 4 dc in first st, drop lp from hook, insert hook in top of first dc of group, pull dropped lp through st, ch 1, sc in last 11 sts.

Rnd 6: Sc in each st around. *(12)*

Rnd 7: Sc in each of first 3 sts, 2 sc in next st, sc in next 5 sts, 2 sc in next st, sc in each of last 2 sts. *(14)*

Rnds 8–13: Sc in each st around. At end of last rnd, join with sl st in first sc. Fasten off. Stuff.

Sew Arms over rnds 10–15 on each side of Body with thumbs pointing up.

Leg (make 2)

Rnds 1–2: Starting at foot, with off-white, repeat rnds 1–2 of Ear. At end of last rnd, **do not fasten off.**

Rnd 3: Ch 1, sc in first 12 sts, 2 sc in next st, sc in each of next 2 sts, 2 sc in next st, sc in next 12 sts, 2 sc in next st, sc in last st, join. *(33)*

Rnd 4: Working this rnd in **back lps** *(see Stitch Guide)*, ch 1, sc in each st around, join.

Rnd 5: Ch 1, sc in each st around, join.

Rnd 6: Ch 1, sc in first 11 sts; for **top of foot,** (dc next 2 sts tog) 4 times; sc in last 14 sts, join. *(29 sts)*

Rnd 7: Ch 1, sc in first 9 sts, (dc next 2 sts tog) 4 times, sc in last 12 sts, join. *(25)*

Rnd 8: Ch 1, sc in first 7 sts, (sc next 2 sts tog) 4 times, sc in last 10 sts, join. *(21)*

Rnd 9: Ch 1, sc in first 5 sts, (sc next 2 sts tog) 4 times, sc in last 8 sts, join. *(17)*

Rnds 10–13: Repeat rnd 5. Stuff.

Rnd 14: Ch 1, sc in each of first 3 sts, sc next 2 sts tog, sc in next 7 sts, sc next 2 sts tog, sc in each of last 3 sts, join. *(15)*

Rnd 15: Repeat rnd 5.

Rnd 16: Ch 1, sc in each of first 3 sts, (sc next 2 sts tog, sc in each of next 2 sts) 3 times, join. Fasten off. *(12)* Stuff.

Sew Legs 1" apart over rnds 5–8 on front of Body with foot tilting slightly outward.

For **paw pads,** cut circles from pink felt according to pattern pieces. Glue or sew to bottom of Arms and Legs according to diagrams.

PAW PADS

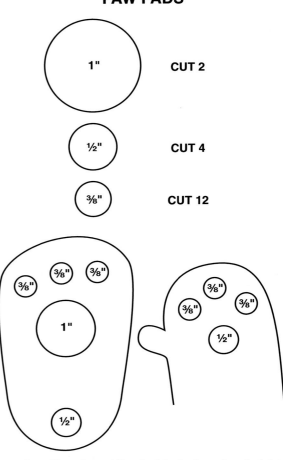

Sew handle of pacifier behind thumb of right Arm. Cut 16" pink ribbon, tie in bow. Sew to handle.

Tail

Rnd 1: With off-white, ch 2, 4 sc in second ch from hook. *(4 sc made)*

Rnds 2–4: Sc in each st around.

Rnd 5: (2 sc in next st, sc in next st) around. *(6)*

Rnds 6–8: Repeat rnd 2. At end of last rnd, join with sl st in first sc. Fasten off. Stuff.

Sew over rnds 7–8 on center back of Body.

BONNET

Rnds 1–3: With pink, repeat rnds 1–3 of Body.

Rnd 4: Sc in first 5 sts, 2 sc in each of last 15 sts. *(35)*

Rnd 5: Sc in each st around, join with sl st in first st, **turn.**

Row 6: For **brim,** working in rows, sc in first 28 sts leaving last 7 sts unworked, turn.

Row 7: Ch 4, tr in each of next 2 sts, dc in next st, hdc in next st, sc in next 18 sts, hdc in next st, dc in next st, tr in each of last 3 sts, turn. *(28 sts)*

Row 8: Ch 1, sc in first 8 sts; (for **ear opening,** ch 7, skip next 3 sts); sc in next 7 sts; repeat between ( ), sc in last 7 sts, turn. *(22 sc, 14 ch)*

Row 9: Ch 3, 3 dc in same st, 4 dc in each st and in each ch across, turn. *(144 dc)*

Rows 10–11: Ch 3, dc in each st across, turn. At end of last row, **do not turn.** Fasten off.

Rnd 12: Working in ends of rows and in sts around outer edge, with right side facing you, join white with sc in top of last dc made, 2 sc in same row, 3 sc in each of next 2 rows; *for **tie,** ch 45, sl st in fifth ch from hook, sl st in next 40 chs, sl st in last sc made*; 3 sc in next row, sc in each of next 2 rows, (sc next 2 sts tog, sc in next st) 2 times, sc in next st, sc in each of next 2 rows, 3 sc in next row; repeat between first and second *, 3 sc in each of next 2 rows, 2 sc in next row, sc in top of ch 3, (ch 4, skip next st, sc in next st) across, join with sl st in first sc. Fasten off.

DIAPER

Rnds 1–4: With white, repeat rnds 1–4 of Body. At end of last rnd, **turn.**

Row 5: For **back,** working in rows, ch 1, sc in first 28 sts leaving last 12 sts unworked, turn. *(28)*

Rows 6–7: Ch 1, sc in each st across, turn.

Row 8: Ch 1, sc in first 12 sts; for **tail opening,** ch 4, skip next 4 sts; sc in last 12 sts, turn. *(24 sc, 4 chs)*

Rows 9–10: Ch 7, sc in second ch from hook, sc in each ch and in each st across, turn. *(34, 40)*

Row 11: Repeat row 6.

Row 12: Ch 1, sc in first 13 sts, sl st in next st leaving last 26 sts unworked. Fasten off.

Row 5: For **front,** with right side facing you, skip next 4 sts on rnd 4, join with sc in next st, sc in each of next 3 sts leaving last 4 sts unworked, turn. *(4)*

Rows 6–8: Repeat row 6 of back.

Row 9: Ch 1, 3 sc in first st, sc in each st across with 3 sc in last st, turn. *(8)*

Row 10: Repeat row 6 of back.

Rows 11–12: Repeat row 9 of front. At end of last row, fasten off. *(16)*

With diaper pins, pin Diaper on Orphan.

SHOE (make 2)

Rnd 1: Starting at sole, with pink, ch 13, sc in

second ch from hook, sc in next 6 chs, hdc in next ch, dc in each of next 3 chs, 6 dc in last ch; working in remaining lps on opposite side of ch, dc in each of next 3 chs, hdc in next ch, sc in next 6 chs, 2 sc in last ch, join with sl st in first sc. *(29 sts made)*

Rnd 2: Ch 1, sc in first 12 sts, 2 sc in each of next 4 sts, sc in next 12 sts, 2 sc in last st, join. *(34 sc)*

Rnd 3: Ch 1, sc in first 14 sts, 2 sc in next st, sc in each of next 2 sts, 2 sc in next st, sc in next 14 sts, 2 sc in next st, sc in last st, join. *(37)*

Rnd 4: Working this rnd in **back lps,** ch 1, sc in each st around, join.

Rnd 5: Ch 1, sc in each st around, join.

Rnd 6: Ch 1, sc in first 13 sts, (dc next 2 sts tog) 4 times, sc in next 16 sts, join. *(33)*

Rnd 7: Ch 1, sc in first 11 sts, (dc next 2 sts tog) 4 times, sc in next 14 sts, join. Fasten off. *(29)*

Rnd 8: For **left Shoe,** join white with sl st in last sc made, ch 1, **reverse sc** *(see Stitch Guide)* in next 8 sts; for **strap,** ch 15, sl st in fifth ch from hook, sl st in next 10 chs, sl st in last reverse sc made, reverse sc around, join with sl st in first st. Fasten off.

Rnd 8: For **right Shoe,** join white with sl st in last sc made, ch 1, reverse sc in next 21 sts; for **strap,** ch 15, sl st in fifth ch from hook, sl st in next 10 ch, sl st in last reverse sc made, reverse sc around, join. Fasten off.

Rnd 9: For **both Shoes,** working this rnd in **front lps** of rnd 4 on sole, with sole facing you, join pink with sl st in any st, sl st in each st around, join. Fasten off.

Sew button opposite strap on each Shoe.

Continued on page 34

Continued from page 33

BASKET
Lining
Rnd 1: With pink, ch 2, 6 sc in second ch from hook. *(6 sc made)*

Rnd 2: 2 sc in each st around. *(12)*

Rnd 3: (2 sc in next st, sc in next st) around. *(18)*

Rnd 4: (2 sc in next st, sc in each of next 2 sts) around. *(24)*

Rnd 5: (2 sc in next st, sc in each of next 3 sts) around. *(30)*

Rnd 6: (2 sc in next st, sc in next 4 sts) around. *(36)*

Rnd 7: (2 sc in next st, sc in next 5 sts) around. *(42)*

Rnd 8: (2 sc in next st, sc in next 6 sts) around. *(48)*

Rnd 9: (2 sc in next st, sc in next 7 sts) around. *(54)*

Rnd 10: (2 sc in next st, sc in next 8 sts) around. *(60)*

Rnd 11: (2 sc in next st, sc in next 9 sts) around, join with sl st in first sc. Fasten off. *(66)*

Rnd 12: For **edging**, join white with sl st in any st, (ch 3, 4 dc) in same st, skip next 2 sts, *(sl st, ch 3, 4 dc) in next st, skip next 2 sts; repeat from * around, join with sl st in bottom of first ch-3. Fasten off.

Sew or glue to bottom of Basket.

Music Box
Cut white felt 1" larger than music box on all edges. Cut hole for wind-up mechanism. Folding corners, glue over box.

Cut 6" pink ribbon, tie in bow; glue to top of box.

Glue to center of Basket Lining.

Holder
Sew ends of elastic together to form ring.

Rnd 1: Working around elastic *(see Stitch Guide)*, join pink with sc, evenly space 97 sc around, join with sl st in first sc. Fasten off. *(98 sc made)*

Rnd 2: Join white with sc in any st, ch 4, skip next st, (sc in next st, ch 4, skip next st) around, join. Fasten off.

Cut six 10" pieces pink ribbon, tie each piece in bow. Tack bows evenly spaced to Holder. Tack Holder inside basket at each bow 1" from top rim.

Ruffle
Rnd 1: With white, ch to fit around top rim of basket ending with even number of chs, sl st in first ch to form ring, ch 3, 3 dc in same ch, (3 dc in next ch, 4 dc in next ch) around, join with sl st in top of ch-3.

Rnds 2–6: Or to desired length; ch 3, dc in each st around, join.

Rnd 7: Ch 5, (skip next 2 sts, sc in next st, ch 4) around, join with sl st in first ch of ch-5.

Rnd 8: Ch 5, (sc in next ch-4 lp, ch 5) around, join. Fasten off.

Divide rnd 6 into twelve equal sections. Cut one piece pink ribbon to fit each section plus 10". Weave one ribbon through sts of first section, weave second ribbon through next section, tie adjoining ends in bow. Repeat with remaining ribbons.

For **top edging**, working on opposite side of starting ch on rnd 1, repeat rnd 2 of Holder.

Wrap and glue or sew white ribbon to Handle. Tie remaining ribbon in large bow, glue or sew to top of Handle. Glue or sew silk flowers in center of bow.

Easing to fit, sew rnd 1 of Ruffle to top rim of basket.

BLANKET
Row 1: With pink, ch 33, dc in fourth ch from hook, dc in each of next 2 chs, *skip next 2 chs, (2 dc, ch 2, 2 dc) in next ch, skip next 2 chs, dc in next 4 chs; repeat from * across, turn. *(28 dc, 3 ch sps made)*

Rows 2–25: Ch 3, dc in each of next 3 sts, *skip next 2 sts, (2 dc, ch 2, 2 dc) in next ch sp, skip next 2 sts, dc in next 4 sts; repeat from * across, turn.

Row 26: Ch 3, dc in each of next 3 sts, (sc in each of next 2 sts, sc in next ch sp, sc in each of next 2 sts, dc in next 4 sts) across, **do not turn.** *(31 sts)*

Rnd 27: Working around outer edge, ch 1, 2 sc in end of each row and sc in each st around with 3 sc in each corner st, join with sl st in first sc. Fasten off. *(174)*

Rnd 28: Repeat rnd 12 of Basket Lining.

PILLOW
Side (make 2)
Rnds 1–10: Repeat rnds 1–10 of Basket Lining. At end of **first Side,** fasten off. At end of **second Side,** do not fasten off.

Rnd 11: Hold Pillow Sides with wrong sides tog; working through both thicknesses, sc in each st around stuffing before closing, join with sl st in first sc. Fasten off.

Rnd 12: Repeat rnd 12 of Basket Lining.

Tie 4" pink ribbon in bow, sew to Pillow on rnd 11. Glue silk flower to center of bow. Pin diaper pins on Pillow. ❧

Wintertime Bear

Design by Katie Morse

Instructions begin on page 36

Wintertime Bear

Finished Size: Approximately 18" tall.

Materials:
- Worsted yarn:
    - 8 oz. brown
    - 4 oz. green
    - 2 oz. red
    - 2 oz. white
- Scrap of each red, black and white felt
- 3" square cardboard
- 6" square plastic
- Polyester fiberfill
- Tapestry needle
- G hook or hook needed to obtain gauge

Gauge: 4 sc = 1"; 4 sc rows = 1".

Basic Stitches: Ch, sl st, sc, dc.

Note: Work in continuous rnds; do not join rnds unless otherwise stated. Mark first st of each rnd.

BEAR

Head

Rnd 1: Starting at top of Head, with brown, ch 2, 6 sc in second ch from hook. *(6 sc made)*

Rnd 2: 2 sc in each st around. *(12)*

Rnd 3: (Sc in next st, 2 sc in next st) around. *(18)*

Rnd 4: (Sc in each of next 2 sts, 2 sc in next st) around. *(24)*

Rnd 5: (Sc in each of next 3 sts, 2 sc in next st) around. *(30)*

Rnd 6: (Sc in next 4 sts, 2 sc in next st) around. *(36)*

Rnd 7: (Sc in next 5 sts, 2 sc in next st) around. *(42)*

Rnd 8: (Sc in next 6 sts, 2 sc in next st) around. *(48)*

Rnds 9–15: Sc in each st around.

Rnd 16: (Sc in next 4 sts, sc next 2 sts tog) around. *(40)*

Rnd 17: Sc in first st; for **cheek**, 2 sc in each of next 6 sts; sc in next 16 sts; for **cheek**, 2 sc in each of next 6 sts; for **front of Head**, sc in last 11 sts. *(52)*

Rnds 18–20: Sc in each st around.

Rnd 21: (Sc in each of next 3 sts, sc next 2 sts tog) 10 times, sc in each of last 2 sts. *(42)*

Rnd 22: (Sc in each of next 2 sts, sc next 2 sts tog) 10 times, sc in each of last 2 sts. *(32)*

Rnd 23: (Sc in each of next 2 sts, sc next 2 sts tog) around. *(24)*

Rnds 24–26: Sc in each st around. At end of last rnd, join with sl st in first sc. Fasten off. Stuff.

Muzzle

Rnds 1–6: With white, repeat rnds 1–6 of Head.

Rnd 7: Sc in each st around.

Rnd 8: Sl st in each st around, join with sl st in first sl st. Fasten off. Stuff.

Sew over rnds 14–23 on front of Head.

From felt, cut eyes, nose and tongue according to pattern pieces. Sew or glue eye pieces according to eye diagram. Sew or glue eyes over rnds 13–14 of Head above muzzle 1¾" apart. Sew or glue nose over rnds 1–3 on top of muzzle and tongue on rnd 3 on bottom of muzzle leaving tip free.

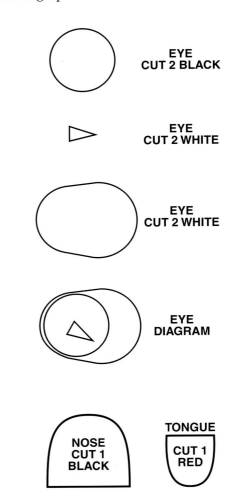

EYE
CUT 2 BLACK

EYE
CUT 2 WHITE

EYE
CUT 2 WHITE

EYE
DIAGRAM

NOSE
CUT 1
BLACK

TONGUE
CUT 1
RED

Body

Rnd 1: Starting at bottom of body, with brown, ch 40, sl st in first ch to form ring, ch 1, sc in each ch around. *(40 sc made)*

Rnds 2–21: Sc in each st around.

Rnd 22: (Sc in each of next 2 sts, sc next 2 sts tog) around. *(30)*

Rnd 23: (Sc in each of next 3 sts, sc next 2 sts tog) around, join with sl st in first sc. Fasten off. Stuff. *(24)*

Flatten rnd 1. Sew opening closed.

Sew rnd 26 of Head to rnd 23 of Body.

Ear Piece (make 2 brown, 2 white)

Rnd 1: Ch 2, 6 sc in second ch from hook. *(6 sc made)*

Rnds 2–4: Repeat rnds 2–4 of Head.

Rnd 5: Sc in each st around, join with sl st in first sc. Fasten off.

For **each Ear,** hold one brown and one white Ear Piece wrong sides together, matching sts; working in **back lps,** *(see Stitch Guide),* sew together. Cup Ear and sew over rnds 6–8 of Head 4" apart.

Mitten & Arm (make 2)

Rnds 1–2: For **Mitten,** with green, repeat rnds 1–2 of Head.

Rnds 3–7: Sc in each st around. At end of last rnd, join with sl st in first sc. Fasten off.

Rnd 8: For **Arm,** join brown with sc in first st, sc in each st around.

Rnds 9–19: Sc in each st around. Flatten rnd 7 of Mitten and sew together. Stuff Arm.

Row 20: Flatten rnd 19; working through both thicknesses, sc in each st across, turn. *(6)*

Rows 21–23: Ch 1, sc in each st across, turn. At end of last row, fasten off.

Sew row 23 of each Arm to rnd 20 on each side of Body.

Leg (make 2)

Rnds 1–4: Starting at bottom of Leg, repeat rnds 1–4 of Head.

Rnds 5–24: Sc in each st around. Stuff.

Row 25: For **hip,** working in rows, sc in first 12 sts leaving last 12 sts unworked, turn. *(12)*

Rows 26–30: Ch 1, sc in each st across, turn. At end of last row, fasten off. Stuff.

Sew rnd 24 and rows 25–30 of each hip over rnds 1–10 on each side of Body.

SWEATER

Side (make 2)

Note: When changing colors (see Stitch Guide), drop first color to wrong side of work; pick up when needed. Fasten off each color when no longer needed.

Row 1: With red, ch 25, sc in second ch from hook, sc in each ch across, turn. *(24 sc made)*

Row 2: Ch 1, sc in each st across changing to white in last st made, turn.

Row 3: Ch 1, sc in each st across, turn.

Row 4: Ch 1, sc in each st across changing to red in last st made, turn.

Row 5: Ch 1, sc in each st across, turn.

Rows 6–21: Repeat rows 2–5 consecutively.

Rows 22–24: Repeat row 5. At end of last row, fasten off.

For **shoulder seam,** with right sides together,

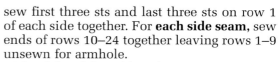

sew first three sts and last three sts on row 1 of each side together. For **each side seam,** sew ends of rows 10–24 together leaving rows 1–9 unsewn for armhole.

For **trim,** join white with sc in any st on row 24, sc in each st around, join with sl st in first sc. Fasten off.

Sleeve (make 2)

Rows 1–9: Repeat rows 1–9 of Sweater Side.

Rows 10–12: Ch 1, sc in each st across, turn. At end of last row, fasten off. Sew ends of rows 1–12 together.

For **trim,** join white with sc in any st on row 12, sc in each st around, join with sl st in first sc. Fasten off.

Easing to fit, sew Sleeves to armholes.

SCARF

Row 1: With green, ch 11, sc in second ch from hook, sc in each ch across, turn. *(10 sc made)*

Rows 2–80: Ch 1, sc in each st across, turn. At end of last row, fasten off.

HAT

Rnd 1: With green, ch 42, sl st in first ch to form ring, ch 1, sc in each ch around. *(42 sc made)*

Rnds 2–4: Sc in each st around.

Rnd 5: (Sc in next 4 sts, sc next 2 sts tog) around. *(35)*

Rnds 6–10: Sc in each st around.

Rnd 11: (Sc in each of next 3 sts, sc next 2 sts tog) around. *(28)*

Rnds 12–15: Sc in each st around.

Rnd 16: (Sc in each of next 2 sts, sc next 2 sts tog) around. *(21)*

Rnds 17–20: Sc in each st around.

Rnd 21: (Sc in next st, sc next 2 sts tog) around. *(14)*

Continued on page 48

Cuddly Cottontails

Design by Lois Lee

Finished Size: Mama is 23" tall.
Babies are 10" tall.

Materials:
- Worsted yarn:
  - 10 oz. tan
  - 6 oz. yellow
  - 3 oz. white
  - 1 oz. each pink and blue
  - 7 yds. brown
  - 1½ yds. bright pink
- Two 15-mm. and four 12-mm. animal eyes with washers
- 1" Velcro fastener
- Two 6" white chenille stems
- Powdered blush
- White acrylic craft paint
- Tiny paintbrush
- 1" and 2" pieces of cardboard
- Polyester fiberfill
- G and I hooks or hooks needed to obtain gauges

Gauges: **G hook,** 4 sc = 1"; 4 sc rows = 1". **I hook,** 3 dc = 1"; 2 dc rows = 1".

Basic Stitches: Ch, sl st, sc, hdc, dc.

Special Stitch: For **shell,** (2 dc, ch 1, 2 dc) in next st.

Notes: Use G hook unless otherwise stated.
Work in continuous rnds; do not join or turn unless otherwise stated. Mark first st of each rnd.

MAMA

HEAD
Rnd 1: Starting at **muzzle,** with white, ch 2, 6 sc in second ch from hook. *(6 sc made)*
Rnd 2: 2 sc in each st around. *(12)*
Rnd 3: Sc in each st around.
Rnd 4: (2 hdc in each of next 2 sts, sc in next 4 sts) 2 times. *(8 hdc, 8 sc)*
Rnd 5: Sc in first st, 2 hdc in each of next 2 sts, sc in next 6 sts, 2 hdc in each of next 2 sts, sc in last 5 sts, join with sl st in first sc. Fasten off. *(12 sc, 8 hdc)*
Rnd 6: Join tan with sc in first st, sc in each st around. *(20 sc)*
Rnd 7: Sc in first 6 sts, 2 sc in each of next 5 sts, sc in last 9 sts. *(25)*
Rnd 8: Sc in each st around.
Rnd 9: (Sl st, ch 3) in first st, dc in next st; *for **cheek,** 2 dc in each of next 4 sts*; sc in next 11 sts; repeat between first *, dc in last 4 sts. *(22 dc, 11 sc)*
Rnd 10: Sc in first 11 sts, 5 sc in next st, sc in next 7 sts, 5 sc in next st, sc in last 13 sts. *(41 sc)*
Rnd 11: Sc in first 16 sts; for **eyelid,** 2 sc in next

st; sc in next 5 sts; for **eyelid,** 2 sc in next st; sc in last 18 sts. *(43)*
Rnds 12–14: Sc in each st around.
Rnd 15: (Sc in next 11 sts; for **back of eye,** skip next 4 sts) 2 times, sc in last 13 sts. *(35)*
Rnds 16–20: Sc in each st around.
Place one 15-mm. eye between eyelid and back of eye between sts on rnd 13, secure with washer. Repeat with other eye.
Rnd 21: (Sc in each of next 3 sts, sc next 2 sts tog) around. *(28)*
Rnd 22: (Sc in each of next 2 sts, sc next 2 sts tog) around. *(21)*
Rnd 23: (Sc in next st, sc next 2 sts tog) around *(14)*. Stuff.
Rnd 24: (Sc next 2 sts tog) around, join with sl st in first sc. Leaving 8" for sewing, fasten off. Sew opening closed.
For **eyebrow,** join tan with sl st around rnd 15 at top of opening at back of eye; working across top of eye, sl st across to rnd 11. Fasten off.
Repeat on other eye leaving eight sts between eyebrows on rnd 11.
For **shaping,** with 12" strand tan and tapestry needle, secure one end of strand on rnd 11 under one eyebrow, insert needle through Head and out at rnd 11 under other eyebrow. Pull slightly to form bridge of nose, secure. Hide loose ends inside Head. Repeat on rnd 15 at back of eye.
For **sparkle,** with paint and brush, paint small dot on eye.
For **top of muzzle,** with tan, using satin stitch *(see Stitch Guide),* embroider 15 sts over rnds 1–5.

NOSE
With brown, ch 2, (3 sc, 3 hdc) in second ch from hook, join with sl st in first sc. Leaving 12" for sewing, fasten off.
Working in **back lps** *(see Stitch Guide),* sew hdc sts over top of rnd 1 with sc sts over rnd 2.
With brown, using straight stitch *(see Stitch Guide),* embroider mouth lines according to face diagram.
Join tan with sl st between rnds 5 and 6 on bottom of muzzle, sl st around muzzle, join with sl st in first sl st. Fasten off.
Brush blush on bottom of muzzle.

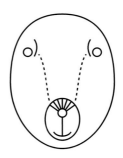

Continued on page 40

Continued from page 39

EAR SIDE (make 2 tan, 2 white)

Rnd 1: Ch 12, 2 sc in second ch from hook, sc in next 9 chs, 4 sc in last ch; working in remaining lps on opposite side of starting ch, sc in next 9 chs, 2 sc in last ch. *(26 sc made)*

Rnd 2: Sc in first st, 3 sc in next st, sc in next 10 sts, 2 sc in next st, sc in next st, 2 sc in next st, sc in next 10 sts, 3 sc in last st. *(32)*

Rnd 3: Sc in each of first 2 sts, 3 sc in next st, (sc in next 13 sts, 3 sc in next st) 2 times, sc in last st. *(38)*

Rnd 4: Sc in each of first 3 sts, (3 sc in next st, sc in next 15 sts) 2 times, 3 sc in next st, sc in each of last 2 sts, join with sl st in first sc. Fasten off.

Center and sew one chenille stem to wrong side of white Ear Side. Fold remaining end of stem up over stitching.

Hold one white and one tan Ear Side wrong sides together with white side facing you; working through both thicknesses in **back lps,** join tan with sc in first st of rnd 4, sc in next 21 sts; for **top,** (sc, ch 2, sl st in second ch from hook, sc) in next st; sc in last 20 sts, join with sl st in first sc. Leaving 12" for sewing, fasten off.

Brush blush on bottom of each white Ear Side, shading lightly out to sides and up center.

Fold bottom of one Ear in half, sew together. Repeat with other Ear.

Sew Ears over rnds 19–22 on Head 1½" apart.

SHOE & LEG (make 2)

Rnd 1: Starting at **sole,** with yellow, ch 10, sc in second ch from hook, sc in next 5 chs, hdc in next ch, 2 hdc in next ch, 5 hdc in last ch; working in remaining lps on opposite side of starting ch, 2 hdc in next ch, hdc in next ch, sc in next 5 chs, 2 sc in last ch. *(13 sc, 11 hdc made)*

Rnd 2: 2 sc in first st, sc in next 8 sts, (2 sc in next st, sc in next st) 3 times, sc in next 7 sts, 2 sc in next st, sc in last st. *(29 sc)*

Rnd 3: 2 sc in first st, sc in next 9 sts, (2 sc in next st, sc in next st) 2 times, (sc in next st, 2 sc in next st) 2 times, sc in next 9 sts, 2 sc in next st, sc in last st. *(35)*

Rnd 4: Working this rnd in **back lps,** sc in each st around.

Rnd 5: Sc in each st around.

Rnd 6: Sc in first 11 sts, sc next 2 sts tog, hdc in next st, (dc next 2 sts tog, dc in next st) 2 times, dc next 2 sts tog, hdc in next st, sc next 2 sts tog, sc in next 8 sts, sc last 2 sts tog, join with sl st in first sc. Fasten off. *(29 sts)*

Rnd 7: Working this rnd in **back lps,** join tan with sc in first st, sc in next 9 sts, (sc next 2 sts tog) 4 times, sc in last 11 sts. *(25)*

Rnd 8: Sc in first 9 sts, (sc next 2 sts tog) 4 times, sc in last 8 sts. *(21)*

Rnd 9: Sc in first 8 sts, sc next 2 sts tog, sc in next st, sc next 2 sts tog, sc in last 8 sts. *(19)*

Rnd 10: Sc in first 8 sts, (sc next 2 sts tog) 2 times, sc in last 7 sts. *(17)*

Rnd 11: 2 sc in first st, sc in each st around. *(18)*

Rnd 12: Sc in each of first 3 sts, 2 sc in next st, sc in each st around. *(19)*

Rnd 13: Sc in each of first 2 sts, 2 sc in next st, sc in each st around *(20)*. Stuff. Continue stuffing as you work.

Rnds 14–21: Sc in each st around.

Rnds 22–24: Sl st in first 10 sts; for **knee,** hdc in last 10 sts.

Rnd 25: Sc in first 4 sts, 2 sc in next st, sc in last 15 sts. *(21)*

Rnd 26: Sc in first 4 sts, 2 sc in each of next 2 sts, sc in last 15 sts. *(23)*

Rnds 27–35: Sc in each st around. At end of last rnd, join with sl st in first sc. Fasten off.

For **strap,** ch 12. Fasten off.

Sew ends to ninth and 23rd sts on rnd 6 of Shoe.

PANTY & BODY

Rnd 1: Starting at **bottom,** with yellow, ch 48, sl st in first ch to form ring, ch 1, sc in first 23 chs; for **center front,** hdc in next ch, sc in next 23 chs; for **center back,** hdc in last ch. *(46 sc, 2 hdc made)*

Rnd 2: Working this rnd in **back lps,** *for **hip,** 2 hdc in first st, (hdc in next st, 2 hdc in next st) 5 times*, sc in next 26 sts; repeat between first and second *. *(34 hdc, 26 sc)*

Rnds 3–13: Sc in each st around. At end of last rnd, join with sl st in first sc. Fasten off.

Rnd 14: Working this rnd in **back lps,** join tan with sc in first st, sc in each st around.

Rnd 15: Sc in each st around.

Rnd 16: (Sc in next 13 sts, sc next 2 sts tog) around. *(56 sc)*

Rnd 17: Sc in each st around.

Rnd 18: (Sc in next 12 sts, sc next 2 sts tog) around. *(52)*

Rnd 19: Sc in each st around.

Rnd 20: (Sc in next 11 sts, sc next 2 sts tog) around. *(48)*

Rnd 21: Sc in each st around.

Rnd 22: (Sc in next 10 sts, sc next 2 sts tog) around. *(44)*

Rnd 23: Sc in each st around.

Rnd 24: (Sc in next 9 sts, sc next 2 sts tog) around. *(40)*

Rnd 25: Sc in each st around.

Rnd 26: (Sc in next 8 sts, sc next 2 sts tog) around. *(36)*

Rnd 27: Sc in each st around.

Rnd 28: (Sc in next 7 sts, sc next 2 sts tog) around. *(32)*

Rnd 29: Sc in each st around.

Rnd 30: (Sc in next 6 sts, sc next 2 sts tog) around. *(28)*

Rnd 31: Sc in each st around.

Rnd 32: (Sc in next 5 sts, sc next 2 sts tog) around, join with sl st in first sc. Leaving 18" for sewing, fasten off. Stuff.

Sew center front and back of rnd 1 on Panty together.

Panty Trim
Working in **front lps** of rnd 2, join white with sl st in any st, (ch 4, skip next st, sl st in next st) around, **turn;** working in skipped sts, (ch 4, sl st in next st) around. Fasten off.

Sew Legs to starting ch on Panty with toes pointing forward.

Sew Head to rnd 32 of Body with hips in back.

RIGHT ARM
Rnd 1: Starting at **hand,** with tan, ch 4, 3 sc in second ch from hook, sc in next ch, 4 sc in last chs; working in remaining lps on opposite side of starting ch, sc in each of next 2 chs. *(10 sc made)*

Rnd 2: Sc in first st, 2 sc in next st, sc in next 5 sts, 2 sc in next st, sc in each of last 2 sts. *(12)*

Rnd 3: Sc in each of first 2 sts, 2 sc in next 6 sts, 2 sc in next st, sc in each of last 2 sts. *(14)*

Rnd 4: Sc in each of first 3 sts, 2 sc in next st, sc in next 6 sts, 2 sc in next st, sc in each of last 3 sts. *(16)*

Rnds 5–7: Sc in each st around. Stuff lightly.

Row 8: For **wrist,** flatten last rnd; working in rows through both thicknesses, ch 1, sc in each st across, turn. *(8)*

Row 9: Working in **front lps,** ch 1, sc in first 8 sts; working on **back lps** of same row, sc in last 8 sts. *(16)*

Rnd 10: Working in rnds, sc in each st around.

Rnd 11: 2 sc in first st, sc in next 7 sts, 2 sc in next st, sc in last 7 sts. *(18)*

Rnds 12–18: Sc in each st around.

Rnds 19–22: Sl st in first 10 sts; for **elbow,** hdc in last 8 sts.

Rnd 23: Sc in each st around.

Rnd 24: 2 sc in first st, sc in next 8 sts, 2 sc in next st, sc in last 8 sts. *(20)*

Rnds 25–29: Sc in each st around.

Rnds 30–32: Sl st in first 6 sts; for **shoulder,** hdc in last 14 sts. At end of last rnd join with sl st in first sc. Fasten off. Stuff.

LEFT ARM
Rnds 1–18: Repeat rnds 1–18 of Right Arm.

Rnds 19–22: For **elbow,** hdc in first 8 sts; sl st in last 10 sts.

Rnds 23–29: Repeat rnds 23–29 of Right Arm.

Rnds 30–32: For **shoulder,** hdc in first 14 sts, sl st in last 6 sts. At end of last rnd, join with sl st in first sc. Fasten off. Stuff.

With elbows curved outward, sew Arms over rnds 24–29 on each side of Body.

Sew Velcro to tips of each Arm.

TAIL
Wrap white around 2" cardboard 100 times; slide loops off cardboard, tie separate 6" strand white tightly around center of all loops; cut

loops. Trim ends to 1¼".

Sew to center back of rnd 7 on Panty.

DRESS
Row 1: Starting at **yoke,** with I hook and yellow, ch 31, dc in fourth ch from hook, dc in each of next 2 chs; (for **sleeve,** 3 dc in next ch, dc in each of next 3 chs, 3 dc in next ch); dc in next 11 chs; repeat between ( ), dc in last 4 chs, turn. *(37 dc made)*

Row 2: Ch 3, dc in next 4 sts, (3 dc in next st, dc in next 5 sts, 3 dc in next st), dc in next 13 sts; repeat between ( ), dc in last 5 sts, turn. *(45)*

Row 3: Ch 3, dc in next 5 sts, (3 dc in each of next 9 sts), dc in next 15 sts; repeat between ( ), dc in last 6 sts, turn. *(81)*

Row 4: Ch 3, dc in each st across, turn.

Row 5: Ch 3, dc in next 6 sts; (for **armhole,** ch 10, skip next 26 sts); dc in next 15 sts; repeat between ( ), dc in last 7 sts, turn. *(29 dc, 20 ch)*

Row 6: Ch 3, dc in each st and in each ch across, turn. *(49 dc)*

Row 7: For **skirt,** ch 1, sc in first st, (2 sc in next st, sc in next st) across, turn. *(73 sc)*

Rnd 8: Working in rnds, ch 3, skip next 2 sts; * for **shell, (2 dc, ch 1, 2 dc)** in next st; skip next 2 sts; repeat from * around to last st, dc in last st, join with sl st in top of ch 3. *(23 shells)*

Rnd 9: Sl st in each of first 2 sts, (sl st, ch 3, dc, ch 1, 2 dc) in first ch 1 sp, shell in ch sp of each shell around, join.

Rnds 10–15: Sl st in next st, (sl st, ch 3, dc, ch 1, 2 dc) in first ch 1 sp, shell in each shell around, join. At end of last rnd, fasten off.

For **skirt trim,** working in **back lps** of rnd 15, work same as Panty Trim.

For **neck trim,** working in remaining lps on opposite side of starting ch, join white with sl st in first ch, (ch 4, skip next ch, sl st in next ch) across, turn; working in skipped chs, (ch 4, sl st in next ch) across. Fasten off.

For **sleeve trim,** working in **front lps** of row 4, join white with sl st in first worked st on back, (ch 4, skip next st, sl st in next st) across, turn;

Continued on page 42

Continued from page 41

working in **back lps** of skipped sts, (ch 4, sl st in next st) across. Fasten off.

Repeat on other sleeve.

For **neck ties,** cut two strands yellow each 7" long. Tie one end of each strand to rnd 1 on back opening.

For **belt,** with white, ch 100. Fasten off. Weave through sts of rnd 6.

FLOWER

Leaving 2" end, with pink, ch 4, sl st in fourth ch from hook, (ch 3, sl st in same ch as first sl st) 4 times. Leaving 2" end, fasten off. Tie loose ends together. *(5 petals)*

Sew to row 2 on left front yoke with loose ends at bottom.

Place Dress on bunny, tie neck ties and belt in bows.

HAT

Rnd 1: With I hook and yellow, ch 2, 8 sc in second ch from hook, join with sl st in first sc. *(8 sc made)*

Rnd 2: Ch 2, hdc in same st, 2 hdc in each st around, join with sl st in top of ch-2. *(16)*

Rnd 3: Ch 3, dc in next st; *for **ear opening,** ch 4, skip next 3 sts*; for **front,** 2 dc in next st, dc in each of next 2 sts, 2 dc in next st; repeat between first and second *, (dc in next st, 2 dc in next st) 2 times, join with sl st in top of ch-3. *(14 dc, 8 chs)*

Rnd 4: Working in sts and in chs, ch 3, 2 dc in next st, (dc in next st, 2 dc in next st) around, join. *(33)*

Rnd 5: Working this rnd in **front lps,** ch 1, 2 sc in first st, (sc in next st, 2 sc in next st) around, join with sl st in first sc. *(50)*

Rnd 6: Ch 3, dc in same st, skip next st, (shell in next st, skip next st) around, join with sl st in top of ch-3. *(24 shells, 2 dc)*

Rnd 7: Ch 3, dc in next st, shell in each shell around, join as before. Fasten off.

Rnd 8: For **trim,** working in **back lps** of sts and chs, ch 4, skip next st, (sl st in next st, ch 4, skip next st) around, sl st in same st as first ch 4, **turn;** working in **front lps** of skipped sts, (ch 4, sl st in next st) around. Fasten off.

For **Flower,** work same as Flower on Dress.

Fold rnd 7 over rnd 3 in back; working through both thicknesses, sew Flower in center leaving ends at bottom.

BOY BUNNY

HEAD

Rnd 1: Starting at **muzzle,** with tan, ch 2, 6 sc in second ch from hook. *(6 sc made)*

Rnd 2: Sc in first st, 2 sc in next st, sc in each of next 2 sts, 2 sc in next st, sc in last st. *(8)*

Rnd 3: For **cheek,** (3 dc in next st; sc in each of next 3 sts) 2 times. *(6 dc, 6 sc)*

Rnd 4: Sc in first 4 sts; for **bridge of nose,** 2 sc in each of next 3 sts, sc in next 4 sts, 2 sc in last st, join with sl st in first sc. *(16)*

Rnd 5: Ch 3, dc in same st, 2 dc in each of next 2 sts; for **eyelid,** 4 sc in next st, sc in next 6 sts, 4 sc in next st, 2 dc in each of next 3 sts, dc in each of last 2 sts. *(14 dc, 14 sc)*

Rnds 6–8: Sc in each st around. *(28)*

Rnd 9: Sc first 2 sts tog, sc in next 4 sts; (for **back of eye,** skip next 4 sts; sc in next 6 sts) 2 times, sc last 2 sts tog. *(18)*

Rnd 10: Sc in each st around.

Rnd 11: Sc first 2 sts tog, sc in each st around to last 2 sts, sc last 2 sts tog. *(16)*

Place one eye between rnds 7 and 8 before back of eye. Secure with washer.

Repeat with other eye.

Rnd 12: Sc in first st, (sc next 2 sts tog, sc in next st) around. Stuff. *(11)*

Rnd 13: Sc in first st, (sc next 2 sts tog) around, join with sl st in first sc. *(6)* Leaving 8" for sewing, fasten off. Sew opening closed.

For **eyebrows,** working from rnd 9 to rnd 6, work same as Mama's eyebrows on page 39.

For **shaping,** working on rnds 6 and 9, work same as shaping for Mama.

Add sparkle to eyes same as Mama's.

For **nose,** split 2 yds. brown into 2-ply; with 2-ply, ch 2, (3 hdc, 3 dc) in second ch from hook, join with sl st in first hdc. Fasten off.

Working in **back lps,** sew hdc sts over bottom of rnd 1 on muzzle with dc sts over rnd 2.

With white, using satin and straight stitches, embroider mouth lines according to face diagram.

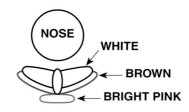

Animal Attractions
42

EAR (make 2)

With tan, ch 10, 4 dc in fourth ch from hook, dc in next ch, hdc in next ch, sc in each of next 3 chs; for **top,** (sc, ch 2, sl st in second ch from hook, sc) in last ch; working in remaining lps on opposite side of starting ch, sc in each of next 3 chs, hdc in next ch, dc in each of last 2 chs, join with sl st in top of ch-3. Fasten off.

Fold bottoms of Ears in half; with ½" between, sew bottoms of Ears to rnds 11–13 on back of Head.

For **headband,** with blue, ch 27, sl st in second ch from hook, sl st in each ch across. Fasten off.

Slip over Ears, sew around Head.

BODY

Rnd 1: Starting at **neck,** with tan, ch 12, sl st in first ch to form ring, ch 1, sc in each ch around. *(12 sc made)*

Rnd 2: (Sc in next st, 2 sc in next st) around. *(18)*

Rnd 3: Sc in each st around.

Rnd 4: (Sc in each of next 2 sts, 2 sc in next st) around. *(24)*

Rnds 5–6: Sc in each st around. At end of last rnd, join with sl st in first sc. Fasten off.

Rnd 7: For **pants,** working this rnd in **back lps,** join blue with sc in first st, sc in each of next 2 sts, 2 sc in next st, (sc in each of next 3 sts, 2 sc in next st) around. *(30)*

Rnds 8–9: Sc in each st around.

Rnd 10: (Sc in each of next 3 sts, sc next 2 sts tog) around. *(24)*

Rnd 11: Working this rnd in **back lps,** (sc in each of next 2 sts, sc next 2 sts tog) around, join with sl st in first sc. Leaving 12" for sewing, fasten off. Stuff.

Flatten last rnd; working through both thicknesses, sew opening closed.

Sew rnds 6–8 on bottom of Head to starting ch at neck.

TAIL

Wrap white around 1" cardboard 50 times; slide loops off cardboard, tie separate 6" strand white tightly around center of all loops; cut loops. Trim ends to ¾".

Sew to rnd 8 on center back of Body.

BIB

Row 1: With blue, ch 6, sc in second ch from hook, sc in each ch across, turn. *(5 sc made)*

Rows 2–3: Ch 1, sc in each st across, turn.

Row 4: Ch 1, sc in each st across; for **first strap,** ch 14. Fasten off.

For **2nd strap,** join with sl st in first st of row 4, ch 14. Fasten off.

Sew starting ch to rnd 7 on front of Body.

Crisscross straps in back, sew ends to rnd 7 on Body with three sts between.

SHOE & LEG (make 2)

Rnd 1: Starting at **sole,** with blue, ch 8, sc in sec-
ond ch from hook, sc in next 4 chs, hdc in next ch, 4 hdc in last ch; working in remaining lps on opposite side of starting ch, hdc in next ch, sc in next 4 chs, 2 sc in last ch. *(11 sc, 6 hdc made)*

Rnd 2: 2 sc in first st, sc in next 5 sts, 2 sc in next st, sc in each of next 2 sts, 2 sc in next st, sc in next 6 sts, 2 sc in last st. *(21)*

Rnd 3: Working this rnd in **back lps,** sc in each st around.

Rnd 4: Sc in first 6 sts, (sc next 2 sts tog) 4 times, sc in next 5 sts, sc last 2 sts tog, join with sl st in first sc. Fasten off. *(16)*

Rnd 5: Working this rnd in **back lps,** join tan with sc in first st, sc in next 5 sts, sc next 2 sts tog, sc in next st, sc next 2 sts tog, sc in last 5 sts. Stuff. Continue stuffing as you work. *(14)*

Rnd 6: Sc in first 6 sts, (sc next 2 sts tog) 2 times, sc in last 4 sts. *(12)*

Rnd 7: (Sc next 2 sts tog, sc in next 4 sts) 2 times. *(10)*

Rnds 8–11: Sc in each st around. At end of last rnd, join as before. Fasten off.

Rnd 12: Working this rnd in **back lps,** join blue with sc in first st, sc in each st around.

Rnds 13–14: Sc in each st around. At end of last rnd, join. Leaving 8" for sewing, fasten off.

For **cuff,** with blue, ch 12. Leaving 8" for sewing, fasten off. Sew to rnd 12.

Flatten last rnd with toes pointing forward; working through both thicknesses, sew opening closed.

Sew Legs side by side to rnd 11 of Body.

RIGHT ARM

Rnd 1: Starting at **hand,** with tan, ch 2, 8 sc in second ch from hook. *(8 sc made)*

Rnds 2–3: Sc in each st around.

Rnd 4: For **wrist,** flatten last rnd; working in rows through both thicknesses, ch 1, sc in each st across, turn. *(4)*

Rnd 5: Working in **front lps,** ch 1, sc in first 4 sts; working in **back lps** of same row, sc in last 4 sts. *(8)*

Rnd 6: Working in rnds, sc in each st around.

Rnd 7: 2 sc in first st, sc in each st around. *(9)*

Rnd 8: Sc in each st around.

Rnds 9–10: Sl st in first 5 sts; for **elbow,** hdc in last 4 sts.

Rnd 11: Sc in each st around.

Rnd 12: Repeat rnd 7. *(10)*

Rnds 13–14: Sc in each st around. Stuff lightly.

Rnd 15: (Sc next 2 sts tog) around, join with sl st in first sc. Leaving 8" for sewing, fasten off. Sew opening closed.

LEFT ARM

Rnds 1–8: Repeat rnds 1–8 of Right Arm.

Rnds 9–10: For **elbow,** hdc in first 4 sts, sl st in last 5 sts.

Rnds 11–15: Repeat rnds 11–15 of right arm.

Continued on page 44

Continued from page 43

With elbows curved outward, sew Arms over rnds 2–4 on each side of Body.

GIRL BUNNY

HEAD
Work same as Boy Bunny's Head on page 42.

EAR (make 2)
Work same as Boy Bunny's Ear on page 43.

HAT
Rnd 1: With pink, ch 28, sl st in first ch to form ring, ch 4, (skip next ch, sl st in next ch, ch 4) around, join with sl st in first ch of first ch 4.

Rnd 2: Sl st in next ch, (sl st in next ch sp, ch 4) around, join with sl st in first sl st. Fasten off. Slip over Ears; sew around Head.

BODY
Rnds 1–6: Repeat rnds 1–6 of Boy Bunny's Body on page 43.

Rnds 7–11: With pink, repeat rnds 7–11 of Boy Bunny's Body.

SKIRT
Rnd 1: Working in **front lps** of rnd 10, join pink with sc in any st, sc in same st, 3 sc in each of next 2 sts, (2 sc in next st, 3 sc in each of next 2 sts) around, join with sl st in first sc.

Rnd 2: Working this rnd in **back lps**, ch 2, (skip next st, sl st in next st, ch 2) around, join with sl st in first ch of first ch-2. Fasten off.

BIB
Row 1: With pink, ch 6, sc in second ch from hook, sc in each ch across, turn. *(5 sc made)*

Rows 2–3: Ch 1, sc in each st across, turn.

Row 4: Ch 1, sc in each st across; for **first strap**, ch 18, sl st in fourth ch from hook, (ch 3, skip next ch, sl st in next ch) across, **turn.** Fasten off.

For **2nd strap**, join with sl st in first st of row 4, ch 18, sl st in fourth ch from hook, (ch 3, skip next ch, sl st in next ch) across. Fasten off.

Sew starting ch of Bib to center of rnd 7 on front of Body.

Sew ends of straps to rnd 7 on center back of Body.

TAIL
Work same as Boy Bunny's Tail on page 43.

SHOE & LEG (make 2)
Rnds 1–4: With pink, repeat rnds 1–4 of Boy Bunny's Shoe & Leg on page 43.

Rnds 5–7: With tan, repeat rnds 5–7 of Boy Bunny's Shoe & Leg.

Rnds 8–14: Sc in each st around. At end of last rnd, join with sl st in first sc. Leaving 8" for sewing, fasten off.

Flatten last rnd with toes pointing forward; working through both thicknesses, sew opening closed. Sew Legs side by side to rnd 11 of Body.

For each **strap**, cut 5" strand pink, place over top of each foot, secure ends.

RIGHT & LEFT ARMS
Work same as Boy Bunny's Arms on page 43.

FLOWER
With blue, work same as Mama's Flower on page 42. Tack to rnd 1 of Left Arm. ❧

Beautiful Dolls from the Inside Out

For crocheted dolls or toys to look truly beautiful, an artful job of stuffing them is essential!

Begin with the correct stuffing material. Shredded foam, quilt batting, cotton and cut-up old nylons tend to bunch and shift, so for a professional finish, rely on polyester fiberfill. It is sold in bulk bags under several brand names. Fiberfill is durable and has a soft resilience which stands up well under use.

Add stuffing a little at a time, spreading evenly into the desired shape. The end of a pencil or your crochet hook can be used to push stuffing into tight places. Small spaces can also be stuffed with scraps and trimmings of yarn such as fluff left over from pom-poms or two to three-inch-long clippings of matching yarn.

Stuff a toy for an older child more firmly than a baby toy, and be sure to stuff arms and legs completely so they will hold their shape. Adjust to your preference before closing the final seam.

If the stuffing shows through because your stitches are too loose or your design is made primarily from double crochets, try lining the crocheted pieces with pieces of the same color nylon hose before stuffing with fiberfill.

For crocheted dolls, beauty really does begin from within! ❧

General Ted E. Bear

Design by Michele Wilcox

Instructions begin on page 46

General Ted E. Bear

Finished size:
Approximately 16" tall.

Materials:
- Worsted yarn:
  - 6½ oz. camouflage
  - 3½ oz. black
  - 3½ oz. lt. brown
- Polyester fiberfill
- Two brown 9-mm. animal eyes with washers
- One black 12-mm. animal nose with washer
- Eight gold 9-mm. star studs
- Tapestry needle
- F hook or hook needed to obtain gauge

Gauge: 9 sc = 2"; 9 sc rows = 2".

Basic Stitches: Ch, sl st, sc, hdc, dc.

Note: Work in continuous rnds; do not join or turn unless otherwise stated. Mark first st of each rnd.

BODY
Rnd 1: Starting at **bottom,** with camouflage, ch 2, 6 sc in second ch from hook. *(6 sc made)*
Rnd 2: 2 sc in each st around. *(12)*
Rnd 3: (Sc in next st, 2 sc in next st) around. *(18)*
Rnd 4: (Sc in each of next 2 sts, 2 sc in next st) around. *(24)*
Rnd 5: (Sc in each of next 3 sts, 2 sc in next st) around. *(30)*
Rnd 6: (Sc in next 4 sts, 2 sc in next st) around. *(36)*
Rnd 7: (Sc in next 5 sts, 2 sc in next st) around. *(42)*
Rnd 8: (Sc in next 6 sts, 2 sc in next st) around. *(48)*
Rnd 9: (Sc in next 7 sts, 2 sc in next st) around. *(54)*
Rnd 10: (Sc in next 8 sts, 2 sc in next st) around. *(60)*
Rnds 11–14: Sc in each st around.
Rnd 15: (Sc in next 8 sts, sc next 2 sts tog) around. *(54)*
Rnds 16–17: Sc in each st around.
Rnd 18: (Sc in next 7 sts, sc next 2 sts tog) around. *(48)*
Rnds 19–20: Sc in each st around.
Rnd 21: (Sc in next 6 sts, sc next 2 sts tog) around. *(42)*
Rnds 22–25: Sc in each st around.
Rnd 26: (Sc in next 5 sts, sc next 2 sts tog) around. *(36)*
Rnds 27–28: Sc in each st around.
Rnd 29: (Sc in next 4 sts, sc next 2 sts tog) around. *(30)*
Rnds 30–31: Sc in each st around.

Rnd 32: (Sc in each of next 3 sts, sc next 2 sts tog) around. *(24)*
Rnd 33: (Sc in each of next 2 sts, sc next 2 sts tog) around, join with sl st in first sc. Fasten off. Stuff.

HEAD
Rnds 1–3: Starting at **nose,** with lt. brown, repeat rnds 1–3 of Body.
Rnds 4–6: Sc in each st around.
Rnds 7–8: Repeat rnds 4 and 5 of Body.
Rnd 9: Sc in each st around.
Rnd 10: For **top of Head,** 2 sc in each of first 12 sts; sc in last 18 sts. *(42)*
Rnds 11–18: Sc in each st around.
With increases of rnd 10 at top, insert animal nose through center of rnd 1. Secure with washer.
Insert eyes between rnds 9 and 10 centered above nose 2" apart. Secure with washers.
Rnd 19: (Sc in next 5 sts, sc next 2 sts tog) around. *(36)*
Rnd 20: (Sc in next 4 sts, sc next 2 sts tog) around. *(30)*
Rnd 21: Sc in each st around. Stuff. Continue stuffing as you work.
Rnd 22: (Sc in each of next 3 sts, sc next 2 sts tog) around. *(24)*
Rnd 23: (Sc in each of next 2 sts, sc next 2 sts tog) around. *(18)*
Rnd 24: (Sc in next st, sc next 2 sts tog) around. *(12)*
Rnd 25: (Sc next 2 sts tog) around, join with sl st in first sc. Leaving 8", fasten off. Weave end through last rnd to close.
For **mouth,** with black, embroider straight stitches *(see Stitch Guide),* over bottom half of rnds 1–5 of Head as shown in photo.
Sew bottom half of rnds 14–20 on Head over rnd 33 of Body.

EAR (make 2)
Rnds 1–3: With lt. brown, repeat rnds 1–3 of Body.
Rnds 4–6: Sc in each st around.
Rnd 7: (Sc in next st, sc next 2 sts tog) around, join with sl st in first sc. Leaving 8", fasten off. Flatten last rnd, sew over rnds 15–17 on each side of Head 3" apart.

ARM (make 2)
Rnds 1–3: Repeat rnds 1–3 of Body.
Rnds 4–17: Sc in each st around. At end of last rnd, join with sl st in first sc. Fasten off.
Rnd 18: Join lt. brown with sc in first st, sc in each st around.
Rnds 19–20: Sc in each st around.
Rnd 21: (Sc in next st, sc next 2 sts tog) around. Stuff. *(12)*
Rnd 22: (Sc next 2 sts tog) around, join as before. Leaving 8", fasten off. Weave end through last rnd to close.

Sew rnds 1–5 of Arm over rnds 25–30 on each side of Body.

LEG (make 2)
Rnds 1–4: Repeat rnds 1–4 of Body.
Rnds 5–15: Sc in each st around. At end of last rnd, join with sl st in first sc. Fasten off.
Rnd 16: Join black with sc in first st, sc in each st around.
Rnds 17–23: Sc in each st around.
Rnd 24: 2 sc in each of first 12 sts, sc in last 12 sts. *(36)*
Rnd 25: Sc in first 9 sts; for **toes,** 2 sc in each of next 6 sts; sc in last 21 sts. *(42)*
Rnds 26–31: Sc in each st around.
Rnd 32: Working this rnd in **back lps,** *(see Stitch Guide),* (sc in next 5 sts, sc next 2 sts tog) around. *(36)*
Rnd 33: (Sc in next 4 sts, sc next 2 sts tog) around. *(30)*
Rnd 34: (Sc in each of next 3 sts, sc next 2 sts tog) around. *(24)*
Rnd 35: (Sc in each of next 2 sts, sc next 2 sts tog) around, join as before. *(18)*
Leaving 8", fasten off. Stuff.
Flatten last rnd lengthwise, sew opening closed.
Sew rnds 1–9 of Leg over rnds 6–14 on Body 3½" apart with toes in front.

HAT
Rnds 1–4: Repeat rnds 1–4 of Body.
Rnd 5: Working this rnd in **back lps,** sc in each st around.
Rnds 6–8: Sc in each st around.
Rnd 9: For **brim,** sl st in first st, 2 sc in next st, 2 hdc in next st, 2 dc in each of next 3 sts, 2 hdc in next st, 2 sc in next st, sl st in next st leaving remaining sts unworked. Fasten off. Stuff.
Sew to top of Head between Ears.

PLACKET
With camouflage, ch 15, sc in second ch from hook, sc in each ch across. Fasten off.
For **buttons,** with black, embroider five French knots *(see Stitch Guide)* evenly spaced down Placket.
Sew Placket over rnds 18–32 on front of Body.

BELT
Row 1: With black, ch 43, sc in second ch from hook, sc in each ch across, turn. *(42 sc made)*
Row 2: Ch 1, sc in each st across. Fasten off.
Sew over rnds 17 and 18 around Body, sewing ends of rows together in back.

SHIRT POCKET (make 2)
Row 1: With camouflage, ch 7, sc in second ch from hook, sc in each ch across, turn. *(6 sc made)*
Rows 2–6: Ch 1, sc in each st across, turn. At end of last row, fasten off.
Sew bottom and sides to Body over rnds 18–24

on each side of Placket.

SHIRT POCKET FLAP (make 2)
Row 1: With camouflage, ch 8, sc in second ch from hook, sc in each ch across, turn. *(7 sc made)*
Row 2: Ch 1, sc in each st across. Fasten off.
Sew row 1 centered above each Shirt Pocket.

SHIRT CUFF (make 2)
Row 1: With camouflage, ch 22, sc in second ch from hook, sc in each ch across, turn. *(21 sc made)*
Rows 2–4: Ch 1, sc in each st across, turn. At end of last row, fasten off.
Sew row 1 over rnd 17 on each Arm, sewing ends of rows together in back.

EPAULET (make 2)
Row 1: With camouflage, ch 11, sc in second ch from hook, sc in each ch across, turn. *(10 sc made)*
Rows 2–3: Ch 1, sc in each st across, turn. At end of last row, fasten off.
Attach four stars evenly spaced across sts. Sew one end to rnd 31 of Body and other end to rnd 5 of Arm.

COLLAR
Row 1: With camouflage, ch 20, sc in second ch from hook, sc in each ch across, turn. *(19 sc made)*
Row 2: Ch 1, 2 sc in first st, sc in each st across to last st, 2 sc in last st, turn. *(21)*
Row 3: Ch 1, sc in each st across, turn.
Row 4: Repeat row 2. Fasten off. *(23)*
Place around neck, tack first and last sts of row 1 to center front of rnd 33 on Body.

PANT POCKET (make 2)
Row 1: With camouflage, ch 8, sc in second ch from hook, sc in each ch across, turn. *(7 sc made)*
Rows 2–6: Ch 1, sc in each st across, turn. At end of last row, fasten off.
Sew bottom and sides over rnds 12–17 of each Leg.

PANT POCKET FLAP (make 2)
Row 1: With camouflage, ch 9, sc in second ch from hook, sc in each ch across, turn. *(8 sc made)*
Rows 2–3: Ch 1, sc in each st across, turn. At end of last row, fasten off.
Sew row 1 centered above each Pant Pocket.

BOOT CUFF (make 2)
Row 1: With black, ch 26, sc in second ch from hook, sc in each ch across, turn. *(25 sc made)*
Rows 2–3: Ch 1, sc in each st across, turn. At end of last row, fasten off.
Sew row 1 to rnd 15 on each Leg, sewing ends of rows together in back. ❖

Wintertime Bear

Continued from page 37

Rnds 22–25: Sc in each st around.

Rnd 26: (Sc in next st, sc next 2 sts tog) 4 times, sc in each of last 2 sts. *(10)*

Rnds 27–30: Sc in each st around.

Rnd 31: (Sc next 2 sts tog) around, join with sl st in first sc. Leaving 6" for sewing, fasten off. Sew rnd 31 closed.

Brim

Row 1: With green, ch 6, sc in second ch from hook, sc in each ch across, turn. *(5 sc made)*

Rows 2–50: Ch 1, sc in each st across, turn. At end of last row, fasten off.

Sew rows 1 and 50 together.

Easing to fit, sew ends of rows on one side of Brim to row 1 of Hat. Tack rnd 27 of Hat to rnd 1 of Hat. Tack Hat to side of Head covering right Ear.

Pom-Pom (make 3)

Wrap white around 3" cardboard 100 times; slide loops off cardboard, tie separate 6" strand white tightly around center of all loops; cut loops. Trim ends.

Sew one Pom-pom to rnd 31 on Hat and one to each end of Scarf. Tie Scarf around neck.

BOOT (make 2)

Rnd 1: Starting at bottom of sole, with white, ch 10, 3 sc in second ch from hook, sc in next 7 chs, 3 sc in last ch; working in remaining lps on opposite side of starting ch, sc in last 7 chs. *(20 sc made)*

Rnd 2: (2 sc in each of next 3 sts, sc in next 7 sts) 2 times. *(26)*

Rnd 3: (Sc in each of next 2 sts, 2 sc in next st) 8 times, sc in each of last 2 sts. *(34)*

Rnd 4: For **toe**, 2 sc in each of first 10 sts, sc in last 24 sts, join with sl st in first sc. *(44)*

Rnd 5: For **sides,** working this rnd in **back lps** *(see Stitch Guide),* ch 1, sc in each st around.

Rnd 6: Sc in each st around.

Rnd 7: (Sc in each of next 2 sts, sc next 2 sts tog) 5 times, sc in last 24 sts. *(39)*

Rnd 8: Sc in each st around, join with sl st in first sc, **turn.**

Row 9: For **top,** working in rows, ch 1, sc in first 24 sts leaving last 15 sts unworked, turn. *(24)*

Rows 10–15: Ch 1, sc in each st across, turn. At end of last row, fasten off.

Instep & Tongue

Row 1: With white, ch 11, sc in second ch from hook, sc in each ch across, turn. *(10 sc made)*

Rows 2–17: Ch 1, sc in each st across, turn. At end of last row, fasten off.

Easing to fit, sew row 1 and end of rows 1–7 of Instep to unworked sts of rnd 8 on Boot.

Boot Laces

Cut two strands red, each 25" long. Lace one through end of rows 9–15 on each top and tie in bow.

With red, using backstitch *(see Stitch Guide),* embroider around rnd 5 and rnd 8 of Boot.

From 6" plastic, using crocheted sole for pattern, cut two pieces. Place one piece inside each Boot. Stuff toe. Place Leg in each Boot, tack in place.

SNOWBALL

Rnds 1–2: With white, repeat rnds 1–2 of Head.

Rnds 3–4: Sc in each st around.

Rnd 5: (Sc next 2 sts tog) around. Leaving 8" for sewing, fasten off. Stuff. Sew opening closed.

Tack to right Mitten. ❖

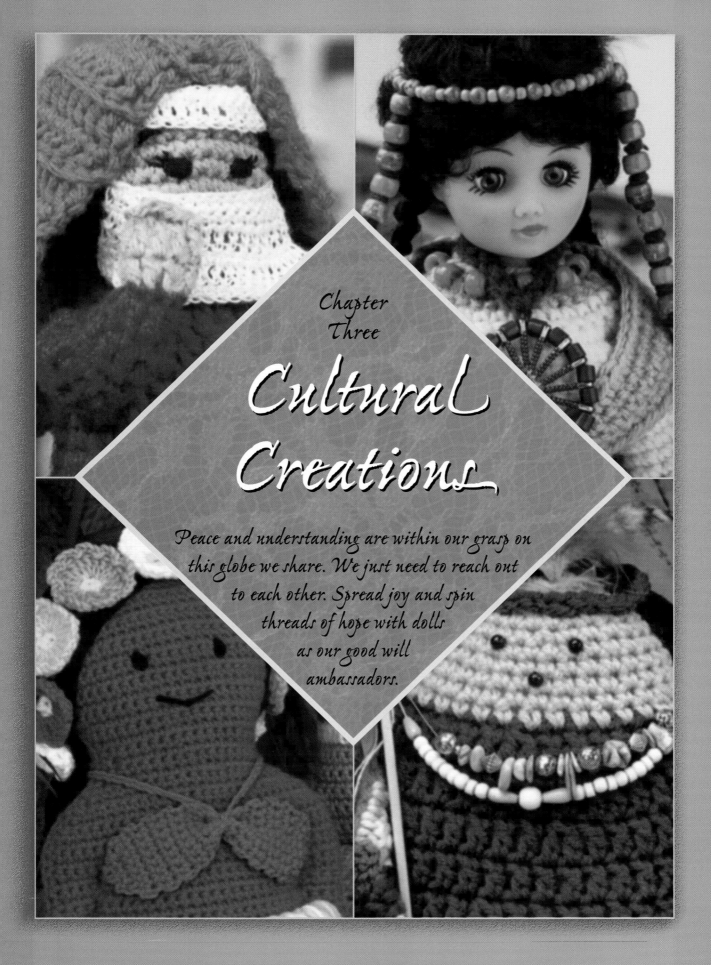

Chapter Three

Cultural Creations

Peace and understanding are within our grasp on
this globe we share. We just need to reach out
to each other. Spread joy and spin
threads of hope with dolls
as our good will
ambassadors.

Indian Brave & Maiden

**Designs by
Maxine Heffelbower**

Indian Maiden
Instructions begin on page 53

Indian Brave

Finished Size: Fits 15" doll.

Materials:
- Worsted yarn:
    - 3 oz. dk. brown
    - 2 oz. med. brown
    - 2 oz. lt. brown
    - 10 yds. turquoise
- 6 × 9-mm. pony beads:
    - 90 turquoise
    - 66 lt. brown
    - 33 med. brown
    - 22 dk. brown
- 34 turquoise 3-mm. barrel beads
- 34 med. brown 5-mm. round beads
- 142 turquoise 4-mm. seed beads
- 24 med. brown 3-mm. round beads
- 192 dk. brown 2-mm. seed beads
- 34 silver 6 × 19-mm. spaghetti beads
- Eight silver 34 × 35-mm. conchos in desired shapes
- Two turquoise feathers
- 24 silver size 00 *(small ¾")* safety pins
- 34 silver size 3 *(large 2")* safety pins
- 26-gauge wire:
    - One 6½" piece
    - One 9½" piece
    - One 10" piece
    - One 11" piece
- Needle-nose pliers
- One 15" boy doll
- One doll stand *(optional)*
- Two 6½"-long braided hair pieces to match doll's hair
- Craft glue
- Six size 4/0 snaps
- Tapestry and sewing needles
- Med. brown sewing thread
- G hook or hook needed to obtain gauge

Gauge: 4 sc = 1"; 4 sc rows = 1".

Basic Stitches: Ch, sl st, sc, hdc, dc.

TUNIC
Row 1: With med. brown, ch 25, sc in second ch from hook, sc in each ch across, turn. *(24 sc made)*

Row 2: Ch 1, sc in each of first 3 sc, 2 sc in next sc, (sc in each of next 3 sc, 2 sc in next sc) 5 times changing to lt. brown in last st made *(see Stitch Guide),* turn. Fasten off med. brown. *(30)*

Row 3: Ch 1, sc in each of first 3 sc, 2 sc in next sc, (sc in each of next 3 sc, 2 sc in next sc) 6 times, sc in each of last 2 sc, turn. *(37)*

Row 4: Ch 1, sc in each sc across, turn.

Row 5: Ch 1, sc in first 4 sc, 2 sc in next sc, (sc in next 4 sc, 2 sc in next sc) 6 times, sc in each of last 2 sc, turn. *(44)*

Rows 6–7: Ch 1, sc in each sc across, turn.

Row 8: Ch 1, sc in first 7 sc; for **armhole**, ch 7, skip next 7 sc; sc in next 16 sc; for **armhole**, ch 7, skip next 7 sc; sc in last 7 sc, turn. *(30 sc, 14 chs)*

Row 9: Ch 1, sc in each sc and in each ch across, turn. *(44 sc)*

Row 10: Ch 1, sc in first 4 sc, sc next 2 sc tog, sc in next 7 sc, sc next 2 sc tog, sc in next 14 sc, sc next 2 sc tog, sc in next 7 sc, sc next 2 sc tog, sc in last 4 sc, turn. *(40)*

Row 11: Ch 1, sc in first 4 sc, sc next 2 sc tog, sc in next 5 sc, sc next 2 sc tog, sc in next 14 sc, sc next 2 sc tog, sc in next 5 sc, sc next 2 sc tog, sc in last 4 sc, turn. *(36)*

Row 12: Ch 1, sc in each sc across, turn.

Row 13: Ch 1, sc in first 12 sc, sc next 2 sc tog, sc in next 8 sc, sc next 2 sc tog, sc in last 12 sc, turn. *(34)*

Row 14: Ch 1, sc in each sc across, turn.

Row 15: Ch 1, sc in first 11 sc, sc next 2 sc tog, sc in next 8 sc, sc next 2 sc tog, sc in last 11 sc, turn. *(32)*

Row 16: Ch 1, sc in first 10 sc, sc next 2 sc tog, sc in next 8 sc, sc next 2 sc tog, sc in last 10 sc, turn. *(30)*

Rows 17–20: Ch 1, sc in each sc across, turn.

Rnd 21: Working in rnds, ch 3 *(counts as first dc),* dc in each sc around, join with sl st in top of ch-3. *(30 dc)*

Rnd 22: Ch 3, skip next dc, (dc in next 6 dc, 2 dc in next dc) 3 times, dc in last 7 dc, join. *(32)*

Rnd 23: Ch 3, skip next dc, dc in next 4 dc, 2 dc in next dc, (dc in next 6 dc, 2 dc in next dc) 3 times, dc in last 4 dc, join. *(35)*

Rnd 24: Ch 3, dc in next dc, (dc in next 6 dc, 2 dc in next dc) 4 times, dc in last 5 dc, join. *(39)*

Rnd 25: Ch 3, skip next dc, dc in next 6 dc, 2 dc in next dc, dc in next 7 dc, 2 dc in next dc, dc in next 8 dc, (2 dc in next dc, dc in next 6 dc) 2 times, join. *(42)*

Rnds 26–27: Ch 3, dc in each dc around, join. At end of last rnd, fasten off.

Sleeves
Working around one armhole on row 8 of Tunic, join lt. brown with sc in third ch of ch-7, sc in each ch and in each sc around, join with sl st in first sc. Fasten off. *(14 sc made)*

Repeat on other armhole.

For **Tunic fringe,** cut 44 strands of dk. brown yarn each 8" long; fold one strand in half, insert hook in st, pull fold through st, pull ends through fold and tighten. Work fringe in each dc of last rnd on Tunic.

For **turquoise pony bead,** thread both strands of fringe through one pony bead, push bead up next to knot, tie a knot next to bottom of bead.

Continued on page 52

Continued from page 51

For **lt. brown pony bead,** thread both strands of fringe through one bead, allowing one bead-length from knot; tie knot next to bottom of bead.

Continue placing beads on fringe, alternating lt. brown and turquoise beads. Trim fringe to desired length.

With sewing thread and needle, sew six snaps evenly spaced down back opening of Tunic. Place Tunic on doll.

PANTS

Rnd 1: With med. brown, ch 30, sl st in first ch to form ring, ch 1, sc in each ch around, join with sl st in first sc. *(30 sc made)*

Rnd 2: Ch 1, sc in each sc around, join.

Rnds 3–4: Ch 2 *(counts as first hdc),* hdc in each st around, join with sl st in top of ch-2. *(30 hdc)*

Rnd 5: Ch 2, hdc in next 9 hdc, 2 hdc in next hdc, hdc in next 8 hdc, 2 hdc in next hdc, hdc in next 10 hdc, join. *(32)*

Rnd 6: Ch 2, hdc in next 9 hdc, 2 hdc in next hdc, hdc in next 10 hdc, 2 hdc in next hdc, hdc in next 10 hdc, join. *(34)*

Rnds 7–9: Ch 2, hdc in each hdc around, join.

Rnd 10: For **right leg,** ch 2, hdc in next 16 hdc leaving remaining sts unworked, join.

Rnds 11–21: Ch 2, hdc in next 16 hdc, join. At end of last rnd, fasten off.

Rnd 10: For **left leg,** join with sl st in first unworked st on rnd 9, ch 2, hdc in each unworked hdc around, join.

Rnds 11–21: Repeat rnds 11–21 of right leg.

Place Pants on doll.

COAT

Row 1: With dk. brown, ch 25, sc in second ch from hook, sc in each ch across, turn. *(24 sc made)*

Row 2: Ch 1, sc in first 4 sc, 2 sc in each of next 16 sc, sc in last 4 sc, turn. *(40)*

Row 3: Ch 1, 2 sc in first sc, sc in each sc across to last sc, 2 sc in last sc, turn. *(42)*

Row 4: Ch 1, sc in each sc across, turn.

Row 5: Ch 1, 2 sc in first sc, sc in each sc across to last sc, 2 sc in last sc, turn. *(44)*

Row 6: Ch 1, sc in each sc across, turn.

Row 7: Ch 1, 2 sc in first sc, sc in each sc across to last sc, 2 sc in last sc, turn. *(46)*

Row 8: Ch 1, sc in first 6 sc, 2 sc in next sc, sc across to last 7 sc, 2 sc in next sc, sc in last 6 sc, turn. *(48)*

Row 9: Ch 1, 2 sc in first sc, sc in each sc across to last sc, 2 sc in last sc, turn. *(50)*

Row 10: Ch 1, sc in first 7 sc; for **armhole,** ch 4, skip next 10 sc; sc in next 16 sc; for **armhole,** ch 4, skip next 10 sc; sc in next 7 sc, turn. *(30 sc, 8 chs)*

Row 11: Ch 1, 2 sc in first sc, sc in each sc and in each ch across to last sc, 2 sc in last sc, turn. *(40 sc)*

Rows 12–26: Ch 1, sc in each sc across, turn. At end of last row, **do not turn.**

Rnd 27: Working around outer edge, ch 1, 3 sc in end of row 26, sc in end of next 14 rows, 2 sc in end of row 11, sc in each row across to corner at neck, 3 sc in corner sc, sc in each st across row 1, 3 sc in end of row 1, sc in next 11 rows, 2 sc in next row, sc in each row to last row, 3 sc in end of row 26, sc in each st across bottom, join with sl st in first sc. Fasten off.

Sleeves

Rnd 1: Working around one armhole on row 10 of Coat, join dk. brown with sc in second ch of ch-4, sc in each ch and in each sc around, join with sl st in first sc. *(14 sc made)*

Rnds 2–8: Ch 1, sc in each sc around, join. At end of last rnd, fasten off.

Repeat on other armhole.

For **Coat fringe,** cut 37 strands of dk. brown each 8" long; fold one strand in half, insert hook in sc worked in end of row 20 on Coat, pull fold through st, pull ends through fold *(this will form knot)* and tighten. Work fringe in each sc from end of row 20 around bottom edge to other end of row 20.

For **beads,** pull both strands of fringe through one lt. brown pony bead, push bead up next to knot; tie a knot next to bottom of bead. Continue placing beads on fringe, alternating lt. brown and turquoise beads. Separate ends of fringe and trim to desired length.

With sewing thread and needle, sew turquoise seed beads between sts on last rnd of Sleeves.

Place Coat on doll.

CONCHOS

For **center front concho,** with med. brown, leaving 3" strand at each end, ch 30. Fasten off. Repeat with turquoise yarn.

With right side of Coat facing you, pull one end of each chain through first st on row 10 of Coat, run through concho and then through last st on row 10, with ends even; pull both ends pulling concho to Coat. Place one lt. brown, one dk. brown and one turquoise pony bead on end of 3" strands, tie a knot in end of strands next to last bead, leaving 1½" for fringe. Separate ends and trim. Repeat on other end of chains.

For **each remaining concho,** cut four 8" turquoise and four 8" med. brown strands of yarn; with tapestry needle and two strands of each color, run through concho, attach to Coat and back out to front of concho, thread beads on ends of strands same as before, making four fringe. Place remaining conchos on Coat as shown in photo.

NECKLACE

For **beaded safety pin** (make 25), open one small safety pin, place eight dk. brown seed beads on safety pin, close pin. Run 6½" wire through hole in one beaded safety pin (this will be next to the neck), place one med. brown round bead on wire next to safety pin. Alternating safety pins and round beads, continue until all safety pins and beads are strung. Place around neck of doll. With needle-nose pliers, twist ends of wire closed.

Beginning at back of neck, run one 9½" piece of wire through head of each beaded safety pin, placing one turquoise pony bead between each safety pin (this is the outside edge of Necklace). Twist ends of wire closed.

HEADDRESS

For **beaded safety pin** (make 34), place one silver spaghetti bead, one med. brown 5-mm. round bead and three turquoise seed beads on one large safety pin, close pin.

Run one 10" piece of wire through hole in each beaded safety pin, placing one turquoise pony bead between each safety pin (this will fit around doll's head). Twist ends of wire closed.

With one med. brown pony bead between each pin, run 11" piece of wire through heads on beaded safety pins. Twist ends of wire around first and last safety pin.

HEADBAND

Rnd 1: With dk. brown, ch 40, sl st in first ch to form ring, ch 1, sc in each ch around, join with sl st in first sc. Fasten off.

Rnd 2: Join turquoise with sc in last sc, sc in each sc around, join. Fasten off.

HAIR

Glue one braid to each side of doll's head, wrap lt. brown yarn approximately 2" from end on each braid. Secure yarn. Glue one feather in end of each braid. Place Headband and Headdress on doll as shown in photo. ❧

Indian Maiden

Finished Size: Fits 15" doll.

Materials:
- Worsted yarn:
  - 3 oz. ecru
  - 2 oz. lt. brown
  - 10 yds. turquoise
  - 10 yds. dk. brown
- 6 × 9-mm. pony beads:
  - 139 turquoise
  - 47 med. brown
  - 37 off-white
- 17 small dk. brown 3-mm. barrel beads
- 23 med. brown 5-mm. round beads
- 22 turquoise 4-mm. seed beads
- 320 dk. brown 2-mm. seed beads
- Two turquoise 11 × 25-mm. oval beads
- Two silver 34 × 35-mm. heart conchos
- Five turquoise feathers
- 40 silver size 00 (small ¾") safety pins
- 9" piece of 26-gauge wire
- Needle-nose pliers
- One 15" girl doll with long hair
- Doll stand (optional)
- Six size 4/0 snaps
- Tapestry and sewing needles
- Sewing thread to match dress
- G hook or hook needed to obtain gauge

Gauge: 4 sc = 1"; 4 sc rows = 1".

Basic Stitches: Ch, sl st, sc, hdc, dc, tr.

BODICE & OVERSKIRT

Row 1: For **Bodice**, with lt. brown, ch 24, sc in second ch from hook, sc in each ch across changing to ecru in last st (see Stitch Guide), turn. Fasten off lt. brown. (23 sc made)

Row 2: Ch 1, sc in each of first 3 sc, (2 sc in next sc, sc in next sc) 8 times, 2 sc in next sc, sc in each of last 3 sc, turn. (32)

Row 3: Ch 1, sc in each sc across, turn.

Row 4: Ch 1, sc in first 5 sc, 2 sc in each of next 22 sc, sc in last 5 sc, turn. (54)

Row 5: Ch 1, sc in each sc across, turn.

Row 6: Ch 1, sc in first 8 sc; for **armhole**, ch 4, skip next 10 sc; sc in next 18 sc; for **armhole**, ch 4, skip next 10 sc; sc in next 8 sc, turn. (34 sc, 8 chs)

Continued on page 54

Continued from page 53

Row 7: Ch 1, sc in each sc and in each ch across, turn. *(42 sc)*

Row 8: Ch 1, sc in each sc across, turn.

Row 9: Ch 1, sc in each of first 3 sc, (sc next 2 sc tog) 18 times, sc in each of last 3 sc, turn. *(24)*

Rows 10–13: Ch 1, sc in each sc across, turn.

Row 14: For **Overskirt**, ch 3 *(counts as first dc throughout)*, dc in same st, dc in each of next 2 sc, (2 dc in next sc, dc in next sc) across, ending with 2 dc in last sc, turn. *(36 dc)*

Rnd 15: Working in rnds, ch 3, dc in same st, dc in each of next 2 dc, 2 dc in next dc, (dc in each of next 3 dc, 2 dc in next dc) across, join with sl st in top of ch-3. *(46)*

Rnds 16–22: Ch 3, dc in each dc around, join.

Rnd 23: Ch 4 *(counts as first tr)*, tr in each dc around, join with sl st in top of ch-4. *(46 tr)*

Rnds 24–25: Ch 1, sc in each st around, join with sl st in first sc. At end of last rnd, fasten off.

Sleeves

Rnd 1: Working around one armhole, join ecru with sl st in second ch of ch-4, sc in same st as joining sl st, sc in each ch and in each sc around, join with sl st in first sc. *(14 sc made)*

Rnds 2–9: Ch 1, sc in first st, sc in each sc around, join; at end of last rnd, change to lt. brown in last st made. Fasten off ecru.

Rnd 10: For **trim**, ch 1, sc in each sc around, join.

Rnd 11: Ch 3, skip next sc, (hdc in next sc, ch 1, skip next sc) around, join with sl st in second ch of ch-3. Fasten off. *(7 hdc)*

Repeat on other armhole.

Trim

For **neck trim**, working in remaining lps on opposite side of starting ch on Bodice, join lt. brown with sl st in first ch, ch 3, skip next ch, hdc in next ch, (ch 1, skip next ch, hdc in next ch) across. Fasten off.

For **neck band trim**, with one 10" strand lt. brown yarn and tapestry needle, secure end at ch-3 on neck trim. Placing one turquoise pony bead in ch-1 sp between each hdc, run yarn through each st and pony bead around. Secure end.

For **sleeve bead trim**, repeat neck bead trim.

For **Overskirt fringe**, cut 46 strands of ecru yarn each 4" long; fold one strand in half, insert hook in st, pull fold through st, pull ends through fold *(this will form knot)*, pull tight. Work fringe in each sc on last rnd of Overskirt.

For **med. brown bead**, thread both strands of fringe through one pony bead, push bead up next to knot; tie a knot next to bottom of bead.

For **off-white bead**, thread both strands of fringe through one pony bead, allowing one bead length from knot; tie a knot next to bottom of bead.

Continue placing beads on fringe, alternating off-white and med. brown pony beads. Separate ends and trim to desired length.

With sewing thread and needle, sew snaps evenly spaced down back opening of bodice. Place Dress on doll.

UNDERSKIRT

Row 1: With lt. brown, ch 25, sc in second ch from hook, sc in each ch across, turn. *(24 sc made)*

Row 2: Ch 3 *(counts as dc)*, dc in same st as ch 3, dc in each st across to last st, 2 dc in last st, turn. *(26 dc)*

Row 3: Ch 4 *(counts as first tr)*, tr in each dc across, turn. *(26 tr)*

Row 4: Ch 4, tr in same st as ch-4, tr in each tr across to last tr, 2 tr in last tr, turn. *(28)*

Rnd 5: Working in rnds, ch 4, tr in each tr around to last tr, 2 tr in last tr, join with sl st in top of ch-4. *(29)*

Rnd 6: Ch 4, tr in same st as ch-4, 2 tr in each tr around, join. *(58)*

Rnds 7–11: Ch 4, tr in each tr around, join.

Rnd 12: Ch 1, 2 sc in each tr around, join with sl st in first sc. *(116 sc)*

Rnd 13: Ch 4, tr in each sc around, join with sl st in top of ch-4. Fasten off.

For **Underskirt bead trim**, with one strand lt. brown yarn and tapestry needle, secure yarn at first ch-4 on rnd 11, place one turquoise pony bead on yarn, skip next st, (run yarn through next st, place one pony bead on yarn, skip next st) around. Secure end.

Place Underskirt on doll. With tapestry needle and lt. brown, sew ends of rows 1–4 together.

CAPE

Rnd 1: With lt. brown, ch 55, sc in second ch from hook, sc in each ch across to last ch, 3 sc in last ch; working in remaining lps on opposite side of starting ch, sc in each ch across to last ch, 3 sc in last ch, join with sl st in first sc. Fasten off.

Row 2: With right side facing you, join lt. brown with sc in 13th sc, sc in next 28 sc leaving remaining sts unworked, turn. *(29 sc)*

Row 3: Skip first sc, sc in next 26 sc, sc last 2 sc tog, turn. *(27)*

Rows 4–14: Skip first sc, sc in each sc across to last 2 sc, sc last 2 sc tog, turn. At end of last row *(5)*.

Row 15: Sc first 2 sc tog, sc in next sc, sc last 2 sc tog. Fasten off.

Rnd 16: Working around outer edge, with lt. brown, join with sc in last sc on last row, sc in each sc and in end of each row around to last sc on row 14, sc in first sc on row 14, 3 sc in next sc, join with sl st in first sc. Fasten off.

CONCHOS

For each **concho,** with dk. brown, leaving 3" strand at each end, ch 30. Fasten off. Repeat with turquoise yarn.

Place one heart Concho centered across rows 11–14 of Cape. Pull both chains through Concho; with ends even, pull both ends on each chain through Cape, pulling Concho to Cape. Place one off-white, one turquoise and one med. brown pony bead on each end of each chain, tie knot in each end, leaving 1½" for fringe. Separate each end and trim to desired length.

For **front Concho,** place at bottom on front of Cape, overlapping front ends of Cape and running chains through both thicknesses on Cape.

BELT

For **beaded safety pin** *(make 20),* open one small safety pin, place eight dk. brown seed beads on safety pin, close pin.

With one 10" piece of lt. brown yarn and tapestry needle, secure yarn to back of Bodice at waist, run yarn through hole in safety pin *(this is top of Belt),* then one turquoise pony bead; alternating safety pins and pony beads, continue until safety pins and pony beads are strung. Secure end.

With one 10" piece of lt. brown yarn and tapestry needle, secure yarn to back of Bodice at waist, run yarn through center of each safety pin, with one turquoise pony bead between each *(this is bottom of Belt).* Secure end.

NECKLACE

Make 17 beaded safety pins same as for Belt.

With small piece of dk. brown yarn and tapestry needle, run yarn through hole in each safety pin, tie ends in knot *(this is center of Necklace).*

With small piece of dk. brown yarn and tapestry needle, run yarn through head of each safety pin with one dk. brown barrel bead between each. Tie ends in knot.

With dk. brown yarn and G hook, ch 30, join with sl st in first ch. Fasten off. Run small piece of dk. brown yarn through head on one safety pin, attach to ch-30. Place around doll's neck.

HEADBAND

Alternating med. brown round beads and small turquoise seed beads, place on 9" wire, with needle-nose pliers twist both ends together forming a circle. Cut 16" piece of dk. brown yarn, fold in half over wire between beads, run both ends of yarn through one med. brown pony bead, tie knot; run ends through turquoise pony bead, tie knot; continue until you have five med. brown beads and four turquoise beads. Place one oval turquoise bead on end of yarn, tie knot, separate ends and trim to desired length. Glue feather in end of oval bead. Repeat on other side of Headband.

HAIR

Make one braid on each side of head, wrap lt. brown yarn around ends of braid, about 2" from end, secure yarn; glue one feather in each end of braid. Glue one feather in hair at back of head, allowing top of feather to stand up over head. ✤

Playing it Safe with Toys

Crochet dolls and toys are tailor-made for giving to loved ones, especially children. But it's wise to carefully consider making these special gifts as safe as possible, especially for little ones under age three.

Faces are the most appealing, but potentially the most dangerous, part of a doll or toy. Never attach anything to a small child's doll or toy that can be pulled or chewed off and swallowed.

Use glue for placement only and always sew features, decorations and buttons, which should not be used at all for young children, securely. Carpet thread is stronger than sewing thread for this use. *(See page 116 for more tips on faces.)*

Chenille stems are not recommended for small children because of their sharp wire ends that can work through stitches.

Crochet toy or doll patterns can be converted into rattles for baby, but keep safety in mind. To use jingle bells, tie a clump together and insert into the middle of the inside stuffing. Or put dried beans or unpopped popcorn into a small plastic container duct-taped securely shut and place deep inside the doll or toy.

When giving the completed toy or doll, it's helpful to include cleaning information. *(See page 72 for tips.)* Specify if your gift is washable by machine or by hand *(it isn't if you used cardboard),* so a beloved toy can be kept fresh for hugging. ✤

Jolly Scotsman

**Design by
Virginia Freas**

Finished Size:
Approximately 11½"
tall.

Materials:
- Worsted yarn:
  1 oz. black
  1 oz. red
  1 oz. green
  1 oz. fleshtone
  1 oz. navy blue
  Small amount
  each white
  and burnt
  orange
- Small amount
  white sport
  yarn
- Rust, gold, blue
  and black
  embroidery
  floss
- Polyester fiberfill
- Tapestry and
  embroidery nee-
  dles
- G, H and I hooks
  or hook needed
  to obtain gauge

Gauge: **G hook and
single strand
worsted yarn,** 4 sc =
1"; 4 sc rows = 1".

Basic Stitches: Ch, sl
st, sc, hdc, dc.

SHOES

Rnd 1: With two strands black and H hook, ch 32, sl st in first ch to form ring, ch 1, sc in each ch around, join with sl st in first sc. *(32 sc made)*

Rnd 2: Ch 3, dc in each st around, join with sl st in top of ch-3. Fasten off.

SOCKS

Rnd 1: With H hook, join single strand white worsted yarn with sl st in top of ch-3 on last rnd; working in **back lps** *(see Stitch Guide)*, ch 3, dc in each st around, join. Fasten off.

Rnd 2: Join single strand red with sl st in top of ch-3 on last rnd, ch 2, hdc in each st around, join with sl st in top of ch-2. Fasten off.

LEGS

Rnd 1: With H hook, join single strand fleshtone with sl st in top of ch-3 on last rnd, ch 3, dc in each st around, join with sl st in top of ch-3.

Rnd 2: Ch 3, dc in each st around, join. Fasten off.

KILT

Rnd 1: With H hook, join single strand red with sl st in top of ch-3 on last rnd, ch 1, sc in same st, sc in each st around, join with sl st in first sc.

Rnd 2: Working this rnd in **back lps**, ch 3, dc in next 6 sts, 2 dc in next st, (dc in next 7 sts, 2 dc in next st) 3 times, join. *(36)*

Rnd 3: Ch 3, dc in each st around, join.

Rnd 4: Ch 1, sc in first 4 sts, sc next 2 sts tog, (sc in next 4 sts, sc next 2 sts tog) 5 times, join. Fasten off. *(30)*

Rnd 5: Turn body upside down; working in remaining lps of rnd 1 on Kilt, join single strand red with sl st in lp at base of ch-3, ch 3, dc in each remaining lp around, join. Fasten off.

Sew through middle of bottom portion to rnd 1 of Kilt, forming legs of equal size and changing yarn colors to match color changes on doll.

Embroider vertical running stitches *(see Stitch Guide)* of navy through Kilt and through red stripes of Socks. Embroider horizontal running stitches of green through Kilt and Socks to create plaid effect *(see photo)*.

SHIRT

Rnd 1: With H hook, join single strand green with sl st in top of ch-3 on last rnd of Kilt, ch 3, dc in next 12 sts, dc next 2 sts tog, dc in next 13 sts, dc next 2 sts tog, join. *(28)*

Rnd 2: Ch 3, dc in next 11 sts, dc next 2 sts tog, dc in next 12 sts, dc next 2 sts tog, join. *(26)*

Rnds 3–4: Ch 3, dc in each st around, join.

Rnd 5: Ch 3, dc in next 10 sts, dc next 2 sts tog, dc in next 11 sts, dc next 2 sts tog, join. *(24)*

Rnd 6: Change to H hook; ch 1, sc in each of first 2 sts, sc next 2 sts tog, (sc in each of next 2 sts, sc next 2 sts tog) 5 times, join. *(18)*

Rnd 7: Ch 1, sc in each st around, join. Fasten off.

SHOE SOLE (make 2)

With two strands black and H hook, ch 4, sl st in first ch to form ring, ch 3, 15 dc in ring, join with sl st in top of ch-3. Fasten off.

With single strand black, working through remaining lps of starting ch on Shoe and both lps on Sole, sc one Sole to bottom of one Leg. Fasten off. Repeat on other Leg.

SLEEVE (make 2)

Rnd 1: With single strand green and H hook, ch 9, sl st in first ch to form ring, ch 3, dc in each ch around, join with sl st in top of ch-3. *(9 dc made)*

Rnds 2–4: Ch 3, dc in each st around, join.

Rnd 5: Sc in first st, hdc in each of next 2 sts, dc in next st, hdc in each of next 2 sts, sc in next st, sl st in next st. Fasten off.

HAND (make 2)

Rnd 1: With single strand fleshtone and G hook, ch 8, sl st in first ch to form ring, ch 3, dc in each ch around, join with sl st in top of ch-3. *(8 dc made)*

Rnd 2: Ch 3, dc in each st around, join.

Rnd 3: To close Hand, fold last rnd in half, matching first four and last four sts; working through both thicknesses, ch 1, sc in next 4 sts. Fasten off. Stuff lightly.

Sew Hand into bottom of Sleeve with single strand green. Sew top of Sleeves to top of rnd 5 on each side of Shirt. Tack Sleeves and Hands in place on sides of body.

HEAD

Rnd 1: With single strand fleshtone and G hook, ch 18, sl st in first ch to form ring, ch 1, sc in each ch around, join with sl st in first sc. *(18 sc made)*

Rnd 2: Ch 1, sc in each of first 2 sts, 2 sc in next

Continued on page 58

Continued from page 57

st, (sc in each of next 2 sts, 2 sc in next st) 5 times, join. *(24)*

Rnd 3: Ch 1, sc in first 5 sts, 2 sc in next st, (sc in next 5 sts, 2 sc in next st) 3 times, join. *(28)*

Rnd 4: Ch 1, sc in first 6 sts, 2 sc in next st, (sc in next 6 sts, 2 sc in next st) 3 times, join. *(32)*

Rnds 5–11: Ch 1, sc in each st around, join.

Rnd 12: Ch 1, sc in each of first 2 sts, sc next 2 sts tog, (sc in each of next 2 sts, sc next 2 sts tog) 7 times, join. *(24)*

Rnd 13: Ch 1, sc first 2 sts tog, (sc next 2 sts tog) 11 times, join. *(12)*

Rnd 14: Ch 1, sc first 2 sts tog, (sc next 2 sts tog) 5 times, join. Stuff firmly. *(6)*

Rnd 15: (Sl st next 2 sts tog) 3 times to close. Fasten off.

With single strand green, sew Head to neck.

TAM

Rnd 1: With single strand navy and F hook, ch 4, sc in second ch from hook, sc in each of next 2 chs; working in remaining lps on opposite side of starting ch, sc in each of next 3 chs, join with sl st in first st. *(6 sc made)*

Rnd 2: Ch 1, 2 sc in each st around, join. *(12)*

Rnd 3: Ch 1, 2 sc in each of first 3 sts, sc in each of next 3 sts, 2 sc in each of next 3 sts, sc in each of last 3 sts, join. *(18)*

Rnd 4: Ch 1, 2 sc in each of first 4 sts, sc in next 5 sts, 2 sc in each of next 4 sts, sc in last 5 sts, join. *(26)*

Rnd 5: Ch 1, sc in first 25 sts, 2 sc in last st, join. *(27)*

Rnd 6: Ch 1, sc in first 26 sts, 2 sc in last st, join. *(28)*

Rnd 7: Ch 1, sc in each st around, join.

Rnd 8: Ch 1, sc in first 27 sts, 2 sc in last st, join. *(29)*

Rnd 9: Ch 1, sc in first 28 sts, 2 sc in last st, join. *(30)*

Rnd 10: Ch 1, sc in first 14 sts, 2 sc in next st, sc in next 14 sts, 2 sc in last st, join. Fasten off. *(32)*

Using single strand red, embroider two rows of running sts in rnds 9 and 10 of Tam. At left front of Tam, embroider four or five satin stitches to resemble feather.

Place Tam on Head in desired position, lightly trace around outer edge with pencil.

HAIR

Cut 15–20 strands burnt orange 12" long. Working with one strand of yarn at a time, sew long straight stitches around head, using circle previously drawn as beginning and ending point. Lengthen and shorten stitches as desired. Pull all loose ends to inside of circle, or inside head. Stuff Tam lightly and sew into place, covering loose ends. Crease Tam down the middle and tack through Tam into Head, to hold crease in place.

BELT

With white sport yarn and G hook, ch 50, sc in second ch from hook, sc in each ch across. Fasten off. Place around waist, tack ends together; tack in place at center back.

With white sport yarn and G hook, ch 40, sc in second ch from hook, sc in each ch across. Fasten off. Tack one end of this piece to belt at left front, place over right shoulder and tack other end to left back.

SPORRAN *(purse hanging from belt)*

Row 1: With white sport yarn and G hook, ch 7, sc in second ch from hook, sc in each ch across, turn. *(6 sc made)*

Row 2: Ch 1, sc in first 5 sts, 2 sc in last st, turn. *(7)*

Row 3: Ch 1, sc in first 6 sts, 2 sc in last st, turn. *(8)*

Row 4: Ch 1, sc in first 7 sts, 2 sc in last st, turn. *(9)*

Rows 5–7: Ch 1, skip first st, sc in next st, sc in each st across, turn. *(8, 7, 6)* At end of last row, fasten off.

Sew Sporran to center front of Belt and tack to body *(see photo)*.

Embroider buckle at center front of Belt with gold embroidery floss.

For each **tassel** *(make 2)*, cut 2 strands black embroidery floss each 2" long, fold in half and tack in place on front of Sporran *(see photo)*.

Using satin stitch and navy yarn, embroider eyes over rnds 6 and 7 at center front of Head about ½" apart. Using outline stitch and 2-ply rust floss, embroider nose over rnd 5 and mouth over rnd 4. ❖

Flamenco Dancer

Design by Frances Morse

Instructions begin on page 60

Flamenco Dancer

Finished Size: Fits 11½" fashion doll.

Materials:
- Size 10 crochet cotton:
    - 500 yds. red
    - 450 yds. black
- Three size 4/0 snaps
- 90 silver 5-mm. sequins
- 90 red seed beads
- Red sewing thread and needle
- No. 7 steel hook or hook needed to obtain gauge

Gauge: 8 dc = 1"; 4 dc rows = 1".

Basic Stitches: Ch, sl st, sc, dc.

Special Stitches: For **double treble crochet (dtr),** yo 3 times, insert hook in st or ch sp, yo, pull through, (yo, pull through 2 lps on hook) 4 times.

For **triple treble crochet (ttr),** yo 4 times, insert hook in st or ch sp, yo, pull through, (yo, pull through 2 lps on hook) 5 times.

BODICE

Row 1: With red, ch 44, dc in fourth ch from hook, dc in next 5 chs, ch 7, skip next 7 chs, dc in next 14 chs, ch 7, skip next 7 chs, dc in last 7 chs, turn. *(28 dc, 14 chs made)*

Row 2: Ch 3 *(counts as first dc),* dc in each st and in each ch across, turn. *(42 dc)*

Row 3: Ch 3, dc in each st across, turn.

Row 4: Ch 3, dc in next 16 sts, dc next 2 sts tog, dc in next 4 sts, dc next 2 sts tog, dc in next 17 sts, turn. *(40)*

Row 5: Ch 3, (dc in each of next 3 sts, dc next 2 sts tog) 7 times, dc in last 4 sts, turn. *(33)*

Row 6: Ch 3, (dc in each of next 2 sts, dc next 2 sts tog) 7 times, dc in last 4 sts, turn. *(26)*

Rows 7–8: Repeat row 3. At end of last row, **do not fasten off.**

SKIRT

Row 1: Ch 3, (dc in each of next 3 sts, 2 dc in next st) 6 times, dc in last st, turn. *(32 dc made)*

Row 2: Ch 3, 2 dc in next st, dc in each of next 2 sts, (2 dc in next st, dc in each of next 3 sts) across, turn. *(40)*

Rnd 3: Working in rnds, ch 3, dc in each st around, join with sl st in top of ch-3.

Rnd 4–6: Ch 3, dc in each st around, join.

Rnd 7: Ch 5, **ttr** *(see Special Stitches)* in same st, 2 ttr in each of next 12 sts, **2 dtr** *(see Special Stitches)* in each of next 14 sts, 2 ttr in each of next 13 sts, join with sl st in top of ch-5. *(80 sts)*

Rnd 8: Ch 3, dc in same st, 2 dc in each of next 25 sts, 2 sc in each of next 28 sts, 2 dc in each of next 26 sts, join. *(160)*

Rnd 9: Working this rnd in **back lps** *(see Stitch Guide),* ch 1, sc in each st around, join with sl st in first sc.

Rnd 10: Ch 5, ttr in same st, (ttr in each of next 3 sts, 2 ttr in next st) 13 times, (dtr in next 5 sts, 2 dtr in next st) 9 times, (ttr in each of next 3 sts, 2 ttr in next st) 13 times, ttr in next st, join. *(196)*

Rnd 11: Ch 3, dc in each of next 3 sts, 2 dc in next st, (dc in next 4 sts, 2 dc in next st) 12 times, (sc in next 4 sts, 2 sc in next st) 13 times, sc in next st, (dc in next 4 sts, 2 dc in next st) 13 times, join. *(235)*

Rnd 12: Repeat rnd 9.

Rnd 13: Ch 5, ttr in next 4 sts, 2 ttr in next st, (ttr in next 5 sts, 2 ttr in next st) 12 times, (dtr in next 5 sts, 2 dtr in next st) 13 times, dtr in next st, (ttr in next 5 sts, 2 ttr in next st) 13 times, join. *(274)*

Rnd 14: Ch 3, (dc in next 5 sts, 2 dc in next st) 15 times, (sc in next 5 sts, 2 sc in next st) 15 times, sc in each of next 2 sts, (dc in next 5 sts, 2 dc in next st) 15 times, dc in last st, join. *(319)*

Rnd 15: Repeat rnd 9.

Rnd 16: Ch 5, ttr in each of next 2 sts, 2 ttr in next st, (ttr in next 5 sts, 2 ttr in next st) 17 times, (dtr in next 5 sts, 2 dtr in next st) 17 times, dtr in next 5 sts, (ttr in next 5 sts, 2 ttr in next st) 17 times, ttr in next 4 sts, join. *(371)*

Rnd 17: Ch 3, dc in each of next 2 sts, (dc in next 5 sts, 2 dc in next st) 20 times, (sc in next 5 sts, 2 sc in next st) 20 times, sc in next 5 sts, (dc in next 5 sts, 2 dc in next st) 20 times, dc in each of next 2 sts, 2 dc in last st, join. *(432)*

Rnd 18: Repeat rnd 9.

Rnd 19: Ch 5, ttr in next 4 sts, 2 ttr in next st, (ttr in next 5 sts, 2 ttr in next st) 23 times, (dtr in next 5 sts, 2 dtr in next st) 24 times, (ttr in next 5 sts, 2 ttr in next st) 24 times, join. *(504)*

Rnd 20: Ch 3, dc in next 6 sts, 2 dc in next st, (dc in next 7 sts, 2 dc in next st) 19 times, dc in next 5 sts, (sc in next 7 sts, 2 sc in next st) 21 times, sc in next 7 sts, (dc in next 7 sts, 2 dc in next st) 20 times, dc in last 4 sts, join. *(565)*

Rnd 21: Repeat rnd 9.

Rnd 22: Ch 5, ttr in next 4 sts, (ttr in next 9 sts, 2 dc in next st) 18 times, dtr in next 5 sts, (dtr in next 10 sts, 2 dtr in next st) 17 times, dtr in next 5 sts, (ttr in next 9 sts, 2 ttr in next st) 18 times, ttr in each of last 3 sts, join. *(618)*

Rnd 23: Ch 3, dc in next 4 sts, (dc in next 9 sts, 2 dc in next st) 19 times, sc in next 4 sts, (sc in next 9 sts, 2 sc in next st) 21 times, sc in next 9 sts, (dc in next 9 sts, 2 dc in next st) 20 times, join. Fasten off. *(678)*

Using red sewing thread, sew 80 sequins and beads evenly spaced on rnd 8 of Skirt.

Continued on page 69

Native American Pals

Designs by Michele Wilcox

Instructions begin on page 62

Native American Pals

Finished Size: Approximately 15" tall.

Basic Materials:
- Worsted yarn:
    Amounts needed for desired doll
- Polyester fiberfill
- Tapestry needle
- G hook or hook needed to obtain gauge

Gauge: 4 sc = 1"; 4 sc rows = 1".

Basic Stitches: Ch, sl st, sc, hdc, dc.

Hawaiian Girl
Materials:
- Worsted yarn:
    5 oz. med. brown
    1 oz. black
    1 oz. lavender
    1 oz. variegated tan
    ¼ oz. yellow
    ¼ oz. pink
    ¼ oz. lt. blue
    ¼ oz. white

Indian Boy
Materials:
- Worsted yarn:
    2½ oz. lt. gold
    2 oz. black
    2 oz. dk. brown
    2 oz. lt. rust
    ½ oz. green
    ¼ oz. red
- Wooden beads:
    Twelve ½" oval
    Three ⅝" round
- 5" feather

Eskimo Girl
Materials:
- Worsted yarn:
    3 oz. dk. green
    1½ oz. gray
    1½ oz. white
    1½ oz. tan
    1½ oz. pink
    10 yds. black
- Powdered blush
- Blush brush
- Wire pet brush

HAWAIIAN GIRL
BODY SIDE (make 2)
Row 1: With med. brown, ch 34, sc in second ch from hook, sc in each ch across, turn. *(33 sc made)*

Row 2: Ch 1, 2 sc in first st, sc in each st across to last st, 2 sc in last st, turn. *(35)*

Rows 3–5: Ch 1, sc in each st across, turn.

Rows 6–8: Ch 1, sc first 2 sts tog, sc in each st across to last 2 sts, sc last 2 sts tog, turn. *(33, 31, 29)*

Rows 9–19: Repeat row 3.

Rows 20–22: Repeat row 2. *(31, 33, 35)*

Rows 23–24: Repeat row 3.

Row 25: Repeat row 6. *(33)*

Row 26: Repeat row 3.

Row 27: Ch 1, sc first 2 sts tog, sc in each of next 3 sts; working in **back lps** *(see Stitch Guide)* sc in next 23 sts; working in both lps, sc in each of next 3 sts, sc last 2 sts tog, turn. *(31)*

Rows 28–37: Repeat row 3.

Rows 38–45: Repeat row 6, ending with 15 sts in last row.

Rows 46–50: Repeat row 2, ending with 25 sts in last row.

Rows 51–60: Repeat row 3.

Rows 61–65: Repeat row 6. At end of last row *(15)*, **do not turn.**

Rnd 66: Working around outer edge, ch 1, sc in end of each row and in each st around, join with sl st in first sc. Fasten off.

FINISHING
With **front lps** of row 26 as right side of work, hold pieces with wrong sides together; working in **back lps** of rnd 66, sew sides together, stuffing before closing.

ARMS & LEGS
For **each Arm,** sew through all thicknesses from first st at one end of row 19 to third st on row 20, then across rows 21–34 four sts over from ends of rows *(see illustration)*. For **Legs,** sew through all thicknesses at center st over rows 1–13.

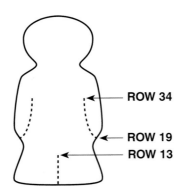

HAIR
Cut 72 strands black each 22" long. Sew center of strands to center of head beginning at row 62 on front and across top of head and down to row 55 on center back of head. Sew Hair in

place across back at neckline and on sides of face. Trim ends even.

FACIAL FEATURES

For **mouth,** with black, sew one 1¼"-long st loosely across center of row 50 and catch into a smile with a small st in the middle on the row below. For **each eye,** with black, using Satin Stitch *(see Stitch Guide)*, embroider over rows 54 and 55, with 7 sts between *(see photo)*.

GRASS SKIRT

Cut 138 strands variegated tan each 10" long. Working in **front lps** on row 26, with 3 strands held together, fold in half, insert hook in st, pull fold through st, pull ends through fold and tighten. Repeat in each st across front and back. Trim ends even with row 9.

BIKINI TOP

Row 1: With lavender, for **tie,** ch 40; 3 sc in second ch from hook, turn. *(3 sc made)*

Rows 2–3: Ch 1, 2 sc in first st, sc in each st across to last st, 2 sc in last st, turn. *(5, 7)*

Rows 4–23: Ch 1, sc in each st across, turn.

Rows 24–25: Ch 1, sc first 2 sts tog, sc in each st across to last 2 sts, sc last 2 sts tog, turn. *(5, 3)*

Row 26: Sc first 3 sts tog; for **tie,** ch 39. Fasten off.

Insert hook from back to front through seam on Body at underarm, pull one tie through to back. Repeat for other tie on opposite seam. Tie in bow at back.

For **neck tie,** with lavender, ch 100. Fasten off. Tie center of neck tie around center of Bikini Top, tie in bow at back of neck under Hair.

FLOWER (make 3 each lavender, pink, white and blue)

Rnd 1: With yellow, ch 2, 6 sc in second ch from hook, join with sl st in first sc. Fasten off. *(6 sc made)*

Rnd 2: Join Flower color with sl st in any st, ch 3, 2 dc in same st, 3 dc in each st around, join with sl st in top of ch-3. *(18)*

Rnd 3: (Ch 3, skip next st, sl st in next st) around, ending with last sl st in same st as first ch-3. Fasten off.

Sew Flowers to head across hairline at edge of face and across back at neckline.

INDIAN BOY

BODY SIDE (make 2)

Rows 1–10: With dk. brown, repeat rows 1–10 of Hawaiian Girl Body Side on page 62. At end of last row, fasten off.

Row 11: Join lt. gold with sc in first st, sc in each st across, turn.

Rows 12–19: Ch 1, sc in each st across, turn.

Rows 20–45: Repeat rows 20–45 of Hawaiian Girl Body Side. At end of last row, fasten off.

Row 46: Join lt. rust with sc in first st, sc in same st, sc in each at across to last st, 2 sc in last st, turn. *(17)*

Rows 47–50: Ch 1, 2 sc in first st, sc in each st across to last st, 2 sc in last st, turn. *(At end of last row, 25)*

Rows 51–65: Repeat rows 51–65 of Hawaiian Girl Body Side.

NOTE: *When changing colors, fasten off color not being used.*

Rnd 66: Working around outer edge, ch 1, sc in end of each row and in each st around changing colors *(see Stitch Guide)* as colors change on piece, join with sl st in first sc. Fasten off.

FINISHING

Sew together, form arms and legs, and embroider face same as Hawaiian Girl.

HAIR

Cut 60 strands black each 28" long. Sew center of strands to center of head beginning at row 65 on front and across top of head and down center back to row 49. Tie 12" strand black around Hair on each side of head at row 49, tack in place to sides of head. Braid hair on each side. Starting ½" from end, wrap red yarn around each braid for 1", secure ends. Trim ends of braid.

With red and green, using backstitch, straight stitch and French knot *(see Stitch Guide)*, embroider design on front of shirt as shown in photo.

SHIRT FRINGE

Cut 46 strands lt. gold each 3" long. Working in **front lps** of row 26, fold one strand in half, insert hook in st, pull fold through st, pull ends through fold, tighten. Repeat in each st across front and back.

HEADBAND

Row 1: With green, ch 62, sc in second ch from hook, sc in each ch across, turn. Fasten off. *(61 sc made)*

Row 2: Working in remaining lps on opposite side of starting ch, join red with sc in first ch, *insert hook in center of next st on row 1, complete as for sc, sc in each of next 2 chs; repeat from * across, turn. Fasten off.

Row 3: Join green with sc in first st, sc in each st across. Fasten off.

Sew ends of rows together. Place around head and place feather in back.

With round beads in center, string beads on yarn, place around neck and tie in back.

ESKIMO GIRL

BACK

Rows 1–13: With gray, repeat rows 1–13 of Hawaiian Girl Body Side on page 62. At end of last row, fasten off.

Continued on page 72

Persian Princess

Design by Virginia Freas

Finished Size: Approximately 10½" tall.

Materials:
- Worsted yarn:
    - 1 oz. lt. blue
    - 1 oz. dk. blue
    - 1 oz. med. blue
    - 1 oz. tan
- Small amount white size 10 crochet cotton
- Small amount gold sport yarn
- Black embroidery floss
- Polyester fiberfill
- Tapestry and embroidery needles
- D, G, H and I hooks or hook needed to obtain gauge

Gauge: G hook and single strand worsted yarn, 4 sc = 1"; 4 sc rows = 1".

Basic Stitches: Ch, sl st, sc, dc.

SKIRT
Rnd 1: With two strands lt. blue held together and I hook, ch 36, sl st in first ch to form ring, ch 3, dc in each ch around, join with sl st in top of ch-3. *(36 dc made)*
Rnd 2: Ch 3, dc in each st around, join.
Rnd 3: Ch 3, dc in each of next 3 sts, dc next 2 sts tog, (dc in next 4 sts, dc next 2 sts tog) 5 times, join. *(30)*
Rnd 4: Ch 3, dc in each st around, join.
Rnd 5: Ch 3, dc in each of next 2 sts, dc next 2 sts tog, (dc in each of next 3 sts, dc next 2 sts tog) 5 times, join. *(24)*
Rnd 6: Ch 3, dc in each of next 3 sts, dc next 2 sts tog, (dc in next 4 sts, dc next 2 sts tog) 3 times, join. Fasten off. *(20)*

BOTTOM
Rnd 1: With two strands lt. blue held together and I hook, ch 4, sl st in first ch to form ring, ch 3, 15 dc in ring, join with sl st in top of ch-3. *(16 dc made)*
Rnd 2: Ch 3, dc in same st, 2 dc in each st around, join. Fasten off. *(32)*
Rnd 3: Join two strands dk. blue held together with sl st in top of ch-3, ch 1, sc in same st, sc in next 6 sts, 2 sc in next st, (sc in next 7 sts, 2 sc in next st) 3 times, join with sl st in first sc. Fasten off. *(36)*
Working through both thicknesses in remaining lps of starting ch on Skirt and both lps of last rnd on Bottom, with single strand dk. blue and I hook, join with sc in first st, sc in each st around, join. Fasten off.

BLOUSE
Rnd 1: Using I hook, join two strands dk. blue held together with sl st in top of ch-3 on last rnd of Skirt, ch 1, sc in same st and in each st around, join with sl st in first sc. *(20 sc made)*
Rnds 2–4: Ch 1, sc in each st around, join.

Rnd 5: Ch 3, dc in each of next 3 sts, 2 dc in next st, (dc in next 4 sts, 2 dc in next st) 3 times, join. *(24 dc)*
Rnd 6: Ch 3, dc in each st around, join. Fasten off one strand of dk. blue.
Rnd 7: Continuing with single strand dk. blue, change to H hook, ch 1, sc in same st, sc in each of next 3 sts, sc next 2 sts tog, (sc in next 4 sts, sc next 2 sts tog) 3 times, join. *(20)*
Rnd 8: Ch 1, sc in same st, sc in next 7 sts, sc next 2 sts tog, sc in next 8 sts, sc next 2 sts tog, join. Fasten off. Stuff firmly. *(18)*

Blouse Trim
Working in last rnd of Skirt, with I hook, join single strand dk. blue with sl st in same st as beginning sc of Blouse, ch 1, sc in same st, ch 6, skip next st, sc in next st, (ch 6, skip next st, sc in next st) 8 times, ch 6, skip last st, sl st in first st. Fasten off.

SLEEVE (make 2)
Rnd 1: With single strand dk. blue and H hook, ch 9, sl st in first ch to form ring, ch 3, dc in each ch around, join with sl st in top of ch-3. *(Bottom of sleeve made—9 dc made)*
Rnds 2–4: Ch 3, dc in each st around, join.
Rnd 5: Sc in first st, hdc in each of next 2 sts, dc in next st, hdc in each of next 2 sts, sc in next st, sl st in last st. Fasten off. Stuff lightly. *(8)*

HAND (make 2)
NOTE: *Separate about 2 yds. of tan into 2-ply strands for Hands.*
Rnd 1: With 2-ply tan and G hook, ch 8, sl st in first ch to form ring, ch 3, dc in each ch around, join with sl st in top of ch-3. *(8 dc made)*

Continued on page 66

Continued from page 65

Rnd 2: Ch 3, dc in each st around, join.

Rnd 3: To close hand, fold last rnd in half, matching first four sts and last four sts; working through both thicknesses, ch 1, sc in next 4 sts. Fasten off. Stuff lightly.

Sew Hand to bottom of Sleeve with dk. blue. Sew top of Sleeves to rnd 6 on each side of Blouse.

HEAD

Rnd 1: With single strand tan and G hook, ch 18, sl st in first ch to form ring, ch 1, sc in each ch around, join with sl st in first sc. *(18 sc made)*

Rnd 2: Ch 1, sc in each of first 2 sts, 2 sc in next st, (sc in each of next 2 sts, 2 sc in next st) 5 times, join. *(24)*

Rnd 3: Ch 1, sc in first 5 sts, 2 sc in next st, (sc in next 5 sts, 2 sc in next st) 3 times, join. *(28)*

Rnd 4: Ch 1, sc in first 6 sts, 2 sc in next st, (sc in next 6 sts, 2 sc in next st) 2 times, join. *(32)*

Rnds 5–11: Ch 1, sc in each st around, join.

Rnd 12: Ch 1, sc in each of first 2 sts, sc next 2 sts tog, (sc in each of next 2 sts, sc next 2 sts tog) 7 times, join. *(24)*

Rnd 13: Ch 1, sc first 2 sts tog, (sc next 2 sts tog) 11 times, join. *(12)*

Rnd 14: Ch 1, sc first 2 sts tog, (sc next 2 sts tog) 5 times, join *(6)*. Stuff firmly.

Rnd 15: (Sl st next 2 sts tog) 3 times to close. Fasten off.

With single strand dk. blue, sew Head to Blouse.

HAIR

Cut 10 strands black each 26" long. Starting at lower back of Head, lay strands flat and tack securely across the ends. Coil Hair around Head once, tacking strands in place at sides, front and back; cover tacked raw ends. Continue coiling around Head until covered. Tack ends securely to center of Head and trim.

HEAD SHAWL

*NOTE: Work in **back lps** only for shawl (see Stitch Guide).*

Row 1: For **Section A,** with single strand med. blue and H hook, ch 32, dc in fourth ch from hook, dc in each ch across, turn. *(30 dc made)*

Rows 2–7: Ch 3, dc in each st across, turn.

Row 8: For **Section B,** ch 3, dc in next 9 sts leaving last 20 sts unworked, turn. *(10)*

Rows 9–16: Ch 3, dc in next 9 sts, turn. At end of last row, fasten off.

Row 17: For **Section C,** working in remaining lps of starting ch on Section A, join single strand med. blue with sl st in first ch, ch 3, dc in next 9 chs leaving last 20 chs unworked, turn. *(10)*

Rows 18–25: Ch 3, dc in each st across, turn. At end of last row, fasten off.

Sew matching edges of Sections B and C to each unworked edge of Section A.

VEIL

Row 1: With white size 10 crochet cotton and D hook, ch 16, sc in second ch from hook, sc in each ch across, turn. *(15 sc made)*

Rows 2–3: Ch 1, sc in each st across, turn.

Row 4: Ch 3, dc in each st across, turn.

Row 5: Ch 1, sc in each st across, turn.

Row 6: Ch 3, dc in same st, (dc in next st, 2 dc in next st) 7 times, turn. *(23)*

Row 7: Ch 1, sc in each st across. Fasten off.

FRONT HEAD PIECE

Row 1: With white size 10 crochet cotton and D hook, ch 16, sc in second ch from hook and in each ch across, turn. *(15 sc made)*

Row 2: Ch 1, sc in each st across, turn.

Row 3: Ch 3, dc in each st across. Fasten off.

Using straight and satin stitches *(see Stitch Guide)* and black floss, embroider eyes over rnds 6 and 7 at center front of Head about ½" apart *(see photo)*. Using gold, embroider lazy-daisy stitch over every fourth st on first and second rnds of Skirt *(see photo)*; and feather stitch *(see Stitch Guide)* across bottom of Head Shawl.

Tack Veil across face at edge of Hair. Tack Headpiece across forehead, overlapping Hair. Tack Shawl to Head, overlapping Veil and Headpiece. Position Hands as desired and tack in place. ❧

Hopi Warrior

Design by Patricia Pogue

Instructions begin on page 68

Hopi Warrior

Finished Size: Approximately 10" tall without feathers.

Materials:
- Worsted yarn:
  - 5 oz. blue
  - 3 oz. blue variegated
  - 1 oz. beige
  - 1 oz. black
- Size 10 crochet cotton thread:
  - 1 yd. black
  - 1 yd. ecru
  - 10" off-white
- Assortment of feathers in various colors and shapes
- Assortment of small beads in silver, wood and stone
- Three 4-mm. black beads for eyes and nose
- 12" length of beading wire
- 9" piece of ⅛" wooden dowel
- Polyester fiberfill
- Small zip-close plastic bag
- Two cups of dried beans
- Glue gun and glue sticks
- Small embroidery needle
- H hook or hook needed to obtain gauge

Gauge: 7 sts = 2"; 7 sc rows = 2"; 2 dc rows = 1".

Basic Stitches: Ch, sl st, sc, dc.

BODY
NOTE: Work in continuous rnds, do not join or turn unless otherwise stated. Mark first st of each rnd.

Rnd 1: Beginning at bottom, with blue, ch 2, 6 sc in second ch from hook. *(6 sc made)*

Rnd 2: 2 sc in each st around. *(12)*

Rnd 3: (2 sc in next st, sc in next st) around. *(18)*

Rnd 4: (2 sc in next st, sc in each of next 2 sts) around. *(24)*

Rnd 5: (2 sc in next st, sc in each of next 3 sts) around. *(30)*

Rnd 6: (2 sc in next st, sc in next 4 sts) around. *(36)*

Rnd 7: (2 sc in next st, sc in next 5 sts) around. *(42)*

Rnd 8: (2 sc in next st, sc in next 6 sts) around. *(48)*

Rnd 9: Working this rnd in **back lps** *(see Stitch Guide)*, ch 3, dc in each st around, join with sl st in top of ch-3.

Rnd 10: Ch 3, dc in same st, dc in next 11 sts, (2 dc in next st, dc in next 11 sts) around, join. *(52)*

Rnd 11: Repeat rnd 9.

Rnd 12: Ch 3, dc in same st, dc in next 12 sts, (2 dc in next st, dc in next 12 sts) around, join. *(56)*

Rnd 13: Repeat rnd 9.

Rnd 14: Ch 3, dc in same st, dc in next 13 sts, (2 dc in next st, dc in next 13 sts) around, join. *(60)*

Rnd 15: Ch 3, dc in next 12 sts, dc next 2 sts tog, (dc in next 13 sts, dc next 2 sts tog) around, join. *(56)*

Rnd 16: Ch 3, dc in each st around, join.

Rnd 17: Ch 3, dc in next 11 sts, dc next 2 sts tog, (dc in next 12 sts, dc next 2 sts tog) around, join. *(52)*

Rnd 20: Ch 3, dc in next 9 sts, dc next 2 sts tog, (dc in next 10 sts, dc next 2 sts tog) around, join. *(44)*

Rnd 21: Ch 3, dc in next 8 sts, dc next 2 sts tog, (dc in next 9 sts, dc next 2 sts tog) around, join. *(40)*

Rnd 22: For **Head**, join beige with sc in first st, sc in each st around. *(Rnd 22 is neckline.)*

Rnd 23: (Sc in next 8 sts, sc next 2 sts tog) around. *(36)*

Rnd 24: Sc in each st around.

Rnd 25: (Sc in next 7 sts, sc next 2 sts tog) around. *(32)*

Rnd 26: Sc in each st around.

Rnd 27: (Sc in next 6 sts, sc next 2 sts tog) around. *(28)*

Rnd 28: Sc in each st around.

Place a thin layer of fiberfill in bottom of Body. Fill plastic bag with beans and seal, place over fiberfill. Lightly stuff the rest of the Body.

Last rnds: (Sc 2 sts tog) until opening is closed. Fasten off.

For **Face**, sew or glue two 4-mm. black beads four stitches apart on rnd 26 for eyes and third bead for nose centered two rows below eyes.

NECKLACES
For **First Necklace**, string 4" of silver and stone beads onto beading wire, place around front of Body and secure at sides by bending wire ends around one st on rnd 22.

For **Second Necklace**, thread embroidery needle with a 15" strand of ecru crochet thread, secure thread in st next to end of First Necklace; string 5" of wooden beads onto crochet thread, bring around front of Body hanging just below First Necklace and secure in st next to other end of First Necklace. Cut off remaining thread.

BLANKET
Row 1: With blue variegated yarn, ch 72, dc in fourth ch from hook, dc in each ch across, turn. *(70 dc made)*

Rows 2–8: Ch 3, dc in each st across, turn. At end of last row, fasten off.

For each **Fringe**, cut a 4" strand of blue variegated yarn; using crochet hook, pull strand through st or end of row to center of strand, tie in knot, separate plys.

Fringe in each st across row 8 and three times evenly spaced across each end of each row.

FINISHING

Sew Blanket around Doll with row 1 at neckline. Fold top corner of Fringed edges back and tack in place on each side.

For **Hair,** cut 28 pieces of black yarn each 18" long; using black crochet thread and embroidery needle, sew center of strands to back and top of Head beginning at rnd 24 and up over top of Head to sixth rnd above eyes.

On each side at neckline, tie separate strand of black crochet thread around Hair strands, stick the end of a brightly colored feather under the thread and glue in place over Hair, glue underside of Hair to neckline covering ends of Necklaces.

For **Headband,** with blue yarn, ch to fit loosely over Hair at rnd 28 of Body, sl st in first ch to form ring. Fasten off. Place Headband on Head and glue in place.

Stick ends of several feathers into top of Head, arrange similar to photo and glue in place.

For **Coup Stick,** thread about five wooden beads onto center of a 10" piece of ecru crochet thread, tie ends together close to beads; wrap thread ends several times around 9" wooden dowel 2" from one end, tie in knot, leave ends long.

Wrap 10" piece of off-white crochet thread several times around 9" wooden dowel 1" from the same end, tie in knot. Tie a feather at each end of the thread and glue to secure; trim thread ends close to knots.

Insert other end of dowel through rnds 13–15 on right side of Body under folded edge of Blanket. ❖

Flamenco Dancer

Continued from page 60

RUFFLES

Rnd 1: Working in **front lps** of rnd 8, join black with sc in first st, ch 3, (sc, ch 3) in each st around, join with sl st in first sc. *(160 ch-3 lps made)*

Rnds 2–3: (Sl st, ch 1, sc, ch 3) in first lp, (sc, ch 3) in each lp around, join. At end of last rnd, fasten off.

Working in **front lps** of rnds 11, 14, 17 and 20, repeat rnds 1–3 making four more ruffles.

Sew snaps evenly spaced down back opening.

SCARF

Row 1: With red, ch 28, dc in fourth ch from hook, dc in each ch across, turn. *(26 dc made)*

Rows 2–9: Ch 3, dc in same st, dc in each st across with 2 dc in last st, turn. At end of last row, fasten off. *(42 dc)*

Rnd 10: Working around outside edge, join black with sc in first st on row 9, sc in each st around with 2 sc in end of each row and in each corner st, join with sl st in first sc, **turn.** *(108)*

Row 11: Working in rows, (ch 3, skip next st, sc in next st) 33 times leaving last 42 sts unworked, turn. *(33 ch-3 lps)*

Row 12: (Sl st, ch 1, sc) in first ch-3 lp, (ch 3, sc) in each ch-3 lp across. Fasten off.

HEADPIECE

Rnd 1: With black, ch 20, sl st in first ch to form ring, ch 3, dc in each ch around, join with sl st in top of ch-3. *(20 dc made)*

Rnd 2: Ch 1, sc in first st, (ch 4, skip next st, sc in next st) 9 times, ch 4, skip next st, join with sl st in first sc. *(10 ch-4 sps)*

Rnd 3: (Sl st, ch 1, sc; for **picot, ch 3, sl st in 3rd ch from hook;** sc) in first ch-4 sp, (sc, picot, sc) in each ch-4 sp around, join as before. Fasten off.

Sew remaining sequins and beads evenly spaced on rnd 1. ❖

Hawaiian Beauty

Design by Frances Morse

Finished Size: Fits 11½" fashion doll.

Materials:
- Size 10 crochet cotton:
    - 90 yds. shaded greens
    - Small amount bright green
    - Small amount variegated pastels
- Two size 3/0 snaps
- Green sewing thread and needle
- No. 7 steel hook or hook needed to obtain gauge

Gauge: 8 dc = 1"; 4 dc rows = 1".

Basic Stitches: Ch, sl st, sc, dc, tr.

TOP

Row 1: With bright green, ch 37, sc in second ch from hook, sc in each ch across, turn. *(36 sc made)*

Row 2: Ch 1, sc in first 12 sts, 2 dc in each of next 3 sts, 3 tr in each of next 2 sts, dc in each of next 2 sts, 3 tr in each of next 2 sts, 2 dc in each of next 3 sts, sc in last 12 sts, turn. *(50 sts)*

Row 3: Ch 1, sc in first 15 sts, (dc next 2 sts tog) 2 times, dc in next st, (dc next 2 sts tog) 2 times, sc next 2 sts tog, (dc next 2 sts tog) 2 times, dc in next st, (dc next 2 sts tog) 2 times, sc in last 15 sts, turn. *(41)*

Row 4: Ch 1, sc in first 18 sts, sc next 2 sts tog, sc in next st, sc next 2 sts tog, sc in last 18 sts. Fasten off. Sew snap to back.

SKIRT & PANTY

Row 1: With shaded greens, ch 25, sc in second ch from hook, sc in each ch across, turn. *(24 sc made)*

Row 2: Ch 1, sc in each of first 3 sts, 2 sc in next st, (sc in each of next 3 sts, 2 sc in next st) 5 times, turn. *(30)*

Row 3: Working this row in **back lps** *(see Stitch Guide)*, ch 3, dc in next st, 2 dc in next st, (dc in each of next 2 sts, 2 dc in next st) across, turn. *(40)*

Row 4: Ch 3, dc in each st across, turn.

Rnd 5: Working in rnds, ch 3, dc in each st around, join with sl st in top of ch-3.

Rnds 6–8: Ch 3, dc in each st around, join. At end of last rnd, leaving 4" for sewing, fasten off. Fold in half, sew beginning ch-2 and 20th st of rnd 8 together to form leg openings of Panty.

For each **fringe**, cut three strands of shaded greens each 13½" long, with all three strands held together, fold in half, insert hook in st, pull fold through st, pull ends through fold and tighten. Work one row of fringe in **front lps** of each st on row 2 of Panty and work one row of fringe around post of each st *(see Stitch Guide)* on row 3.

Sew snap to top of back opening on Panty.

LEI

Rnd 1: With variegated pastels, ch 50, sl st in first ch to form ring, ch 1, sc in first ch, ch 4, (sc in next ch, ch 4) around, join with sl st in first sc. Fasten off. *(50 sc made)*

Rnd 2: Working in remaining lps on opposite side of starting ch, join with sc in first ch, ch 4, (sc in next ch, ch 4) around, join as before. Fasten off. ✤

Row 14: Join white with sc in first st, sc in each st across, turn.

Row 15: Ch 1, sc in each st across, turn. Fasten off.

Row 16: Join green with sc in first st, sc in each st across, turn.

Rows 17–19: Ch 1, sc in each st across, turn.

Rows 20–65: Repeat rows 20–65 of Hawaiian Girl Body Side on page 62.

Rnd 66: Repeat rnd 66 of Indian Boy Body Side on page 63.

FRONT

Rows 1–19: Repeat rows 1–19 of Eskimo Girl Back.

Rows 20–45: Repeat rows 20–45 of Hawaiian Girl Body Side. At end of last row, fasten off.

Row 46: Join tan with sc in first st, sc in same st, sc in each st across with 2 sc in last st, turn. *(17)*

Rows 47–50: Repeat row 2 of Hawaiian Girl Body Side, ending with 25 sts in last row.

Rows 51–65: Repeat rows 51–65 of Hawaiian Girl Body Side.

Rnd 66: Repeat rnd 66 of Indian Boy Body Side.

FINISHING

Sew together, form arms and legs, and embroider face same as Hawaiian Girl. Dust cheeks with blush.

JACKET TRIM

Holding doll with feet toward you, working in **front lps** of row 26 on front, join white with sc in first st, sc in each st across. Fasten off. Repeat on back.

FUR TRIM

Working around each st in a 1" border around edge of face and using white yarn, work in same manner as Shirt Fringe of Indian Boy on page 63. Separate plys of each yarn strand and brush to fluff.

SCARF

Row 1: With pink, ch 7, sc in second ch from hook, sc in each ch across, turn. *(6 sc made)*

Rows 2–85: Ch 1, sc in each st across, turn. At end of last row, fasten off.

Cut 24 strands pink each 3" long. With two strands held together, fringe in each st across each end of Scarf. Tie Scarf around neck. ❖

Suds 'n' Such: Keeping Dolly Clean

Once a crocheted doll or toy project is completed, the next challenge becomes how to keep dolls and toys clean or wash them when they become soiled.

Begin with the yarn. Yarns for use in dolls and toys should be washable by hand or machine. Check yarn wrappers for specific care guidelines before starting your project.

Then help prevent soiling in the first place by treating the doll or toy with a spray-on fiber protectant for invisible protection. Look for a formulation that protects without changing the feel of the yarn.

Remove dust, fur and lint by wrapping your hand with masking tape, sticky side out, and patting the item to freshen it. Sticky-faced lint rollers are also handy for quick clean-ups.

Spot clean small soiled areas as soon as you notice them. Use mild dishwashing liquid diluted with lukewarm water to sponge on and then blot off. Avoid leaving a ring by using light strokes to feather away all traces of the cleaning solution.

If you choose to wash the entire doll or toy, check to make sure all parts are washable and secure and repair or reinforce if needed. (Dolls containing cardboard are not washable.)

For machine washing use a gentle cycle and a mild detergent that does not contain bleach. Machine dry on a permanent press or gentle cycle and use fabric softener in the washer or dryer. Do not dry with towels, flannel or other fluffy fabrics that may cause the yarn to attract lint or to pill.

For hand washing, use mild soap flakes or detergent and fill a basin with warm water. Let the item soak for a few minutes, then gently squeeze suds through without rubbing or twisting. Squeeze gently to remove excess water and roll in a heavy towel to press out moisture. Place on a towel on a flat surface out of direct sunlight to dry, turning and reshaping as necessary until completely dry. ❖

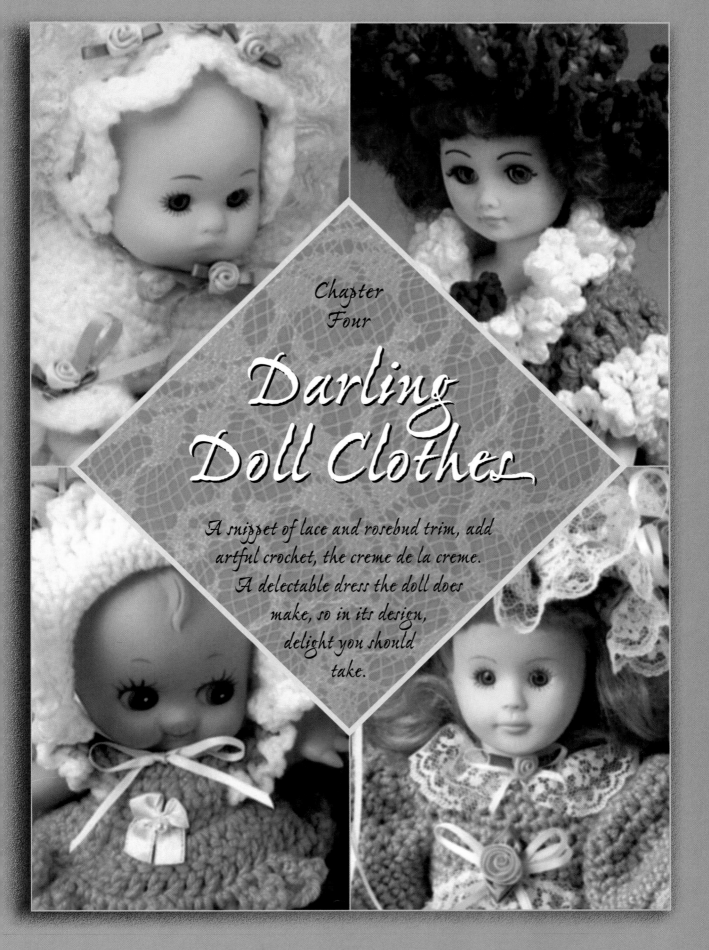

Chapter
Four

Darling
Doll Clothes

A snippet of lace and rosebud trim, add
artful crochet, the creme de la creme.
A delectable dress the doll does
make, so in its design,
delight you should
take.

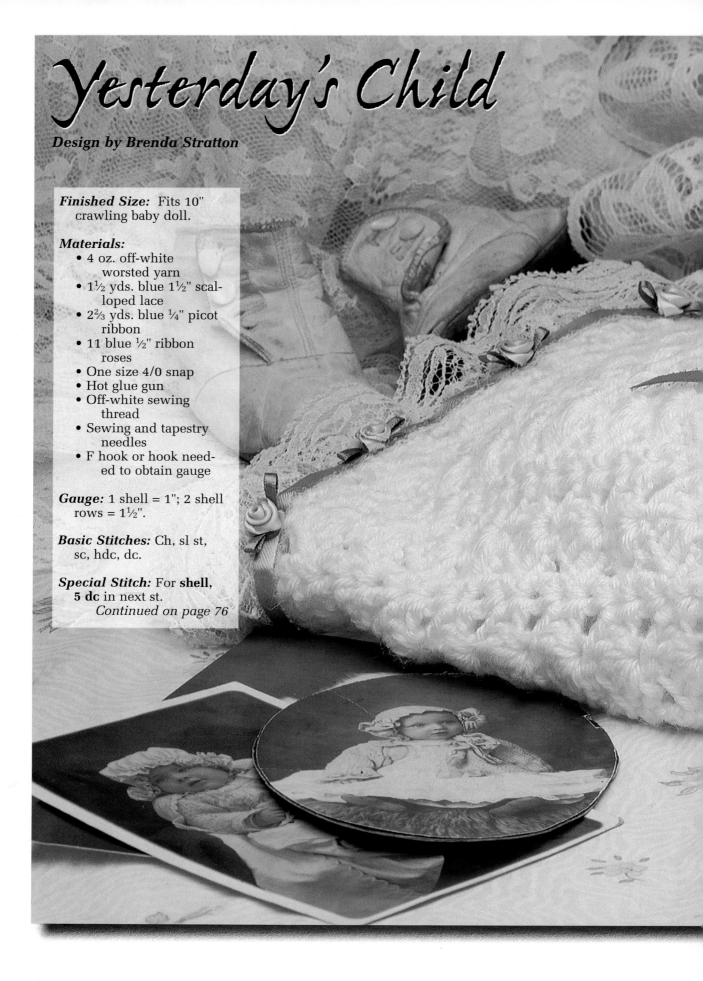

Yesterday's Child

Design by Brenda Stratton

Finished Size: Fits 10" crawling baby doll.

Materials:
- 4 oz. off-white worsted yarn
- 1½ yds. blue 1½" scalloped lace
- 2⅔ yds. blue ¼" picot ribbon
- 11 blue ½" ribbon roses
- One size 4/0 snap
- Hot glue gun
- Off-white sewing thread
- Sewing and tapestry needles
- F hook or hook needed to obtain gauge

Gauge: 1 shell = 1"; 2 shell rows = 1½".

Basic Stitches: Ch, sl st, sc, hdc, dc.

Special Stitch: For **shell**, **5 dc** in next st.

Continued on page 76

Yesterday's Child

Continued from page 74

DRESS

Row 1: Starting at neckline of bodice, ch 25, sc in second ch from hook, sc in each ch across, turn. *(24 sc made)*

Row 2: Ch 1, sc in each of first 2 sts, 2 sc in next st, (sc in each of next 2 sts, 2 sc in next st) 3 times, (2 sc in next st, sc in each of next 2 sts) 4 times, turn. *(32 sc—Front of row 2 is right side of work.)*

Row 3: Ch 1, sc in each of first 3 sts, 2 sc in next st, (sc in each of next 3 sts, 2 sc in next st) 3 times, (2 sc in next st, sc in each of next 3 sts) 4 times, turn. *(40)*

Row 4: Ch 1, sc in each st across, turn. Fasten off.

Row 5: For **Front,** skip first 15 sts, join with sc in next st, sc in next 9 sts leaving last 15 sts unworked, turn. *(10)*

Rows 6–11: Ch 1, sc in each st across, turn. At end of last row, **do not turn.** Fasten off.

Row 12: Join with sc in first st on row 4, sc in next 7 sts; for **armhole,** ch 9, skip next 7 sts; sc in next 10 sts on Front; for **armhole,** ch 9, skip next 7 sts on row 4, sc in last 8 sts, turn.

Rnd 13: Working in rnds, ch 1, sc in first 6 sts, hdc in next st, dc in next 39 chs and sts, hdc in next st, sc in last 6 sts, join with sl st in first sc. *(44 sts)*

Rnd 14: For **skirt,** ch 3, dc in each st around, join with sl st in top of ch-3. *(Ch-3 counts as first dc.)*

Rnd 15: Ch 1, sc in first st, skip next st, **shell** *(see Special Stitch)* in next st, skip next st, (sc in next st, skip next st, shell in next st, skip next st) around, join with sl st in first sc.

Rnd 16: (Ch 3, dc) in first st, ch 2, sc in center st of next shell, ch 2, (2 dc in next sc, ch 2, sc in center st of next shell, ch 2) around, join with sl st in top of ch-3.

Rnd 17: Ch 1, (sc, ch 2, sc) in sp between first 2 sts, shell in next sc, *(sc, ch 2, sc) in sp between next 2 dc, shell in next sc; repeat from * around, join with sl st in first sc.

Rnd 18: (Sl st, ch 3, dc) in first ch-2 sp, ch 2, sc in center st of next shell, ch 2, (2 dc in next ch-2 sp, ch 2, sc in center st of next shell, ch 2) around, join with sl st in top of ch-3.

Rnds 19–34: Repeat rnds 17 and 18 alternately.

Rnd 35: Ch 3, dc in each st around with 2 dc in each ch-2 sp, join. Fasten off.

Row 36: For **facing,** join with sc in end of fifth row worked on left back, ch 1, sc in next 4 rows; working in remaining lps on opposite side of starting ch on row 1 of Bodice, sl st in each ch across. Fasten off.

Lap facing over right back, tack together at bottom. Sew snap to each end of row 1.

Sleeves

Rnd 1: Join with sc in center st at underarm, evenly space 23 more sc around armhole, join with sl st in first sc. *(24 sc made)*

Rnd 2: Ch 1, sc in first st, skip next 2 sts, shell in next st, skip next 2 sts, (sc in next st, skip next 2 sts, shell in next st, skip next 2 sts) around, join.

Rnd 3: (Ch 3, dc) in first st, ch 2, sc in center of next shell, ch 2, (2 dc in next sc, ch 2, sc in center st of next shell, ch 2) around, join with sl st in top of ch-3.

Rnd 4: Ch 1, (sc, ch 2, sc) in sp between first 2 sts, shell in next sc, *(sc, ch 2, sc) in sp between next 2 dc, shell in next sc; repeat from * around, join with sl st in first sc.

Rnd 5: (Sl st, ch 3, dc) in first ch-2 sp, ch 2, sc in center st of next shell, ch 2, (2 dc in next ch-2 sp, ch 2, sc in center st of next shell, ch 2) around, join with sl st in top of ch-3.

Rnd 6: Repeat rnd 4. Fasten off.

Repeat for other armhole.

Finishing

Cut two pieces of lace each 18" long. Glue straight edge of one piece around bottom of rnd 35 on Skirt. Glue straight edge of other piece around bottom of rnd 34 on Skirt. Glue an 18" piece of ribbon over straight edge of lace on rnd 34. Glue four ribbon roses evenly spaced across back of Dress over ribbon.

Place Dress on doll.

Cut two pieces of ribbon each 15" long. Beginning and ending at top, weave one piece through ch sps of rnd 5 on one Sleeve. Tie ends in bow. Repeat with other piece of ribbon on other Sleeve. Glue ribbon rose to center of each bow.

Starting and ending at back, weave a 24" piece of ribbon through sts of rnd 14 on Dress. Tie ends in bow. Glue a ribbon rose to center of bow.

BONNET

NOTE: *Work in continuous rnds; do not join or turn unless otherwise stated. Mark first st of each rnd.*

Rnd 1: Ch 2, 6 sc in second ch from hook. *(6 sc made)*

Rnd 2: 2 sc in each st around. *(12)*

Rnd 3: (Sc in next st, 2 sc in next st) around. *(18)*

Rnd 4: (Sc in each of next 2 sts, 2 sc in next st) around. *(24)*

Rnd 5: (Sc in each of next 3 sts, 2 sc in next st) around. *(30)*

Row 6: (Sc in next st, skip next 2 sts, shell in next st, skip next 2 sts) 4 times, sc in next st leaving last 5 sts unworked for **bottom,** turn.

Continued on page 79

Vintage Finery

Design by Carol Alexander

Finished Size: Fits 16" soft body porcelain-look doll.

Materials:
- 11 oz. lt. green worsted yarn
- 2¼ yds. ecru ⅛" satin ribbon
- 2¼ yds. ecru 2½" ruffled double-edge beaded lace with lt. green ribbon
- 3¾ yds. ecru 1⅜" ruffled lace
- One 10-mm. ribbon rose
- Three 18-mm. ribbon roses
- Four size 4/0 snaps
- Craft glue
- Ecru sewing thread
- Sewing and tapestry needles
- G hook or hook needed to obtain gauge

Gauge: 4 sts = 1"; 4 sc rows = 1"; 2 dc rows = 1".

Basic Stitches: Ch, sl st, sc, hdc, dc.

Special Stitches:
For **beginning V stitch (beg V st)**, ch 4, dc in first st.
For **V stitch (V st)**, (dc, ch 1, dc) in next st.

Continued on page 78

Vintage Finery

Continued from page 77

DRESS
Bodice & Overskirt

Row 1: For **Bodice**, starting at neck, ch 25, sc in second ch from hook, sc in next ch, 2 sc in next ch, (sc in each of next 2 chs, 2 sc in next ch) 3 times, (2 sc in next ch, sc in each of next 2 chs) 4 times, turn. *(32 sc made)*

Row 2: Ch 1, sc in first 10 sts, (2 sc in next st, sc in next 10 sts) 2 times, turn. *(34)*

Row 3: Ch 1, sc in first 10 sts, (2 sc in next st, sc in next 11 sts) 2 times, turn. *(36)*

Row 4: Ch 1, sc in each st across, turn.

Row 5: Ch 1, sc in first 8 sts, (2 sc in next st, sc in next 8 sts) 2 times, 2 sc in next st, sc in last 9 sts, turn. *(39)*

Row 6: Ch 1, sc in each of first 2 sts, 2 sc in next st, sc in next 3 sts; (for **armhole**, ch 9, skip next 8 sts); sc in next 5 sts, 2 sc in next st, sc in next 5 sts; repeat between ( ), sc in each of next 3 sts, 2 sc in next st, sc in each of last 2 sts, turn. *(26 sc, 18 chs)*

Row 7: Ch 2 *(counts as first hdc throughout)*, hdc in next 4 sts, hdc next 2 sts tog *(see Stitch Guide)*, sc in next 9 chs, (sc in each of next 2 sts, 2 sc in next st) 3 times, sc in each of next 3 sts, sc in next 9 chs, hdc next 2 sts tog, hdc in last 5 sts, turn. *(45)*

Row 8: Ch 2, hdc in next 6 sts, sc in next 31 sts, hdc in last 7 sts, turn.

Row 9: Ch 1, sc in first 7 sts, (sc in next 6 sts, sc next 2 sts tog) 3 times, sc in last 14 sts, turn. *(42 sc)*

Row 10: Ch 1, sc in first 7 sts, (sc in next 5 sts, sc next 2 sts tog) 3 times, sc in last 14 sts, turn. *(39)*

Row 11: Ch 1, sc in first 8 sts, (sc in next 4 sts, sc next 2 sts tog) 3 times, sc in last 13 sts, turn. *(36)*

Rows 12–15: Ch 1, sc in each st across, turn.

Rnd 16: Working in rnds, ch 1, sc in each st around, join with sl st in first sc.

Rnd 17: For **Overskirt**, working in **front lps** *(see Stitch Guide)*, ch 3, *(counts as first dc throughout)*, 2 dc in same st, 3 dc in each st around, join with sl st in top of ch-3. *(108 dc)*

Rnds 18–20: Ch 3, dc in each st around, join.

Rnd 21: Ch 3, dc in next st, 2 dc in next st, (dc in each of next 2 sts, 2 dc in next st) around, join *(144)*

Rnd 22: Ch 3, dc in each st around, join.

Rnd 23: Ch 3, dc in next 62 sts, hdc in next 4 sts, sc in next 4 sts, hdc in next 4 sts, dc in last 69 sts, join. *(144 sts)*

Rnd 24: Ch 3, dc in next 61 sts, hdc in each of next 3 sts, sc in next 6 sts, hdc in each of next 3 sts, dc in last 70 sts, join.

Rnd 25: Ch 3, dc in next 60 sts, hdc in each of next 2 sts, sc in each of next 3 sts, sl st in each of next 3 sts, sc in each of next 3 sts, hdc in each of next 2 sts, dc in last 70 sts, join. Fasten off.

For **right back edging**, starting at neck edge on right back Bodice, join with sc in end of row 1, sc in end of each row across to waist. Fasten off.

For **left back edging**, starting at waist on left back Bodice, join with sc in end of row 15, sc in end of each row across to neck edge. Fasten off.

Underskirt

Rnd 1: Working in unworked **back lps** of row 16 on Bodice, join with sl st in first st, ch 3, dc in same st, 2 dc in each st around, join with sl st in top of ch-3. *(72 dc made)*

Rnd 2: Ch 3, dc in each of next 2 sts, 2 dc in next st, (dc in each of next 3 sts, 2 dc in next st) around, join. *(90)*

Rnds 3–4: Ch 3, dc in each st around, join.

Rnd 5: Ch 3, dc in each of next 3 sts, 2 dc in next st, (dc in next 4 sts, 2 dc in next st) around, join. *(108)*

Rnds 6–7: Ch 3, dc in each st around, join.

Rnd 8: Ch 3, dc in next 4 sts, 2 dc in next st, (dc in next 5 sts, 2 dc in next st) around, join. *(126)*

Rnds 9–10: Ch 3, dc in each st around, join.

Rnd 11: Working this rnd in **front lps, beg V st** *(see Special Stitches)* in first st, **V st** *(see Special Stitches)* in next st, V st in each st around, join with sl st in third ch of first ch-4. *(126 V sts)*

Rnd 12: Ch 5, (sc, ch 4) in ch-1 sp of each V st around, join with sl st in ch-5 sp. *(126 ch sps)*

Rnd 13: Beg V st in first ch sp, ch 2, (V st, ch 2) in each ch sp around, join with sl st in third ch of first ch-4.

Rnd 14: Ch 3, (V st, ch 2) in next ch-2 sp, *(sc, ch 2) in next V st, (V st, ch 2) in next ch-2 sp; repeat from * around, join with sl st in ch-3 sp.

Rnd 15: Ch 3, (sc, ch 2) in next V st, *(V st, ch 2) in next sc, (sc, ch 2) in next V st; repeat from * around, join. Fasten off.

Sleeves

NOTE: *Work in continuous rnds; do not join or turn at end of each rnd. Mark first st of each rnd.*

Rnd 1: For **first sleeve**, working around one armhole on Bodice, join with sc in fifth ch of ch-9, sc in same st as joining sc, sc in next 4 chs, 2 sc in end of next row, 3 hdc in next st, 2 hdc in each of next 6 sts, 3 hdc in next st, 2 sc in end of next row, sc in next 4 chs. *(32 sts)*

Rnds 2–4: Sc in each sc and hdc in each hdc around.

Rnds 5–10: Sc in each st around.

Rnd 11: (Sc next 2 sts tog) around. *(16 sc)*

Rnd 12: (Sc in each of next 3 sts, sc next 2 sts tog) 3 times, sc in next st. *(13)*

Rnds 13–16: Sc in each st around.

Rnd 17: Sc in each st around, join with sl st in next st. Fasten off.

For **second sleeve,** repeat rnds 1–17 of first sleeve on other armhole.

Finishing

Cut a 4" piece of 2½" lace; overlapping ends, sew lace to right side of Sleeve around wrist edge with ¾" of lace extending over edge *(see photo)*. Repeat for other Sleeve.

Cut a 41" piece of 2½" lace; overlapping ends, sew lace to bottom side of Overskirt around bottom edge with ¾" of lace extending over edge.

Cut a 112" piece of 1⅜" lace. Gathering to fit, sew bound edge of lace to wrong side of Underskirt around bottom edge.

Cut two 6½" pieces of 1⅜" lace. Gathering to fit, sew one piece of lace to Bodice beginning with bound edge of one end at center front and ending with bottom edge of other end at right back waist leaving ¼" extending over back edging; fold extended lace to inside and tack in place. Trim center front edges. Repeat with other piece of lace, ending at left back waist.

Cut two 4" pieces of 1⅜" lace. Gathering to fit, sew bound edge of one piece of lace to right side of Bodice around neck edge from center front to right back edging. Trim center front edge. Repeat with other piece of lace from center front to left back edging.

Cut a 5½" piece of ⅛" ribbon; tie in a bow leaving 1" ends. Glue 10-mm. ribbon rose centered on top of bow. Glue bow to center front neck edge of Bodice *(see photo)*.

Cut two pieces of ⅛" ribbon each 17" long; hold both pieces together and tie in a bow leaving 6" ends for streamers. Glue one 18-mm. ribbon rose centered to top of bow. Glue bow to center front of Bodice over bound edge of lace.

Sew snaps evenly spaced down back opening of Bodice.

HAT

Rnd 1: Ch 2, 6 sc in second ch from hook. *(6 sc made)*

Rnd 2: 2 sc in each st around. *(12)*

Rnd 3: (Sc in next st, 2 sc in next st) around. *(18)*

Rnd 4: (Sc in each of next 2 sts, 2 sc in next st) around. *(24)*

Rnd 5: (Sc in each of next 3 sts, 2 sc in next st) around. *(30)*

Rnd 6: (Sc in next 4 sts, 2 sc in next st) around. *(36)*

Rnd 7: (Sc in next 8 sts, 2 sc in next st) 4 times. *(40)*

Rnd 8: Sc in each st around.

Rnd 9: Sc in each st around, join with sl st in **front lp** of next st.

Rnd 10: For **brim,** working this rnd in **front lps,** ch 3 *(counts as first dc)*, dc in same st as ch-3, 2 dc in each st around, join with sl st in top of ch-3. *(80 dc)*

Rnd 11: Ch 3, 2 dc in next st, (dc in next st, 2 dc in next st) around, join. Fasten off.

Cut a 27" piece of 2½" lace; overlapping ends, sew lace to right side of Hat around outer edge with ¾" of lace extending over edge.

Cut two pieces of ⅛" ecru ribbon each 17" long; holding both pieces together, tie in a bow, leaving 6" ends for streamers. Glue one 18-mm. ribbon rose centered to top of bow. Glue bow to one side of Hat. Repeat for other side. ❖

Yesterday's Child
Continued from page 76

Row 7: (Ch 3, dc) in first st, (sc in center st of next shell, 2 dc in next sc) across, turn.

Row 8: Ch 1, (sc, ch 2, sc) in sp between first 2 sts, *shell in next sc, (sc, ch 2, sc) in sp between next 2 dc; repeat from * across, turn.

Row 9: (Sl st, ch 3, dc) in first ch sp, (sc in center st of next shell, 2 dc in next ch-2 sp) across, turn.

Row 10: Repeat row 8, **do not turn.**

Row 11: Working in ends of rows and in unworked sts on rnd 5, sc evenly spaced across bottom edge of Bonnet. Fasten off.

Finishing

Gather straight edge of remaining lace to fit row 8 on Bonnet and glue gathered edge across center of row 8. Glue three ribbon roses evenly spaced across row 8 at top of Bonnet in front of lace *(see photo)*.

Weave remaining ribbon through sts of row 9. Tie ends of ribbon in bow below doll's chin. Glue a ribbon rose to center of bow. ❖

Ice Skater's Delight

Design by Sandra McCubbins

Finished Size: Fits 11½" fashion doll.

Materials:
- Size 10 crochet cotton thread: 160 yds. yellow 2 yds. silver
- ⅜" × 29½" strip white fake fur
- Four sets size 2/0 snaps
- Fabric stiffener
- Tapestry needle
- No. 2 steel hook or hook needed to obtain gauge

Gauge: 8 sc = 1"; 8 sc rows = 1".

Basic Stitches: Ch, sl st, sc, hdc, dc.

DRESS

Rnd 1: For **panties,** with yellow, ch 32, sl st in first ch to form ring; for **crotch,** ch 4, sl st in 16th ch of ring, **turn,** ch 1, hdc in each ch of ch-4, sc in next sl st *(joining sl st on ring);* sc in each ch and in each sl st around ring, join with sl st in first sc. *(32 sc made)*

Rnd 2: Ch 1, sc in first st, 2 sc in each of next 2 sts, sc in next 26 sts, 2 sc in each of next 2 sts, sc in last st, join. *(36)*

Rnds 3–5: Ch 1, sc in each st around, join.

Rnd 6: Ch 1, sc in first 8 sts, sc next 2 sts tog *(see Stitch Guide),* sc in next 16 sts, sc next 2 sts tog, sc in next 7 sts leaving last st unworked, **do not join.** *(33)*

Rnd 7: Ch 1, sc last st on rnd 6 and first st on rnd 6 tog *(this is center back),* sc in next 5 sts, sc next 2 sts tog, sc in next 18 sts, sc next 2 sts tog, sc in last 5 sts, join. *(31)*

Rnd 8: Ch 1, sc in first 10 sts, sc next 2 sts tog, sc in next 7 sts, sc next 2 sts tog, sc in last 10 sts, join. *(29)*

Rnd 9: Ch 1, sc first 2 sts tog, sc in next 27 sts, join. *(28)*

Row 10: Working in rows, ch 1, sc in each of first 2 sts, **turn** *(back opening)*; sc in first st, sc in next 27 sts, turn.

Row 11: Ch 1, sc in first 9 sts, sc next 2 sts tog, sc in next 6 sts, sc next 2 sts tog, sc in last 9 sts, turn. *(26)*

Row 12: For **skirt,** working in **front lps** *(see Stitch Guide),* ch 1, sc in first st, 2 sc in next st, (sc in next st, 2 sc in next st) across, turn. *(39)*

Row 13: Ch 1, sc in first st, (2 sc in next st, sc in next st) across, turn. *(58)*

Rnd 14: Working in rnds, ch 1, sc in first st, 2 sc in next st, (sc in next st, 2 sc in next st) around. **Do not join.** *(87)*

Rnd 15: Skip ch-1, sc in first st, (2 sc in next st, sc in next st) around. **Do not join.** *(130)*

Rnds 16–26: Sc in each st around. At end of last rnd, join with sl st in first sc. Fasten off.

Bodice

Row 1: Working beside sts on row 11, join yellow with sc in first st, sc in each of next 2 sts, sc next 2 sts tog, sc in next 16 sts, sc next 2 sts tog, sc in each of last 3 sts, turn. *(24 sc made)*

Rows 2–5: Ch 1, sc in each st across, turn.

Row 6: Ch 1, sc in first 7 sts, 2 sc in next st, sc in next 8 sts, 2 sc in next st, sc in last 7 sts, turn. *(26)*

Row 7: Ch 1, sc in first 11 sts, 2 sc in next st, sc in each of next 2 sts, 2 sc in next st, sc in last 11 sts, turn. *(28)*

Row 8: Ch 1, sc in first 5 sts, 2 sc in next st, sc in next 5 sts, 2 sc in next st, sc in next 4 sts, 2 sc in next st, sc in next 5 sts, 2 sc in next st, sc in last 5 sts, turn. *(32)*

Row 9: Ch 1, sc in first 6 sts, 2 sc in next st, sc in next 4 sts, 2 sc in next st, sc in next 8 sts, 2 sc in next st, sc in next 4 sts, 2 sc in next st, sc in last 6 sts, turn. *(36)*

Row 10: Ch 1, sc in first 5 sts, 2 sc in next st, sc in next 8 sts, 2 sc in next st, sc in next 6 sts, 2 sc in next st, sc in next 8 sts, 2 sc in next st, sc in last 5 sts, turn. *(40)*

Row 11: Ch 1, sc in first 4 sts, 2 sc in next st, sc in next 10 sts, 2 sc in next st, sc in next 8 sts, 2 sc in next st, sc in next 10 sts, 2 sc in next st, sc in last 4 sts, turn. *(44)*

Row 12: Ch 1, sc in first 21 sts, sc next 2 sts tog, sc in last 21 sts, turn. *(43)*

Row 13: Ch 1, sc in first 18 sts, sc next 2 sts tog, sc in each of next 2 sts, sc next 2 sts tog, sc in last 19 sts, turn. *(41)*

Row 14: Ch 1, sc in first 19 sts, (sc next 2 sts tog) 2 times, sc in last 18 sts, turn. *(39)*

Row 15: Ch 1, sc in first 16 sts, (sc next 2 sts tog) 3 times, sc in last 17 sts, turn. *(36)*

Row 16: For **right back,** ch 1, sc in first 8 sts leaving remaining sts unworked, turn.

Rows 17–23: Ch 1, sc in each st across, turn. At end of last row, fasten off.

Row 16: For **left back,** join yellow with sc in beginning st on row 15, sc in next 7 sts, turn.

Rows 17–23: Ch 1, sc in each st across, turn. At end of last row, fasten off.

Row 16: For **front,** skip next 3 unworked sts on row 15, join with sc in next st, sc in next 13 sts leaving remaining sts unworked, turn.

Rows 17–21: Ch 1, sc in each st across, turn.

Rows 22–23: Ch 1, sc in first 6 sts, sl st in each of next 2 sts, sc in last 6 sts, turn. At end of last row, **do not turn.**

Row 24: Sc in first st on last row of left back to join at shoulder, sc in next 7 sts, turn.

Row 25: Ch 1, sc in first 14 sts, sl st in each of next 2 sl sts, sc in next 6 sts, pick up right back, sc in next 8 sts, turn.

Row 26: Ch 1, sc in first 8 sts, sl st in next st. Fasten off.

Sleeves (make 2)

Row 1: With yellow, ch 16, sc in second ch from hook, sc in each ch across, turn. *(15 sc made)*

Row 2: Ch 1, sc in each st across, turn.

Row 3: Ch 1, sc first 3 sts tog, sc in next 10 sts, sc last 2 sts tog, turn.

Rows 4–26: Ch 1, sc in each st across, turn. At end of last row, fasten off leaving 15" for sewing.

Sew rows 1 and 26 together for underarm. Sew ends of rows to armhole.

HAT

Rnd 1: With yellow, ch 2, 6 sc in second ch from hook, join with sl st in first sc. *(6 sc made)*

Rnd 2: Ch 1, 2 sc in each st around, join. *(12)*

Rnd 3: Ch 1, sc in first st, 2 sc in next st, (sc in next st, 2 sc in next st) around, join. *(18)*

Rnd 4: Ch 1, sc in each of first 2 sts, 2 sc in next

Continued on page 88

Mary Elizabeth Bed Doll

Design by Mary Layfield

Finished Size: Fits 15" fashion doll. Skirt is approximately 20" in diameter.

Materials:
- Worsted yarn:
    12 oz. pale purple
    6 oz. bright purple
    6 oz. white
- 15" fashion doll
- Tapestry needle
- E hook or hook needed to obtain gauge

Gauge: 5 sc = 1"; 5 sc rows = 1".

Basic Stitches: Ch, sl st, sc, dc, tr.

DRESS

Bodice

Row 1: Beginning at waist, with pale purple, ch 35; working in **back bar of ch** *(see Stitch Guide),* sc in second ch from hook, sc in each ch across, turn. *(34 sc made)*

Rows 2–5: Ch 1, sc in each st across, turn.

Row 6: For **first back,** ch 1, sc in first 6 sts leaving remaining sts unworked, turn. *(6)*

Rows 7–8: Ch 1, sc in each st across, turn.

Row 9: For **shoulder,** ch 1, sc in first 3 sts leaving remaining sts unworked for neck, turn. *(3)*

Row 10: Ch 1, sc in each st across, turn.

Row 11: Ch 1, sc in each st across. Fasten off.

Row 6: Skip next 5 sts on row 5 for underarm; for **front,** join pale purple with sc in next st on row 5, sc in next 11 sts leaving remaining 5 sts unworked, turn. *(12)*

Rows 7–8: Ch 1, sc in each st across, turn.

Row 9: For **first front shoulder,** ch 1, sc in each of first 3 sts leaving remaining sts unworked, turn. *(3)*

Row 10: Ch 1, sc in each st across, turn.

Row 11: Ch 1, sc in each st across. Fasten off.

Row 9: For **second front shoulder,** skip next 6 sts on row 8, join pale purple with sc in next st, sc in each of last 2 sts, turn. *(3)*

Row 10: Ch 1, sc in each st across, turn.

Row 11: Ch 1, sc in each st across. Fasten off.

Row 6: Skip next 5 unworked sts on row 5 for underarm; for **second back,** join pale purple with sc in next st, sc in last 5 sts, turn. *(6)*

Rows 7–8: Ch 1, sc in each st across, turn.

Row 9: For **shoulder,** ch 1, sc in each of first 3 sts leaving remaining st unworked for neck, turn. *(3)*

Row 10: Ch 1, sc in each st across, turn.

Row 11: Ch 1, sc in each st across. Fasten off. Sew shoulder seams.

Skirt

Row 1: With wrong side of Bodice facing you, working in **back lps** *(see Stitch Guide)* of starting ch on row 1, join pale purple with sl st in first ch, ch 3 *(counts as first dc),* dc in same ch as sl st, 2 dc in each ch across, turn. *(68 dc made—Back of row 1 is right side of work.)*

Row 2: Ch 3, dc in next st, (ch 5, skip next 2 sts, sc in next st, ch 5, skip next 2 sts, dc in next st) across, turn. *(22 ch sps, 11 sc, 13 dc)*

Row 3: Ch 6, sc in next ch sp, 3 dc in next sc, sc in next ch sp, (ch 6, skip next dc, sc in next ch sp, 3 dc in next sc, sc in next ch sp) across, ch 3, skip next dc, dc in top of ch-3, turn. *(12 ch sps, 33 dc)*

Rnd 4: Working in rnds, (ch 6, sc in next ch sp, ch 6, sc in next sc, ch 6, sc in second dc of next 3-dc group, ch 6, sc in next sc) 11 times, ch 6, sc in last ch sp, ch 2, join with dc in first ch of first ch-6, **do not turn.** *(Ch-2 and dc count as joining ch sp—46 ch sps)*

Rnds 5–8: (Ch 6, sc in next ch sp) around, ch 2, dc in joining dc of last rnd.

Rnd 9: (Ch 3, dc) in joining ch sp, 3 dc in each ch sp around to joining ch sp, dc in joining ch sp, join with sl st in top of ch-3. *(138 dc)*

Rnd 10: For **ruffle,** sl st in next st, sc in next space between 3-dc groups, (ch 8, sc in next space between 3-dc groups) around, ch 4, join with tr in first ch of first ch-8. *(Ch-4 and tr count as joining ch sp—46 ch sps)*

Rnd 11: Ch 8, *(sc, ch 4, sc) in next ch sp, ch 8; repeat from * around to joining ch sp, sc in joining ch sp, ch 4, sc in joining tr.

Rnd 12: Sl st in each of next 2 chs, (sc, ch 6, sc) in first ch sp, ch 6, sc in next ch sp, ch 6, *(sc, ch 6, sc) in next ch sp, ch 6, sc in next ch sp, ch 6; repeat from * around, join with sl st in first sc.

Rnd 13: (Sc, ch 6, sc, ch 6) in each ch sp around, join. Fasten off.

Rnd 14: Join bright purple with sc in first ch sp, ch 6, (sc in next ch sp, ch 6) around, join. Fasten off.

Rnd 15: Working behind ruffle into sts of rnd 9, join pale purple with sc in second dc of any 3-dc group at back of Skirt, ch 8, (sc in second dc of next 3-dc group, ch 8) around, join with sl st in first sc. *(46 ch sps)*

Rnds 16–17: Sl st in next 4 chs, sc in first ch sp, ch 8, (sc in next ch sp, ch 8) around, join.

Rnd 18: Sl st in each of next 2 chs, (sc in first ch sp, ch 6) 3 times, *sc in next ch sp, ch 6, (sc in same ch sp as last sc made, ch 6) 2 times; repeat from * around, join.

Rnds 19–20: Sl st in each of next 3 chs, sc in first ch sp, ch 6, (sc in next ch sp, ch 6) around, join.

Rnd 21: Ch 1, sc in first ch sp, (ch 6, sc in same ch sp as last sc made) 2 times, *ch 6, sc in next ch sp, (ch 6, sc in same ch sp as last sc made) 2 times; repeat from * around, ending with ch 3, join with dc in first sc.

Rnd 22: Ch 6, (sc in next ch sp, ch 6) around, join with sl st in first ch of first ch-6. Fasten off.

Rnd 23: Join bright purple with sc in first ch sp, ch 6, (sc in next ch sp, ch 6) around, join with sl st in first sc. Fasten off.

Underskirt

Row 1: With wrong side of Bodice facing you, working in unworked **front lps** of starting ch on row 1 of Bodice, join pale purple with sl st in first ch, (ch 3, dc) in same ch as sl st, 2 dc in each ch across, turn. Fasten off. *(68 dc made)*

Row 2: Join bright purple with sl st in first st, ch 4, (dc in next st, ch 1) across with dc in last st, turn.

Row 3: Ch 3, dc in next st, (ch 1, dc) in each st across, turn.

Rnd 4: Working in rnds, ch 3, dc in first ch sp, ch 2, (skip next dc, dc in next ch sp, ch 2)

Continued on page 84

Continued from page 83

around, join with sl st in top of ch-3, **do not turn.**

Rnd 5: Ch 3, (dc, ch 2) in each st around, join.

Rnd 6: Ch 3, (dc, ch 1) in each ch sp and in each st around, join.

Rnds 7–11: Ch 3, (dc, ch 1) in each st around, join. At end of last rnd, fasten off.

Rnd 12: Join white with sc in first st, sc in each st and in each ch sp around, join with sl st in first sc.

Rnd 13: Ch 5, (dc in next st, ch 2) around, join with sl st in third ch of ch-5.

Rnd 14: Ch 1, sc in first st, (ch 6, sc) in each st and in each ch sp around, ending with ch 3, join with dc in first sc.

Rnd 15: Ch 1, sc in first ch sp, ch 6, (sc in next ch sp, ch 6) around, join with sl st in first sc. Fasten off.

Collar

Row 1: With white, ch 44, dc in fourth ch from hook, ch 1, (dc in next ch, ch 1) 3 times, (dc, ch 1, dc, ch 1) in next ch, (dc in next ch, ch 1) 11 times, (dc, ch 1, dc, ch 1) in next ch, (dc in next ch, ch 1) 6 times, (dc, ch 1, dc, ch 1) in next ch, (dc in next ch, ch 1) 11 times, (dc, ch 1, dc, ch 1) in next ch, (dc in next ch, ch 1) 4 times, dc in last ch, turn.

Row 2: Ch 1, sc in first st, *ch 4, sc in next ch sp, (ch 4, sc) 2 times in next st; repeat from * across. Fasten off.

Matching ends of row 1 to corners at back neck edge on Bodice, easing to fit, sew starting ch of row 1 to neck edge on Bodice.

Sleeve (make 2)

Row 1: With pale purple, beginning at elbow, ch 17, sc in second ch from hook, sc in each ch across, turn. *(16 sc made)*

Row 2: Ch 4 *(counts as dc and ch-1)*, dc in next st, (ch 1, dc in next st) across, turn. *(17 dc, 16 ch sps)*

Row 3: Ch 4, dc in next ch sp, (ch 1, dc in next ch sp) across to last st, ch 1, dc in last st, turn. *(17 dc, 16 ch sps)*

Row 4: Sl st in first st, (skip next ch sp, sl st in next st) 2 times, dc in next 11 ch sps, sl st in next st, (skip next ch sp, sl st in next st) 2 times. Fasten off.

Sew ends of rows 1–4 together for Sleeve seam

Rnd 5: For **ruffle,** working in remaining lps on opposite side of starting ch on row 1, join pale purple with sc in first ch past Sleeve seam, ch 3, (sc in next ch, ch 3) around, join with sl st in first sc. Fasten off.

Rnd 6: Join white with sc in first ch sp, (ch 3, sc)

2 times in same ch sp as last sc made, ch 3, sc in next st, *(ch 3, sc) 3 times in next ch sp, ch 3, sc in next st; repeat from * around, ch 3, join. Fasten off.

Turn piece so right side of sts on row 1 are on outside of Sleeve. Matching Sleeve seam to center of underarm on Bodice, sew row 4 of Sleeve to edge of armhole, easing to fit.

HAT

Rnd 1: With pale purple, ch 12, sl st in first ch to form ring, ch 3, 29 dc in ring, join with sl st in top of ch-3. *(30 dc made)*

Rnd 2: Ch 3, dc in each st around, join.

Rnd 3: Ch 1, sc in each st around, join with sl st in first sc.

Rnd 4: (Ch 3, dc) in first st, 2 dc in each st around, join with sl st in top of ch-3. *(60 dc)*

Rnd 5: Ch 4, (dc in next st, ch 1) around, join with sl st in third ch of ch-4.

Rnd 6: Ch 1, (sc in next ch sp, ch 4, sc in next st, ch 4) around, join with sl st in first sc. Fasten off.

Rnd 7: With bright purple, join with sc in any ch sp, ch 4, (sc in next ch sp, ch 4) around, join. Fasten off.

BASKET

Rnd 1: With white, ch 4, sl st in first ch to form ring, ch 3, 14 dc in ring, join with sl st in top of ch-3. *(15 dc made)*

Rnds 2–3: Ch 1, sc in each st around, join with sl st in first sc.

Rnd 4: Ch 5, (sc in next st, ch 5) around, join with sl st in first ch of first ch-5; for **handle,** ch 25, sl st in sc at center of rnd 4. Fasten off.

FINISHING

Place Dress on doll; overlap edges at back of Bodice and tack together.

For **tie belt,** with bright purple, ch to measure 30". Fasten off. Tie around waist with a bow at front.

For **hatband,** with bright purple, ch to measure 24". Fasten off. Weave through sts of rnd 3 on Hat, tie ends in bow.

Place Hat on head.

For **flower** *(make 6)*, with bright purple, ch 3, sl st in first ch, (ch 3, sl st in first ch of first ch-3) 4 times. Fasten off.

Sew one Flower to center front of Collar.

Wind a small ball of white yarn and tack to inside of Basket; tack five Flowers to inside of Basket, covering ball of yarn.

Place Basket Handle over doll's arm. With bright purple, ch to measure 12". Fasten off. Tie in bow around Handle and arm to hold Basket in place.✤

Cupie Doll Cuties

Designs by Mary Layfield

Instructions begin on page 86

Blue Pinafore

Finished Size: Fits 8" Cupie doll.

Materials:
- Worsted yarn:
  - ½ oz. blue
  - ½ oz. white
- One small snap
- One small bow appliqué
- 20" white ⅛"-wide ribbon
- Sewing and tapestry needles
- Blue sewing thread
- G hook or hook needed to obtain gauge

Gauge: 4 dc = 1"; 2 dc rows = 1".

Basic Stitches: Ch, sl st, sc, hdc, dc.

PINAFORE
Skirt
Row 1: With blue, ch 30, sc in second ch from hook, sc in each ch across, turn. *(29 sc made)*

Row 2: Ch 3, (dc in next st, 2 dc in next st) across, turn. *(43 dc)*

Row 3: Ch 3, dc in each st across, turn.

Rnd 4: Working in rnds, (ch 4, sc in next st) across, join with sl st in first ch of beginning ch-4.

Rnd 5: Ch 1, sc in first ch sp, ch 4, (sc in next ch sp, ch 4) around, join with sl st in first sc. Fasten off.

Bodice
Row 1: For **bib,** working in remaining lps on opposite side of starting ch on row 1 of Skirt, skip first 11 chs, join blue with sc in next ch, sc in next 6 chs leaving remaining chs unworked, turn. *(7 sc made)*

Rows 2–4: Ch 1, sc in each st across, turn.

Row 5: For **first shoulder strap,** ch 15, sc in second ch from hook, sc in next 6 chs, ch 2, 2 hdc in next 7 chs, sc in first st on row 4, **do not turn.** Fasten off.

Row 6: Skip first 6 sts on strap, join white with sc in next st, ch 3, sc in next ch-2 sp, (ch 3, sc in next st) 15 times, sl st in end of row 5, turn. Fasten off.

Row 5: For **second shoulder strap,** with blue, ch 14, sc in first st at end of row 4 on bib opposite first strap, **turn,** sl st in first st, 2 hdc in next 7 chs, ch 2, sc in last 7 chs, **do not turn.** Fasten off.

Row 6: Join with sl st in first hdc, (ch 3, sc in next st) 13 times, ch 3, sc in next ch-2 sp, ch 3, sc in next st leaving remaining 6 sts unworked. Fasten off.

Tack each strap to inside back of Skirt with yarn and tapestry needle.

With sewing thread and needle, sew snap to back opening of Skirt. Sew appliqué to center front of bib at waist. Place on doll.

BONNET
Row 1: With white, ch 28, dc in fourth ch from hook, dc in each ch across, turn. *(26 dc made)*

Rows 2–5: Ch 1, sc in each of first 3 sts, hdc in next 20 sts, sc in each of last 3 sts, turn.

Rnd 6: Ch 1, sc in each of first 5 sts, (sc next 2 sts tog) 8 times, sc in each of last 5 sts, ch 6, join with sl st in first sc. Fasten off.

Row 7: For **brim,** working in remaining lps on opposite side of starting ch on row 1, join white with sc in first ch, sc in each of next 2 chs, (dc in next ch, 2 dc in next ch) 10 times, sc in each of last 3 chs, turn. *(36 sts)*

Row 8: Ch 1, sc in each of first 3 sts, (2 dc in next st, dc in next 4 sts) 6 times, sc in each of last 3 sts, turn.

Row 9: (Ch 4, sc in next st) across. Fasten off.

Weave ribbon through sts of row 2, leaving even amount at each end for ties. Tie Bonnet on doll. Fold brim up. ❧

Nautical Outfit

Finished Size: Fits 8" Cupie doll.

Materials:
- Worsted yarn:
  - ½ oz. red
  - ½ oz. white
- Four small snaps
- One small nautical appliqué
- Sewing and tapestry needles
- White sewing thread
- G hook or hook needed to obtain gauge

Gauge: 4 dc = 1"; 2 dc rows = 1".

Basic Stitches: Ch, sl st, sc, dc.

TOP
Row 1: Starting at neckline, with red, ch 28, sc in second ch from hook, sc in each ch across, turn. Fasten off. *(27 sc made)*

Row 2: Join white with sl st in first st, (ch 3, dc) in same st, dc in next st, (2 dc in next st, dc in next st) across to last st, 2 dc in last st, turn. *(41 dc)*

Row 3: For **first back,** (ch 3, dc) in first st, (dc in next st, 2 dc in next st) 3 times; ch 3, skip next 7 sts *(armhole made);* for **front,** 2 dc in next st, (dc in next st, 2 dc in next st) 6 times; ch 3, skip next 7 sts *(armhole made);* for **second back,** 2 dc in next st, (dc in next st, 2 dc in next st) across, turn.

Row 4: Ch 3, dc in each st and in each ch across, turn.

Row 5: Ch 3, dc in each st across, turn.

Row 6: (Ch 4, sc in next st) across. Fasten off.

With sewing thread and needle, sew two snaps evenly spaced on back opening. Sew nautical appliqué to center front of Top. Place on doll.

PANTS SIDE (make 2)

Row 1: Starting at waist, with red, ch 18, sc in second ch from hook, sc in each ch across, turn. *(17 sc made)*

Rows 2–7: Ch 1, sc in each st across, turn.

Rows 8–9: Ch 2, sc in second ch from hook, sc in each st across, turn. *(18, 19)*

Rows 10–11: Ch 1, sc in each st across, turn. At end of last row, leaving 6" for sewing, fasten off.

Fold Pants Side in half; with tapestry needle and red yarn, sew ends of last two rows together to form leg opening.

Sew ends of rows 1–10 on each Pants Side together to form front seam. Sew opposite ends of rows 7–10 on each Pants Side together leaving rows 1–6 open.

Waistband

Row 1: Working in remaining lps on opposite side of starting ch on row 1 of assembled Pants, join red with sc in first ch, sc in each ch across, turn.

Row 2: Ch 1, sc in each st across. Fasten off.

With sewing needle and thread, sew two snaps evenly spaced down opening. Place on doll.

VISOR

Rnd 1: With red, ch 32, sl st in first st to form ring, ch 1, sc in each ch around, join with sl st in first sc. *(32 sc made)*

Row 2: Ch 1, sc in each of first 2 sts, (dc in next st, 2 dc in next st) 3 times, sc in each of next 2 sts leaving remaining sts unworked, turn.

Row 3: Ch 1, sc in each st across. Fasten off. Place on doll. ✤

Pink Dress

Finished Size: Fits 8" Cupie doll.

Materials:
- 1 oz. pink worsted yarn
- Two small snaps
- Two small flower appliqués
- Small ribbon roses:
    One pink
    One blue
- 26" pink ⅛"-wide ribbon
- sewing and tapestry needles
- pink sewing thread
- G hook or hook needed to obtain gauge

Gauge: 4 dc = 1"; 2 dc rows = 1".

Basic Stitches: Ch, sl st, sc, dc, tr.

DRESS

Row 1: Ch 28, sc in second ch from hook, sc in each ch across, turn. *(27 sc made)*

Row 2: For **first back,** (ch 3, dc) in first st, dc in next st, 2 dc in each of next 2 sts leaving remaining sts unworked, turn. *(7 dc)*

Row 3: Ch 3, 2 dc in next st, (dc in next st, 2 dc in next st) 2 times leaving ch-3 unworked, **do not turn.** Fasten off. *(9)*

Row 2: For **second back,** join with sl st in first unworked st on row 1, (ch 3, dc) in same st, dc in next st, 2 dc in each of next 2 sts leaving remaining sts unworked, turn. *(7)*

Row 3: Repeat row 3 of first back.

Row 2: For **front,** skip next 5 unworked sts on row 1, join with sl st in next st, (ch 3, dc) in same st, (dc in next st, 2 dc in next st) 4 times leaving remaining 5 sts unworked, turn. *(14)*

Row 3: (Ch 3, dc) in first st, (dc in next st, 2 dc in next st) across leaving ch-3 unworked, turn. Fasten off. *(20)*

Row 4: Working across row 3 of both backs and front, join with sl st in first st on back, ch 3, dc in each st across, turn. *(38)*

Row 5: (Ch 3, dc) in first st, dc in next st, (2 dc in next st, dc in next st) across, turn. *(57)*

Row 6: (Ch 4, skip next st, sc in next st) across, turn. *(Front of row 6 is right side of work.)*

Row 7: Ch 4; working in skipped sts of row 6, sc in next st, (ch 4, sc in next st) across. Fasten off.

Row 8: Working in remaining lps on opposite side of starting ch around neckline, join with *Continued on page 88*

Continued from page 87

sc in first ch, (ch 6, sc in next ch) across. Fasten off.

Sew appliqué to center front of Dress with sewing needle and thread. With sewing needle and thread, sew two snaps evenly spaced down back opening.

Armhole Ruffle

Working in five skipped sts of row 1 on Dress, join with sc in first st, (ch 4, sc) in each of last 4 sts. Fasten off. Repeat on other armhole opening. Place on doll.

BONNET

Row 1: Ch 29, dc in fourth ch from hook, dc in each ch across, turn. *(27 dc made)*

Rows 2–4: Ch 1, sc in each of first 3 sts, dc in next st, tr in next 19 sts, dc in next st, sc in each of last 3 sts, turn.

Rnd 5: Ch 1, sc in each of first 3 sts, dc in next st, tr in next 19 sts, dc in next st, sc in each of last 3 sts, ch 9, join with sl st in first sc; **turn,** sc in each ch of ch-9, sl st in last st just before ch-9. Fasten off.

Row 6: For brim, working in remaining lps on opposite side of starting ch on row 1, join with sc in first chs, sc in each of next 2 chs, dc in next ch, (2 dc in next ch, dc in next ch) 10 times, sc in each of last 3 chs, turn.

Row 7: Ch 1, sc in first st, (ch 3, sc in next st) across. Fasten off.

Cut 6" piece from ribbon. Folding two pleats to gather last row at back opening of Bonnet, weave first end of ribbon through first pleat and other end of ribbon through second pleat. Tighten and tie in bow. Sew appliqué over bow. Weave 20" ribbon through sts of row 2, leaving even amount at each end for ties. Sew ribbon roses over row 1 on left side of Bonnet *(see photo).* Tie Bonnet on doll. Fold brim up. ✤

Ice Skater's Delight

Continued from page 81

st, (sc in each of next 2 sts, 2 sc in next st) around, join. *(24)*

Rnd 5: Ch 1, sc in each of first 3 sts, 2 sc in next st, (sc in each of next 3 sts, 2 sc in next st) around, join. *(30)*

Rnd 6: Ch 1, sc in first 4 sts, 2 sc in next st, (sc in next 4 sts, 2 sc in next st) around, join. *(36)*

Rnd 7: Ch 1, sc in each st around, join.

Rnd 8: Ch 1, sc in first 5 sts, 2 sc in next st, (sc in next 5 sts, 2 sc in next st) around, join. *(42)*

Rnd 9: Ch 1, sc in each st around, join. Fasten off.

SKATE (make 2)

Rnd 1: With yellow, ch 7, sc in second ch from hook, sc in next 4 chs, 2 sc in last ch; working in remaining lps on opposite side of starting ch, sc in next 4 chs, 2 sc in last ch *(toe),* join with sl st in first sc.

Rnd 2: Working this rnd in **back lps** only, ch 1, sc in each st around, join.

Rnd 3: Ch 1, sc first 2 sts tog, sc in next 9 sts, sc next 2 sts tog, join.

Row 4: Working in rows, sl st in next st, sc in next 9 sts, turn.

Rows 5–10: Ch 1, sc in each sc across, turn. At end of last row, fasten off.

Row 11: For **tongue,** join yellow with sc in same st as last sc worked on row 4, sc in each of next 2 sl sts, sc in same st as first sc worked on row 4, turn. *(4 sc)*

Rows 12–15: Ch 1, sc in each st across, turn. At end of last row, fasten off.

Blade

Row 1: With silver thread, ch 8, sc in second ch from hook, sc in next 6 chs, turn.

Row 2: Ch 5, skip first 2 sts, dc in next st, ch 2, skip next 2 sts, dc in next st leaving last st unworked. Leaving 5" for sewing, fasten off.

Sew seven sts of Blade to center bottom of Skate. Cut 9" length of yellow thread and lace up front of Skate. Stiffen Blades with fabric stiffener; shape and let dry.

Finishing

Cut fur to fit bottom of Skirt, bottom of Sleeves, around outer edge of Hat and around neck. Tack each to appropriate section.

Sew snaps to back opening of Dress. ✤

Chapter
Five

Childhood
Treasures

Those gentle days we learned social graces at mama's
knee, then practiced them with dolly. Recall,
in crochet, mother's tender mercies,
teatime's cordial leisures and
friendship's bountiful
measures.

Rag Doll Twins

Designs by Katie Morse

Instructions begin on page 92

Rag Doll Twins

Finished Size: About 29" tall.

Materials:
- Worsted yarn:
  - 20 oz. white
  - 12 oz. blue
  - 9 oz. rust
  - 15 oz. fleshtone
  - 4 oz. black
  - Small amount of each red, pink and brown
- Polyester fiberfill
- 12" white ribbon
- Pink, red and black felt
- Eight white ¾" buttons
- Craft glue
- Tapestry needle
- J hook or hook needed to obtain gauge

Gauge: J hook and two strands held together, 5 sc = 2"; 3 sc rows = 1".

Basic Stitches: Ch, sl st, sc, dc.

Notes: Dolls are made using two strands held together; clothes are made using single strand.

All Body parts are for both girl and boy dolls.

Work in continuous rnds; do not join rnds unless otherwise stated. Mark first st of each rnd.

HEAD
Rnd 1: With two strands fleshtone, ch 2, 6 sc in second ch from hook. *(6 sc made)*
Rnd 2: 2 sc in each st around. *(12)*
Rnd 3: (Sc in next st, 2 sc in next st) around. *(18)*
Rnd 4: (Sc in each of next 2 sts, 2 sc in next st) around. *(24)*
Rnd 5: (Sc in each of next 3 sts, 2 sc in next st) around. *(30)*
Rnd 6: (Sc in next 4 sts, 2 sc in next st) around. *(36)*
Rnd 7: (Sc in next 5 sts, 2 sc in next st) around. *(42)*
Rnd 8: (Sc in next 6 sts, 2 sc in next st) around. *(48)*
Rnds 9–15: Sc in each st around.
Rnd 16: (Sc next 2 sts tog, sc in each of next 2 sts) around. *(36)*
Rnd17: Sc in each st around.
Rnd 18: 2 sc in each of next 6 sts *(cheek made)*, sc in next 4 sts, 2 sc in each of next 6 sts *(cheek made)*, sc in each remaining st around. *(48)*
Rnds 19–21: Sc in each st around.
Rnd 22: (Sc next 2 sts tog) around. Stuff and shape Head, pushing out cheeks. *(24)*
Rnd 23: (Sc in next st, sc next 2 sts tog) around. *(16)*

Rnds 24–25: Sc in each st around.
Rnd 26: (Sc in next st, 2 sc in next st) around. *(24)*
Rnd 27: Sc in each st around. Fasten off.

BODY
Rnd 1: With two strands white, ch 51, sl st in first ch to form ring, ch 1, sc in each ch around. *(51 sc made)*
Rnds 2–6: Sc in each st around.
Rnd 7: (Sc in each of next 3 sts, sc next 2 sts tog) around to last st, sc in last st. *(41)*
Rnds 8–16: Sc in each st around. At end of last rnd, join with sl st if first sc. Fasten off.
Rnd 17: Join fleshtone with sc in first st, sc in each st around.
Rnd 18: Sc in each st around.
Rnd 19: (Sc in each of next 2 sts, sc next 2 sts tog) around to last st, sc in last st. *(31)*
Rnds 20–23: Sc in each st around.
Rnd 24: (Sc in each of next 2 sts, sc next 2 sts tog) around to last 3 sts, sc in each of last 3 sts. *(24)*
Rnds 25–28: Sc in each st around. At end of last rnd, join. Fasten off.
Flatten rnd 1, sew edges together, closing bottom end of Body. Tuck each corner of bottom seam in about 1", tack in place to secure. Stuff and shape. Sew Head to rnd 28 of Body.

ARM (make 2)
Rnd 1: With two strands fleshtone, ch 2, 6 sc in second ch from hook. *(6 sc made)*
Rnd 2: 2 sc in each st around. *(12)*
Rnds 3–6: Sc in each st around.
Rnd 7: Ch 3, skip next 3 sts, sc in last 9 sts.
Rnd 8: Sc in each of next 3 chs, sc in last 9 sts *(Thumb opening made)*.
Rnds 9–25: Sc in each st around.
For wrist, press arm flat just above Thumb opening, sew together through both thicknesses across rnd 10. Stuff upper Arm firmly.
Row 26: Flatten rnd 25; working in rows through both thicknesses, ch 1, sc in each st across, turn.
Rows 27–30: Ch 1, sc in each st across, turn. At end of last row, fasten off.
Sew rows 26–30 to each side of upper Body.

Thumb
Rnd 1: Join two strands fleshtone with sc in any st of Thumb opening, sc in each st and each ch around. *(6 sc made)*
Rnd 2: Sc in each st around.
Rnd 3: (Skip next st, sc in next st) around, join with sl st in first st. Fasten off.

LEG (make 2)
Rnd 1: With two strands white, ch 2, 6 sc in second ch from hook. *(6 sc made)*
Rnd 2: 2 sc in each st around. *(12)*
Rnd 3: (Sc in next st, 2 sc in next st) around. *(18)*
Rnds 4–27: Sc in each st around. Stuff Leg firmly.

Row 28: Flatten last rnd; working in rows through both thicknesses, ch 1, sc in each st across, turn.

Rows 29–33: Ch 1, sc in each st across, turn. At end of last row, fasten off.

Sew Legs to bottom of Body.

SHOE (make 2)
Sole & Side
Rnd 1: With two strands black, ch 6, 3 sc in second ch from hook, sc in each of next 3 chs, 3 sc in last ch; working on opposite side of starting ch, sc in each of next 3 chs. *(12 sc made)*

Rnd 2: 2 sc in each of first 3 sts, sc in each of next 3 sts, 2 sc in each of next 3 sts, sc in each of last 3 sts. *(18)*

Rnd 3: (Sc in next st, 2 sc in next st) around. *(27)*

Rnd 4: Sc in first st, 2 sc in each of next 8 sts *(toe end of shoe)*, sc in each remaining st around. *(35)*

Rnd 5: Working this rnd in **back lps** *(see Stitch Guide)*, sc in each st around.

Rnd 6: Sc in each st around.

Rnd 7: Sc in each of first 2 sts, (sc next 2 sts tog) 6 times, sc in each remaining st around. *(29)*

Rnd 8: Sc in each st around, join with sl st in first sc. Fasten off.

Top
Rnd 1: With two strands black, ch 2, 6 sc in second ch from hook. *(6 sc made)*

Rnd 2: 2 sc in each st around. *(12)*

Rnd 3: (Sc in next st, 2 sc in next st) around, join with sl st in first sc. Leaving about 8" end, fasten off.

With 8" end, sew six stitches on edge of Top to matching center stitches on rnd 8 at toe end of Shoe.

With red, using backstitch *(see Stitch Guide)*, embroider a circle over rnd 2 of Top.

With red, embroider around bottom of Shoe with backstitches *(see photo)*.

Stuff toe of Shoe. Insert end of Leg into Shoe, sew top edge of Shoe in place.

DRESS SIDE (make 2)
Row 1: With single strand blue, ch 16, sc in second ch from hook and in each ch across, turn. *(15 sc made)*

Rows 2–14: Ch 1, sc in each st across, turn.

Row 15: Ch 3, dc in same st as ch-3, 2 dc in each st across, turn. *(30 dc)*

Row 16: Ch 3, dc in each st across, turn.

Row 17: Ch 3, dc in each of next 2 sts, (2 dc in next st, dc in each of next 3 sts) 6 times, 2 dc in next st, dc in each of last 2 sts, turn. *(37)*

Rows 18–26: Ch 3, dc in each st across, turn. At end of last row, fasten off.

Hold Dress Sides together, matching ends of rows; sew ends of rows 15–26 together forming side seams.

Bottom Ruffle
Rnd 1: Join single strand white with sc in any st of last row on Dress, sc in each st around, join with sl st in first sc. Fasten off.

Rnd 2: Join blue with sl st in first st, ch 1, *(sc, dc, sc) in next st, ch 1, skip next st; repeat from * around, join. Fasten off.

Put Dress on Doll, sew matching three stitches at each end of row 1 together, forming shoulder seams.

SLEEVE (make 2)
Row 1: With single strand blue, ch 26, sc in second ch from hook and in each ch across, turn. *(25 sc made)*

Row 2: Ch 1, sc in each st across, turn.

Rows 3–15: Ch 3, dc in each st across, turn. At end of last row, fasten off.

Fold Sleeve in half, matching ends of rows; sew edges together, forming underarm seam.

Sleeve Ruffle
Working in remaining lps on opposite side of starting ch on Sleeve, repeat Bottom Ruffle of Dress. Sew top edges of Sleeves into armholes of Dress, easing to fit.

Run strand of blue through row 1 of Sleeve, pull to tighten around Arm. Secure ends of gathering strand.

APRON
Bib
Row 1: With single strand white, ch 13, sc in second ch from hook and in each ch across, turn. *(12 sc made)*

Rows 2–10: Ch 1, sc in each st across, turn.

Row 11: Ch 1, sc in each of first 3 sts leaving remaining sts unworked, turn. *(3)*

Rows 12–38: Ch 1, sc in each st across, ch 1, turn. At end of last row, fasten off *(first strap made)*.

Row 11: For **second strap**, skip next 6 unworked sts on row 10, join white with sc in next st, sc in each of last 2 sts, turn. *(3)*

Rows 12–38: Ch 1, sc in each st across, turn. At end of last row, fasten off.

Skirt
Row 1: With single strand white, ch 20; working in remaining lps on opposite side of starting ch on Bib, join with sc in first st, sc in each st across, ch 20, turn. *(12 sc and 40 chs made)*

Row 2: Sc in second ch from hook, sc in each ch and in each st across to other end of first ch-20, turn. *(51 sc made)*

Row 3: Ch 3, dc in same st as ch-3, dc in each of next 2 sts, (2 dc in next st, dc in each of next 2 sts) across, turn. *(68 dc)*

Row 4: Ch 3, dc in each st across, turn.

Row 5: Ch 3, dc in same st as ch-3, dc in each of next 3 sts, (2 dc in next st, dc in each of next

Continued on page 94

Continued from page 93

3 sts) across, turn. *(85)*
Rows 6–12: Ch 3, dc in each st across, turn.
Row 13: *Ch 1, skip next st, (sc, dc, sc) in next st; repeat from * across. Fasten off.
With pink, embroider French knots *(wrap yarn four times around needle—see Stitch Guide)* in each dc on row 13.

Neck & Shoulder Ruffle
Leaving about 3" unworked at end of each shoulder strap, working in ends of rows and in sts around neck edge, join single strand white with sc in next row, (dc, sc) in same row, ch 1, skip next row or st, (sc, dc, sc) in next row or st; repeat from * around straps and neck edge. Fasten off.
Embroider French knots across Ruffle same as on row 13 of Skirt.
Put Apron on doll over Dress, matching ends of rows on Skirt and crossing straps in back. Sew ends of rows 2–13 together, forming center back seam. Sew ends of crossed straps to top edge of Apron at back.

PANTALOONS SIDE (make 2)
Row 1: Starting at top, with single strand white, ch 21, sc in second ch from hook and in each ch across, turn. *(20 sc made)*
Row 2: Ch 1, sc in each st across, turn.
Row 3: Ch 3, dc in same st as ch-3, dc in each of next 3 sts, (2 dc in next st, dc in each of next 3 sts) across, turn. *(25)*
Row 4: Ch 3, dc in each of next 3 sts, (2 dc in next st, dc in each of next 2 sts) across, turn. *(32)*
Rows 5–11: Ch 3, dc in each st across, turn.
Row 12: For **first leg,** ch 3, dc in same st as ch-3, (dc in each of next 2 sts, 2 dc in next st) 5 times leaving remaining sts unworked, turn. *(22)*
Rows 13–24: Ch 3, dc in each st across, turn. At end of last row, fasten off.
Row 12: For **second leg,** join white with sl st in 17th st of row 11, ch 3, dc in same st as ch-3, (dc in each of next 2 sts, 2 dc in next st) 5 times leaving remaining sts unworked, turn. *(22)*
Rows 13–24: Ch 3, dc in each st across, turn. At end of last row, fasten off.
Hold both Sides together, matching ends of rows; sew side edges together.

Trim
Working around bottom of one leg, join single strand white with sc in any st, (dc, sc) in same st as first sc, ch 1, skip next st, *(sc, dc, sc) in next st, ch 1, skip next st; repeat from * around, join. Fasten off.
Repeat on other leg.
Put Pantaloons on doll, sew to doll around

waist. Run strand of yarn through bottom of each Pant Leg, pull to tighten around Legs. Secure ends of gathering strands.

SHIRT SIDE (make 2)
Row 1: With single strand white, ch 16, sc in second ch from hook and in each ch across, turn. *(15 sc made)*
Rows 2–12: Ch 1, sc in each st across, turn.
Row 13: Ch 3, dc in same st as ch-3, 2 dc in each st across, turn. *(30 dc)*
Rows 14–15: Ch 3, dc in each st across, turn. At end of last row, fasten off. Leaving rows 1–9 open for Sleeves, sew side edges of Shirt Sides together.
With lt. blue, embroider 3 French knots on front of Shirt. Put Shirt on doll, sew top edges together on each side, forming shoulder seams.

Sleeve (make 2)
Row 1: With single strand white, ch 26, sc in second ch from hook and in each ch across, turn. *(25 sc made)*
Row 2: Ch 1, sc in each st across, turn.
Rows 3–14: Ch 3, dc in each st across, turn. At end of last row, fasten off.

Trim
Working in remaining lps on opposite side of starting ch on Sleeve, join single strand blue with sl st in first ch, ch 1, *(sc, dc, sc) in next ch, ch 1, skip next ch; repeat from * across. Fasten off.
Sew ends of rows on each Sleeve together, forming underarm seam.
Sew Sleeves into armholes, easing to fit. Sew buttons through back and front of Sleeve at wrist *(see photo)*.

Collar
Row 1: With single strand blue, ch 36, sc in second ch from hook and in each ch across, turn. *(35 sc made)*
Row 2: Ch 3, dc in same st as ch-3, 2 dc in each st across, turn. *(70 dc)*
Row 3: Ch 3, dc in each st across, turn.
Row 4: Ch 1, (sc, dc, sc) in first st, *ch 1, skip next st, (sc, dc, sc) in next st; repeat from * across to last st, sl st in last st. Fasten off.
Run about 25" of blue yarn through row 1 of Collar; put Collar around neck, tie ends in bow at front. Tack edge of Collar around neckline of Shirt.

PANTS
With single strand blue, work same as for Pantaloons.

Waist Trim
Working in remaining lps on opposite side of starting ch on Waist, join single strand blue

with sc in first ch, (dc, sc) in same ch as first sc, ch 1, skip next ch, *(sc, dc, sc) in next ch, ch 1, skip next ch; repeat from * around, join. Fasten off.

Sew two buttons on waist of front and back, *(see photo)*.

Put Pants on doll, tuck Shirt in; sew top edge to doll around waist. Sew a button at bottom of each Pant Leg.

HAT

Rnd 1: With single strand blue, ch 2, 6 sc in second ch from hook. *(6 sc made)*

Rnd 2: 2 sc in each st around. *(12)*

Rnd 3: (Sc in next st, 2 sc in next st) around. *(18)*

Rnd 4: (Sc in each of next 2 sts, 2 sc in next st) around. *(24)*

Rnd 5: (Sc in each of next 3 sts, 2 sc in next st) around. *(30)*

Rnd 6: (Sc in next 4 sts, 2 sc in next st) around. *(36)*

Rnd 7: (Sc in next 5 sts, 2 sc in next st) around. *(42)*

Rnd 8: (Sc in next 6 sts, 2 sc in next st) around. *(48)*

Rnd 9: (Sc in next 7 sts, 2 sc in next st) around. *(54)*

Rnd 10: (Sc in next 8 sts, 2 sc in next st) around. *(60)*

Rnds 11–21: Sc in each st around. At end of last rnd, join with sl st in first sc. Fasten off.

Rnd 22: Join white with sc in first st, sc in each st around.

Rnds 23–26: Sc in each st around.

Rnd 27: (Sc in each of next 3 sts, 2 sc in next st) around. *(75)*

Rnds 28–31: Sc in each st around. At end of last rnd, join with sl st in first sc.

Rnd 32: Ch 1, skip first st, *(sc, dc, sc) in next st, ch 1, skip next st; repeat from * around, join with sl st in first sc. Fasten off.

HAIR

Cut about 500 strands of rust, each 5" long. For each **fringe,** fold two strands rust in half, insert hook around st, pull fold through, pull ends of yarn through fold and tighten.

Work fringe in each st around top and back of Head. Trim for desired length.

Tie bow in Girl's Hair with white ribbon.

FACE

Cut felt facial features according to full-size pattern pieces; glue or sew in place as shown in photo.

For **freckles,** with brown, randomly embroider several French knots on face. ❖

FACIAL FEATURES

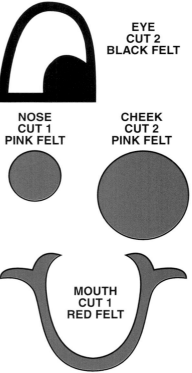

EYE
CUT 2
BLACK FELT

NOSE
CUT 1
PINK FELT

CHEEK
CUT 2
PINK FELT

MOUTH
CUT 1
RED FELT

Bride and Beau

Designs by Barbara Anderson

Finished Size: Approximately 8" tall.

Materials:
- Sport yarn:
  - 1 oz. gray
  - 1 oz. black
  - 1 oz. white
  - 1 oz. brown
- 1 oz. peach baby yarn
- 1½ oz. white pompadour yarn
- Small amount green worsted yarn
- Pink and black embroidery floss
- 1", 3", 5" and 7" squares cardboard
- Four black ¼" rounded shank buttons
- Seven small artificial flowers
- Powdered blush
- Polyester fiberfill
- Tapestry needle
- C and D hooks or hooks needed to obtain gauges

Gauges: C hook, 7 sc = 1"; 7 sc rows = 1".
D hook, 6 sc = 1"; 6 sc rows = 1".

Basic Stitches: Ch, sl st, sc, hdc, dc.

Special Stitches: For **triple picot,** (sc, ch 3, sc, ch 4, sc, ch 3, sc) in next st or ch sp.
For **beginning shell (beg shell),** (ch 3, dc, ch 2, 2 dc) in same st or ch sp.
For **shell,** (2 dc, ch 2, 2 dc) in next st or ch sp.

Note: Work in continuous rnds; do not join rnds unless otherwise stated. Mark first st of each rnd.

BRIDE

HEAD & BODY
Rnd 1: Starting at top of Head, with C hook and peach, ch 2, 6 sc in second ch from hook. *(6 sc made)*
Rnd 2: 2 sc in each st around. *(12)*
Rnd 3: (2 sc in next st, sc in next st) around. *(18)*
Rnd 4: (2 sc in next st, sc in each of next 2 sts) around. *(24)*
Rnd 5: Sc in each st around.
Rnd 6: Repeat rnd 4. *(32)*
Rnds 7–15: Sc in each st around.
Rnd 16: *Sc in next st, (sc next 2 sts tog) 2 times; repeat from * 5 times, sc in each of last 2 sts. *(20)*
Rnd 17: (Sc next 2 sts tog) around. Stuff. *(10)*
Rnds 18–19: Sc in each st around.
Rnd 20: Repeat rnd 3, join with sl st in first sc. Fasten off. *(15)*
Rnd 21: (2 sc in next st, sc in each of next 2 sts) around. *(20)*
Rnd 22: Sc in each st around.
Rnd 23: (2 sc in next st, sc in next 4 sts) around. *(24)*
Rnds 24–30: Sc in each st around. At end of last rnd, join with sl st in first sc. Fasten off.

Rnd 31: For **panties,** working this rnd in **back lps** *(see Stitch Guide),* with D hook and white pompadour, join with sc in first st, sc in each st around.
Rnds 32–34: Sc in each st around.
Rnd 35: (Sc next 2 sts tog, sc in next st) around, join. *(16)*
Leaving 8" for sewing, fasten off. Stuff. Flatten last rnd, sew together.

BODICE
NOTE: *Use D hook for remainder of pattern unless otherwise stated.*
Rnd 1: With white pompadour, ch 20, sl st in first ch to form ring, ch 3, dc in each ch around, join with sl st in top of ch-3. *(20 dc made)*
Rnd 2: Ch 3, dc in each st around, join.
Rnd 3: Ch 1, sc in each of first 3 sts; (for **armhole,** ch 6, skip next 3 sts); dc in next st, hdc in next st, sc in next 4 sts, hdc in next st, dc in next st; repeat between ( ), sc in each of last 3 sts, join with sl st in first sc. Fasten off.
Rnd 4: (Ch 3, sl st in next st) 2 times, (ch 3, sl st in next ch) 6 times, ch 3, skip next dc; **triple picot** *(see Special Stitches)* in next st, skip next st, sl st in each of next 2 sts, skip next st, triple picot in next st, skip next dc, sl st in next ch, (ch 3, sl st in next ch) 5 times, (ch 3, sl st in next st) 3 times, join with sl st in joining sl st of last rnd. Fasten off.
Slip over Body, tack starting ch to bottom of rnd 30 on Body.

LEG (make 2)
Rnd 1: With C hook and peach, ch 10, sl st in first ch to form ring, ch 1, sc in each ch around. *(10 sc)*
Rnds 2–14: Sc in each st around.
Rnds 15–16: Sc in each of first 2 sts; for **foot,** (sc next 2 sts tog) 2 times; sc in each of next 2 sts, 2 sc in each of last 2 sts.
Rnd 17: (Sc next 2 sts tog) around, join with sl st in first sc. *(5)* Leaving 8" for sewing, fasten off. Stuff. Sew rnd 17 closed. Flatten rnd 1 with foot pointing forward, sew together.
Sew rnd 1 to rnd 35 on Body.
For **garter,** with white pompadour, ch 15, sl st in first ch to form ring, ch 3, (sl st in next ch, ch 3) around, join with sl st in first sl st. Fasten off. Slide onto middle of Leg.

SHOE (make 2)
Rnd 1: With white, ch 6, 2 sc in second ch from hook, sc in each of next 3 chs, 5 hdc in next ch; working on opposite side of ch, sc in each of next 3 chs, 3 sc in last ch. *(16 sts)*
Rnd 2: Sc in each st around.
Rnd 3: Sc in first 5 sts, hdc in next st, (hdc next 2 sts tog) 2 times, hdc in next st, sc in last 5 sts, join with sl st in first sc. Fasten off. *(14)*

Continued on page 98

Continued from page 97

ARM (make 2)

Rnd 1: With white pompadour, ch 2, 10 sc in second ch from hook, join with sl st in first sc. *(10 sc)*

Rnds 2–4: Ch 3, dc in each st around, join with sl st in top of ch-3. *(10 dc)*

Rnd 5: Ch 3, dc next 2 sts tog, dc in next st, 2 dc in each of next 3 sts, dc in next st, dc last 2 sts tog, join. *(11)*

Rnd 6: Ch 3, (dc next 2 sts tog) 2 times, 2 dc in each of next 2 sts, (dc next 2 sts tog) 2 times, join. *(9)*

Rnd 7: Repeat rnd 2, **do not fasten off.**

Rnd 8: For **cuff,** working this rnd in **front lps,** (ch 3, sl st in next st) around, join with sl st in first ch-3 sp. *(8 ch-3 sps)*

Rnd 9: (Ch 2, sl st in next ch-3 sp) 3 times, ch 1, triple picot in next ch-3 sp, (ch 2, sl st in next ch-3 sp) 3 times, join with sl st in first ch of first ch-2. Fasten off.

Rnd 10: For **hand,** working this rnd in **back lps** of rnd 7, with C hook and peach, join with sc in fifth st, sc in each st around.

Rnd 11: Sc in each st around.

Rnd 12: Sc in each of first 2 sts; for **thumb,** ch 2, sl st in second ch from hook; sc in last 7 sts.

Rnd 13: Skipping thumb, sc in each st around. *(9)*

Rnd 14: (Sc next 2 sts tog, sc in next st) around, join with sl st in first sc. Leaving 8" for sewing, Fasten off. Stuff. Sew opening closed.

Sew side of rnd 1 of Arm to rnds 22–24 on side of Body covering armhole.

SKIRT

Rnd 1: Working in **front lps** of rnd 30 on Head & Body, join white pompadour with sl st in first sc, (ch 3, dc) in same st as sc, dc in each of next 2 sts, (2 dc in next st, dc in each of next 2 sts) around, join with sl st in top of ch-3. *(32 dc made)*

Rnds 2–3: Ch 3, dc in each st around, join.

Rnd 4: Ch 3, dc in same st as ch-3, 2 dc in each st around, join. *(64 dc)*

Rnds 5–7: Ch 3, dc in each st around, join. At end of last rnd, fasten off.

Row 8: For **train,** working in rows, join white pompadour with sc in 53rd st of rnd 7, sc in each of next 2 sts, hdc in each of next 3 sts, (2 dc in next st, dc in next st) 6 times, 2 dc in next st, hdc in each of next 3 sts, sc in each of next 3 sts leaving remaining sts unworked, turn. *(32 sts)*

Row 9: Ch 1, skip first st, sc in each of next 3 sts, hdc in each of next 3 sts, (2 dc in next st, dc in next st) 9 times, hdc in each of next 3 sts, sc in each of next 3 sts leaving last st unworked, turn. *(39)*

Row 10: Ch 1, skip first st, sc in each of next 3 sts, hdc in each of next 3 sts, (2 dc in next st, dc in next 4 sts) 5 times, hdc in each of next 3 sts, sc in each of next 3 sts leaving last st unworked, turn. *(42)*

Row 11: Ch 1, skip first st, sc in each of next 3 sts, hdc in each of next 3 sts, dc in next 28 sts, hdc in each of next 3 sts, sc in each of next 3 sts leaving last st unworked, turn. *(40)*

Row 12: Ch 1, skip first st, sc in each of next 3 sts, hdc in each of next 3 sts, dc in next 26 sts, hdc in each of next 3 sts, sc in each of next 3 sts leaving last st unworked, **do not turn.** *(38)*

Rnd 13: Working in ends of rows and in sts around outer edge, sl st in end of row 12, ch 1, sc in same row, 2 sc in each of next 4 rows, sc in next 39 sts on rnd 7, 2 sc in each of next 5 rows, sc in next 38 sts on row 12, join with sl st in first sc. *(96 sc)*

Rnd 14: Ch 5, dc in same st, skip next st, *(dc, ch 2, dc) in next st, skip next st; repeat from * around, join with sl st in third ch of ch-5.

Rnd 15: Sl st in first ch sp, **beg shell** *(see Special Stitches),* in same ch sp, ch 1, (sc, ch 1) in next ch sp; ***shell,** (see Special Stitches) in next ch sp, ch 1, (sc, ch 1) in next ch sp; repeat from * around, join with sl st in top of ch-3.

Rnd 16: Sl st in next st, sl st in next ch-2 sp, beg shell, ch 1, sc in next ch-1 sp, ch 2, sc in next ch-1 sp, ch 1, (shell in next ch-2 sp, ch 1, sc in next ch-1 sp, ch 2, sc in next ch-1 sp, ch 1) around, join.

Rnd 17: Sl st in next st, (sl st, ch 1, triple picot) in first ch-2 sp, *[sc in next ch-1 sp, (sc, ch 3, sc) in next ch-2 sp, sc in next ch-1 sp], triple picot in next ch-2 sp; repeat from * 22 more times; repeat between [ ], join with sl st in first sc. Fasten off.

VEIL

Row 1: With white pompadour, ch 11, sc in second ch from hook, (sc in next ch, ch 3) 2 times, skip next ch, (sc, ch 4, sc) in next ch, skip next ch, (sc in next ch, ch 3) 2 times, sc in each of last 2 chs; working in remaining lps on opposite side of starting ch, ch 1, sl st in first ch, (ch 4, sl st in next ch) 9 times, turn.

Row 2: (Ch 4, sc) in each ch sp across, turn. *(9 ch-4 sps)*

Row 3: (Ch 4, sc) 2 times in each ch sp across, turn. *(18 ch-4 sps)*

Rows 4–16: Repeat row 2. At end of last row, fasten off.

FACIAL FEATURES

For **nose,** with peach, using satin stitch *(see Stitch Guide),* embroider three horizontal stitches over rnd 11.

For **eyes,** thread tapestry needle with 18" strand peach; leaving 6" end, insert needle between rnds 9 and 10 at side of Head, pull needle out ⅜" from nose between rnds 9 and 10, put button on needle, insert needle between next 2 sts, pull needle out ⅜" from opposite side of nose between rnds 9 and 10, put button on needle; working back toward nose, insert needle between next 2 sts coming out in same place as 6" end, tighten thread until eyes are ½" apart, tie ends in knot. Hide ends in stuffing.

With two strands black floss, embroider three eyelashes above each eye.

For **mouth,** with six strands pink floss, using satin stitch *(see Stitch Guide),* embroider "V" over rnd 13.

HAIR

Wrap brown around 7" cardboard 15 times, slide loops off cardboard, tie separate 6" strand brown tightly around center of all loops. Tack center of loops to rnds 1–4 on front of Head. Spread loops evenly around back and sides of Head. Tack strands to back and sides of Head 1¼" from center tie.

Tack Veil 1" from front hairline.

Brush cheeks with blush.

BOUQUET

For **leaves,** wrap green around 1" cardboard three times, slide off cardboard. Arrange leaves and six artificial flowers; wrap 3" strand white pompadour around end of flowers and leaves, tie. Tack to Bride's hands.

BEAU

HEAD & BODY

Rnds 1–20: Repeat rnds 1–20 of Bride's Head & Body on page 97.

Rnd 21: For **shirt,** working this rnd in **back lps,** join white sport yarn with sc in first st, sc in same st, sc in each of next 2 sts, (2 sc in next st, sc in each of next 2 sts) around. *(20)*

Rnd 22: Sc in each st around.

Rnds 23–30: Repeat rnds 23–30 of Bride's Head & Body.

Rnd 31: Join black with sc in first st, sc in each st around.

Rnds 32–34: Sc in each st around.

Rnd 35: Repeat rnd 35 of Bride's Head & Body.

LEG (make 2)

Rnd 1: With D hook and black sport yarn, ch 12, sl st in first ch to form ring, ch 1, sc in each ch around. *(12 sc made)*

Rnds 2–14: Sc in each st around. At end of last rnd, join with sl st in first sc. Fasten off.

SHOE (make 2)

Rnd 1: With black, ch 5, 2 sc in second ch from hook, sc in next ch, hdc in next ch, 5 hdc in last ch; working in remaining lps on opposite side of starting ch, hdc in next ch, sc in next ch, 2 sc in last ch, join with sl st in first sc. *(13 sts made)*

Rnd 2: Working this rnd in **back lps,** ch 1, sc in each st around, join.

Rnd 3: Ch 1, sc in each of first 3 sts; working in **back lps,** (sc next 2 sts tog) 4 times; working in **both lps,** sc in each of last 2 sts, join. *(9)*

Rnd 4: Ch 1, sc in each of first 2 sts, (sc next 2 sts tog) 3 times, sc in last st, join. Leaving 8" for sewing, fasten off. *(6)*

Easing to fit, sew to **back lps** of rnd 14 on each Leg. Stuff Leg and Shoe. Flatten rnd 1 of Leg, sew together; sew to rnd 35 of Body.

For **Leg trim,** working in **front lps** of rnd 14 on Leg, join black with sl st in any st, sl st in each st around, join with sl st in first sl st. Fasten off. Repeat on other Leg.

ARM (make 2)

Rnd 1: With gray, ch 2, 5 sc in second ch from hook. *(5 sc made)*

Rnd 2: 2 sc in each st around. *(10)*

Rnds 3–7: Sc in each st around.

Rnd 8: Sc in each of first 3 sts; for **elbow,** dc in next 4 sts; sc in each of last 3 sts.

Rnd 9: 2 sc in each of next 2 sts, hdc in next st, (hdc next 2 sts tog) 2 times, hdc in next st, 2 sc in each of last 2 sts. *(12 sts)*

Rnd 10: Sc in first 4 sts, (sc next 2 sts tog) 2 times, sc in last 4 sts. *(10)*

Rnds 11–13: Sc in each st around. At end of last rnd, join with sl st in first sc. Fasten off.

Rnd 14: Working this rnd in **back lps,** join white sport yarn with sl st in first st, ch 1, sc first 2 sts tog, sc in each st around, join with sl st in first st. Fasten off. Stuff. *(9)*

Rnd 15: For **hand,** working this rnd in **back lps,** with C hook and peach, join with sc in first st, sc in each st around.

Rnd 16: Sc in each of first 2 sts; for **thumb,** ch 2, sl st in second ch from hook; sc in last 7 sts.

Rnd 17: Skipping thumb, sc in each st around. *(9)*

Rnd 18: (Sc next 2 sts tog, sc in next st) around, join with sl st in first sc. Leaving 8" for sewing, fasten off. Stuff. Sew opening closed.

Sew rnds 1–3 of Arm over Rnds 22–24 on each side of Body with elbows pointing toward back.

COLLAR

Row 1: With Head pointing away from you, working in **front lps** of rnd 20 on Head & Body, join white sport yarn with sc in tenth st, sc in same st, sc in each of next 2 sts, (2 sc in next st, sc in each of next 2 sts) around, turn. *(20 sc made)*

Row 2: Ch 2, hdc in same st, sc in each st across to last st, (hdc, ch 2, sl st) in last st. Fasten off.

BOW TIE

With black, ch 7, hdc in third ch from hook, sc in next ch, sl st in next ch, sc in next ch, (hdc, ch 2, sl st) in last ch. Fasten off.

Sew to center front of Collar.

Continued on page 100

Continued from page 99

JACKET

Row 1: Starting at top, with gray, ch 21, sc in second ch from hook, sc in next ch; (for **armhole**, ch 4, skip next 4 chs), sc in next 8 chs; repeat between ( ), sc in each of last 2 chs, turn. *(12 sc made)*

Row 2: Ch 1, sc in each st and in each ch across, turn. *(20)*

Row 3: Ch 1, sc in each st across, turn.

Rows 4–6: Ch 1, 2 sc in first st, sc in each st across with 2 sc in last st, turn. *(22, 24, 26)*

Row 7: Repeat row 3.

Rows 8–12: Ch 1, sc first 2 sts tog, sc in each st across to last 2 sts, sc last 2 sts tog, turn. At end of last row *(16)*.

Rnd 13: Working around outer edge, ch 1, 3 sc in first st, sc in next 14 sts, 3 sc in last st, sc in end of next 12 rows; working in remaining lps on opposite side of starting ch, sc in next 6 chs, hdc in next 8 chs, sc in next 6 chs, sc in end of next 6 rows, mark last st made, sc in end of next 6 rows, join with sl st in first sc. Fasten off. *(64 sts)*

For **collar**, with wrong side facing you, working in **back lps** of rnd 13, join gray with sl st in marked st, sc in each of next 2 sts, hdc in next st, (dc, ch 3, sl st) in next st, (sl st, ch 2, hdc) in next st, sc in next 20 sts, (hdc, ch 2, sl st) in next st, (sl st, ch 3, dc) in next st, hdc in next st, sc in each of next 2 sts, sl st in last st. Fasten off.

Fold collar back. With black, using chain stitch *(see Stitch Guide)*, embroider trim around edge of Collar *(see photo)*.

With black, using satin stitch *(see Stitch Guide)*, embroider button between rows 7 and 8 on right side of Jacket. Place Jacket on Body, tack together in front. Tack armholes in place around Arms.

With green, make one small loop. Tie 3" strand green around end of loop and one artificial flower. Tack flower to left side of Collar.

FACIAL FEATURES

Work same as Bride's nose and eyes on page 98.

For **mouth**, with six strands pink floss, using fly stitch *(see Stitch Guide)*, embroider mouth over rnd 13.

HAIR

For **back and sides**, wrap brown around 5" cardboard 15 times, slide loops off cardboard, tie separate 6" strand brown tightly around center of all loops. Tack center of loops to rnd 1 of Head. Spread loops around back and sides of Head, tack bottom of each loop in place.

For **bangs**, wrap brown around 3" cardboard 10 times, slide loops off cardboard, tie separate 6" strand brown around center of all loops. Tack center of loops to rnd 3 at right side on top of Head. Spread loops to form part, tack bottom of each loop in place on sides of face.

Brush cheeks with blush. ✣

Great Hair—a Doll's Crowning Glory

The best-dressed dolls have fabulous tresses, and there are lots of fun ways to make doll's hair yourself!

Try this: cut several strands of yarn, sew the middle of each strand to the center of the doll's head forming the part; continue until the head is covered. Then the hair can be pulled to each side and braided or tied with ribbons.

You can also tack hair in place around the doll's hairline with a tapestry needle and the same yarn, then pull the ends to the back and twist to keep it in place. Or just trim the yarn ends evenly around for a Dutch boy cut.

Maybe you prefer a curly hairdo. Wrap yarn around your finger six times, insert a tapestry needle threaded with the same yarn through the loops on your finger and then tie the loops together with a tight knot. Slip the loops off your finger and sew the curls to the doll's head. Repeat until the head is covered.

You can also work loop stitches around the stitches on the doll's head until it is completely covered with curls.

For boy dolls, embroider the hair with a tapestry needle and yarn using long, straight satin stitches. Cover the sides and back of the head with close up-and-down stitches; then cover the top of the head with side-to-side stitches. Add sideburns, mustaches and beards the same way.

Use your imagination and your dolls will never have a bad hair day! ✣

Country Cousins

Designs by Michele Wilcox

Instructions begin on page 102

The Little Goose Girl

Finished Size: Approximately 16" tall.

Materials:
- Worsted yarn:
    - 1½ oz. gold
    - 1½ oz. black
    - 1 oz. tan
    - 1 oz. white
    - 1 oz. rust
    - 1 oz. off-white
    - Small amount each red, brown and green
- ½ yd. of ¼" satin ribbon
- ½ yd. of ecru 1½" Cluny lace
- Ecru sewing thread
- 4" diameter plastic lid
- Polyester fiberfill
- Tapestry and sewing needles
- F hook or hook needed to obtain gauge

Gauge: 9 sc = 2"; 9 sc rows = 2".

Basic Stitches: Ch, sl st, sc, dc.

Note: Work in continuous rnds; do not join rnds unless otherwise stated. Mark first st of each rnd.

GIRL

Head & Body
Rnd 1: Starting at top of head, with tan, ch 2, 6 sc in second ch from hook. *(6 sc made)*
Rnd 2: 2 sc in each st around. *(12)*
Rnd 3: (Sc in next st, 2 sc in next st) around. *(18)*
Rnd 4: (Sc in each of next 2 sts, 2 sc in next st) around. *(24)*
Rnd 5: Sc in each st around.
Rnd 6: (Sc in each of next 3 sts, 2 sc in next st) around. *(30)*
Rnd 7: Sc in each st around.
Rnd 8: (Sc in next 4 sts, 2 sc in next st) around. *(36)*
Rnds 9–12: Sc in each st around.
Rnd 13: Sc in first 10 sts; for **cheek,** 3 sc in each of next 2 sts; 2 sc in next st, sc in next 10 sts, 2 sc in next st; for **cheek,** 3 sc in each of next 2 sts; sc in last 10 sts. *(46)*
Rnds 14–15: Sc in each st around.
Rnd 16: Sc in first 9 sts, (sc next 2 sts tog) 5 times, sc in next 8 sts, (sc next 2 sts tog) 5 times, sc in last 9 sts. *(36)*
Rnd 17: (Sc in next 4 sts, sc next 2 sts tog) around. *(30)*
Rnd 18: (Sc in each of next 3 sts, sc next 2 sts tog) around. *(24)*

Rnd 19: (Sc in each of next 2 sts, sc next 2 sts tog) around. Stuff. Continue stuffing as you work. *(18)*
Rnd 20: (Sc in next st, sc next 2 sts tog) around. *(12)*
Rnds 21–23: Sc in each st around.
Rnd 24: (Sc in next st, 2 sc in next st) around. *(18)*
Rnd 25: 2 sc in each st around, join with sl st in first sc. Fasten off. *(36)*
Rnd 26: For **body suit,** join black with sc in first st, sc in each st around.
Rnds 27–40: Sc in each st around.
Rnd 41: Sc in each st around; sc in next 29 sts, move marker to last st made, this is now beginning of rnd.
Rnd 42: For **first leg,** skip first 18 sts, sc in each st around to marked st. *(18)*
Rnd 43: Place marker in last st made on rnd 42, skip next 18 unworked sts on rnd 41, sc in each st around to marker *(marked st is counted as first st of rnd 43).* *(18)*
Rnds 44–49: Sc in each st around. At end of last rnd, join with sl st in first sc. Fasten off.
Rnd 42: For **second leg,** join black with sc in first skipped st on rnd 41, sc in each st around. *(18)*
Rnd 43: Sc in each st around.
Rnds 44–49: Sc in each st around. At end of last rnd, join with sl st in first sc. Fasten off.

Boot (make 2)
Rnd 1: Starting at **sole,** with brown, ch 6, sc in second ch from hook, sc in each of next 3 chs, 3 sc in last ch; working in remaining lps on opposite side of starting ch, sc in each of next 3 chs, 2 sc in last ch. *(12)*
Rnd 2: 2 sc in first st, sc in each of next 3 sts, 2 sc in each of next 3 sts, sc in each of next 3 sts, 2 sc in each of last 2 sts. *(18)*
Rnd 3: (Sc in each of next 2 sts, 2 sc in next st) around. *(24)*
Using crocheted piece as pattern, cut piece from plastic lid.
Rnd 4: Working this rnd in **back lps** *(see Stitch Guide),* sc in each st around.
Rnd 5: Sc in each st around. Place plastic piece inside.
Rnd 6: Sc in first 9 sts, (sc next 2 sts tog) 3 times, sc in last 9 sts. *(21)*
Rnd 7: Sc in first 8 sts, (sc next 2 sts tog) 3 times, sc in last 7 sts. *(18)*
Rnds 8–12: Sc in each st around.
Rnd 13: Working this rnd in **front lps,** (sc in next 5 sts, 2 sc in next st) around. *(21)*
Rnd 14: Sc in each st around, join with sl st in first sc. Fasten off. Stuff firmly.
Sew **back lps** of rnd 12 to bottom of Leg with toes pointing forward.
For **shoestring,** using 18" strand off-white, lace through sts on toe *(see photo),* tie in bow at top.

Arm (make 2)

Rnd 1: Starting at **hand,** with tan, ch 2, 6 sc in second ch from hook. *(6 sc made)*

Rnd 2: 2 sc in each st around. *(12)*

Rnds 3–4: Sc in each st around. At end of last rnd, join with sl st in first sc. Fasten off.

Rnd 5: For **sleeve,** join black with sc in first st, sc in each st around.

Rnds 6–22: Sc in each st around. At end of last rnd, join. Leaving 8" for sewing, fasten off. Stuff.

Flatten last rnd, sew together. Sew at slight angle over rnds 26 and 27 on side of Body.

With brown, using satin stitch *(see Stitch Guide),* embroider eyes as shown in photo over rnds 11 and 12 on Head. With red, using fly stitch *(see Stitch Guide),* embroider mouth over rnds 13 and 14.

Hair

Cut 60 strands gold each 24" long.

Using backstitch *(see Stitch Guide),* starting at rnd 1, sew center of strands in place down center back of Head to rnd 14, forming part.

Starting 3" from center part, braid Hair on each side of Head. Tie separate 6" strand gold around top and bottom of each braid to secure. Trim ends. Tack top of braids to sides of Head.

Cut ¼" ribbon in half. Tie one piece in bow around bottom of each braid.

CLOTHES

Skirt

Rnd 1: Starting at **waist,** with rust, ch 36, sl st in first ch to form ring, ch 1, sc in each ch around, join with sl st in first sc. *(36 sc made)*

Rnd 2: Ch 3, dc in same st, 2 dc in each st around, join with sl st in top of ch-3. *(72)*

Rnds 3–10: Ch 3, dc in each st around, join. At end of last rnd, fasten off.

Sew lace to wrong side of rnd 9 so it hangs just below hemline. Sew waist to rnd 34 of Body.

Vest

Row 1: With green, ch 37, sc in second ch from hook, sc in each ch across, turn. *(36 sc made)*

Rows 2–3: Ch 1, sc in each st across, turn.

Row 4: Ch 1, sc first 2 sts tog, sc in each st across to last 2 sts, sc last 2 sts tog, turn. *(34)*

Row 5: For **right front,** ch 1, sc first 2 sts tog, sc in next 4 sts, sc next 2 sts tog leaving last 26 sts unworked, turn. *(6)*

Row 6: Ch 1, sc in each st across, turn.

Row 7: Repeat row 4. *(4)*

Rows 8–11: Ch 1, sc in each st across, turn. At end of last row, fasten off.

Row 5: For **armhole,** skip next 2 unworked sts on row 4; for **back,** join with sl st in next st, ch 1, sc first 2 sts tog, sc in next 10 sts, sc next 2 sts tog leaving last 10 sts unworked, turn. *(12)*

Row 6: Ch 1, sc in each st across, turn.

Row 7: Repeat row 4. *(10)*

Rows 8–11: Ch 1, sc in each st across, turn.

Row 12: Ch 1, sc in first 4 sts, sl st in each of next 2 sts, sc in last 4 sts, turn. Fasten off. *(8)*

Row 5: For **armhole,** skip next 2 unworked sts on row 4; for **left front,** join with sl st in next st, ch 1, sc first 2 sts tog, sc in next 4 sts, sc last 2 sts tog, turn. *(6)*

Rows 6–11: Repeat rows 6–11 of right front.

Match and sew shoulders together, forming seams.

Working around armhole, join green with sc in any st at bottom of armhole, sc in each st and in end of each row around, join with sl st in first sc. Fasten off. Repeat on other armhole.

Working around outer edge of Vest, join green with sc in any st, sc in each st and in end of each row around with 3 sc in each corner, join with sl st in first sc. Fasten off.

Place Vest on Girl. Using 12" strand red yarn, starting at row 3, lace through sts at ends of rows on of front edges down to row 1; tie ends in bow at bottom.

Apron

Row 1: Starting at **waist,** with off-white, ch 19, sc in second ch from hook, sc in each ch across, turn. *(18 sc made)*

Row 2: Ch 1, 2 sc in first st, sc in next st, (2 sc in next st, sc in next st) across, turn. *(27)*

Rows 3–17: Ch 1, sc in each st across, turn. At end of last row, **do not turn.**

Rnd 18: Working around outer edge, ch 1, 2 sc in end of row 17, sc in end of each row across to row 1; for **first sash,** *ch 40, sc in second ch from hook, sc in each ch across*; (sc next 2 chs tog) across opposite side of starting ch; for **second sash,** repeat between first and second *, sc in end of each row across to row 17, 2 sc in row 17, join with sl st in first sc. Fasten off.

Tie Apron around waist with sashes tied in a bow at back.

Scarf

Row 1: With red, ch 65, sl st in second ch from hook, (sc in next ch, hdc in next ch, dc in each of next 2 chs, hdc in next ch, sc in next ch), sl st in next 6 chs, sc in next 38 chs, sl st in next 6 chs; repeat between ( ), sl st in last ch, turn. Fasten off.

Row 2: Join red with sl st in 15th st, ch 3, dc next 2 sts tog, dc in next 32 sts, dc next 2 sts tog, dc in next st leaving last 13 sts unworked, turn. *(36)*

Row 3: Ch 1, sc in first st, sc next 2 sts tog, sc in each st across to last 3 sts, sc next 2 sts tog, sc in last st, turn. *(34)*

Row 4: Ch 3, dc next 2 sts tog, dc in each st across to last 3 sts, dc next 2 sts tog, dc in last st, turn. *(32)*

Continued on page 104

Continued from page 103

Rows 5–17: Repeat rows 3 and 4 alternately, ending with row 3. At end of last row *(6 sc)*.

Row 18: Ch 1, sc first 2 sts tog, (sc next 2 sts tog) across, turn. *(3)*

Row 19: Ch 1, sc 3 sts tog. Fasten off. Place around Head and tie under chin.

GOOSE

Head & Body

Rnd 1: With white, repeat rnds 1–3 of Girl's Head & Body on page 102.

Rnds 4–8: Sc in each st around.

Rnd 9: (Sc in next st, sc next 2 sts tog) around. *(12)*

Rnds 10–17: Sc in each st around.

Rnd 18: (Sc in next st, 2 sc in next st) around. *(18)*

Rnd 19: Sc in first 4 sts; for **back,** 2 sc in each of next 5 sts; sc in last 9 sts. *(23)*

Rnd 20: Sc in each st around.

Rnd 21: Sc in first 7 sts, 2 sc in each of next 2 sts, 3 sc in next st, 2 sc in each of next 2 sts, sc in last 11 sts. *(29)*

Rnd 22: Sc in each st around.

Rnd 23: Sc in first 9 sts, 2 sc in each of next 2 sts, 3 sc in next st, 2 sc in each of next 2 sts, sc in last 15 sts. *(35)*

Rnds 24–26: Sc in each st around.

Rnd 27: Sc in first 12 sts; for **tail shaping,** (sc next 2 sts tog) 3 times; sc in last 17 sts. *(32)*

Rnd 28: Sc in first 10 sts, (sc next 2 sts tog) 4 times, sc in last 14 sts. *(28)*

Rnd 29: Sc in first st, (sc next 2 sts tog, sc in next st) around. *(19)*

Rnd 30: Sc in first st, (sc next 2 sts tog) around. Stuff. *(10)*

Rnd 31: (Sc next 2 sts tog) around, join with sl st in first sc. Leaving 8" for sewing, fasten off. Sew opening closed.

Wing (make 2)

Row 1: Starting at **tip,** with white, ch 2, 3 sc in second ch from hook. *(3 sc made)*

Row 2: Ch 1, sc in each st across, turn.

Row 3: Ch 1, 2 sc in first st, sc in each st across to last st, 2 sc in last st, turn. *(5)*

Rows 4–6: Repeat rows 2 and 3 alternately, ending with row 2. At end of last row *(7 sc)*.

Rows 7–8: Ch 1, sc first 2 sts tog, sc in each st across to last 2 sts, sc last 2 sts tog, turn. *(5, 3)*

Rnd 9: Working around outer edge, ch 1, sc in end of each row and in each st around with 3 sc in tip, join with sl st in first sc. Leaving 12" for sewing, fasten off.

With row 8 at top, sew Wings to Body sides over

rnds 20–22 at slight angle 2½" apart in front. Using satin stitch and black, embroider eyes over rnd 4 on each side of Head.

Beak

Rnd 1: With gold, ch 2, 6 sc in second ch from hook. *(6 sc made)*

Rnds 2–4: Sc in each st around.

Rnd 5: (2 sc in next st, sc in each of next 2 sts) around, join with sl st in first sc. Leaving 8" for sewing, fasten off. Stuff lightly.

Sew over rnds 3 and 4 on front of Head.

Leg (make 2)

Row 1: Starting with **toes,** with gold, (ch 4, sl st in second ch from hook, sc in next ch, hdc in last ch) 3 times, **do not turn.** *(3 toes)*

Row 2: Ch 1, 2 sc in side of hdc on each toe across, turn. *(6)*

Row 3: Ch 1, sc first 2 sts tog, (sc next 2 sts tog) across, turn. *(3)*

Row 4: Ch 1, sc 3 sts tog; for **leg,** ch 9, sc in second ch from hook, sc in each ch across, join with sl st in top of first sc. Leaving 8" for sewing, fasten off.

Sew Legs to bottom of Body 1" apart. Place Goose in Girl's Arms, tack rnd 1 of hands together. ✤

Boy & Bear

Finished Size: Approximately 17" tall.

Materials:
- Worsted yarn:
    1½ oz. gold
    1½ oz. brown
    1 oz. tan
    1 oz. white
    1 oz. black
    1 oz. green
    Small amount red
- 1 oz. gray sport yarn
- Three ⅜" buttons
- Black sewing thread
- 4"-diameter plastic lid
- Polyester fiberfill
- Sewing and tapestry needles
- F hook or hook needed to obtain gauge

Gauge: 9 sc = 2"; 9 sc rows = 2".

Basic Stitches: Ch, sl st, sc, hdc.

Note: Work in continuous rnds; do not join rnds unless otherwise stated. Mark first st of each rnd.

BOY
Head & Body
Rnd 1: Starting at top of **head,** with tan, ch 2, 6 sc in second ch from hook. *(6 sc made)*

Rnd 2: 2 sc in each st around. *(12)*

Rnd 3: (Sc in next st, 2 sc in next st) around. *(18)*

Rnd 4: (Sc in each of next 2 sts, 2 sc in next st) around. *(24)*

Rnd 5: Sc in each st around.

Rnd 6: (Sc in each of next 3 sts, 2 sc in next st) around. *(30)*

Rnd 7: Sc in each st around.

Rnd 8: (Sc in next 4 sts, 2 sc in next st) around. *(36)*

Rnds 9–12: Sc in each st around.

Rnd 13: Sc in first 10 sts; for **cheek,** 3 sc in each of next 2 sts; 2 sc in next st, sc in next 10 sts, 2 sc in next st; for **cheek,** 3 sc in each of next 2 sts; sc in last 10 sts. *(46)*

Rnds 14–15: Sc in each st around.

Rnd 16: Sc in first 9 sts, (sc in next 2 sts tog) 5 times, sc in next 8 sts, (sc next 2 sts tog) 5 times, sc in last 9 sts. *(36)*

Rnd 17: (Sc in next 4 sts, sc next 2 sts tog) around. *(30)*

Rnd 18: (Sc in each of next 3 sts, sc next 2 sts tog) around. *(24)*

Rnd 19: (Sc in each of next 2 sts, sc next 2 sts tog) around. Stuff. Continue stuffing as you work. *(18)*

Rnd 20: (Sc in next st, sc next 2 sts tog) around. *(12)*

Rnds 21–23: Sc in each st around.

Rnd 24: (Sc in next st, 2 sc in next st) around, join with sl st in first sc. Fasten off. *(18)*

Rnd 25: For **shirt,** join white with sc in first st, sc in same st, 2 sc in each st around. *(36)*

Rnds 26–37: Sc in each st around. At end of last rnd, join with sl st in first sc. Fasten off.

Rnd 38: For **stockings,** join black with sc in first st, sc in each st around.

Rnds 39–40: Sc in each st around.

Rnd 41: Sc in each st around; sc in next 29 sts, move marker to last st made, this is now beginning of rnd.

Rnd 42: For **first leg,** skip first 18 sts, sc in each st around to marked st. *(18)*

Rnd 43: Place marker in last st made on rnd 42, skip next 18 unworked sts on rnd 41, sc in each st around to marker *(marked st is counted as first st of rnd 43). (18)*

Rnds 44–62: Sc in each st around. At end of last rnd, join with sl st in first sc. Fasten off.

Rnd 42: For **second leg,** join black with sc in first skipped st on rnd 41, sc in each st around. *(18)*

Rnds 43–62: Sc in each st around. At end of last rnd, join with sl st in first sc. Fasten off.

Boot (make 2)
Rnd 1: Starting at **sole,** with brown, ch 6, sc in second ch from hook, sc in each of next 3 chs, 3 sc in last ch; working in remaining lps on opposite side of starting ch, sc in each of next 3 chs, 2 sc in last ch. *(12 sc made)*

Rnd 2: 2 sc in first st, sc in each of next 3 sts, 2 sc in each of next 3 sts, sc in each of next 3 sts, 2 sc in each of last 2 sts. *(18)*

Rnd 3: (Sc in each of next 2 sts, 2 sc in next st) around. *(24)*

Using crocheted piece as pattern, cut piece from plastic lid.

Rnd 4: Working this rnd in **back lps** *(see Stitch Guide),* sc in each st around.

Rnd 5: Sc in each st around. Place plastic piece inside.

Rnd 6: Sc in first 9 sts, (sc next 2 sts tog) 3 times, sc in last 9 sts. *(21)*

Rnd 7: Sc in first 8 sts, (sc next 2 sts tog) 3 times, sc in last 7 sts. *(18)*

Rnds 8–12: Sc in each st around.

Rnd 13: Working this rnd in **front lps,** (sc in next 5 sts, 2 sc in next st) around. *(21)*

Rnd 14: Sc in each st around, join with sl st in first sc. Fasten off. Stuff firmly.

Sew **back lps** of rnd 12 to bottom of leg with toes pointing forward.

For **shoestring,** using 18" strand white yarn, lace through sts on toe *(see photo),* tie in bow at top.

Arm (make 2)
Rnd 1: Starting at **hand,** with tan, ch 2, 6 sc in second ch from hook. *(6 sc made)*

Rnd 2: 2 sc in each st around. *(12)*

Rnds 3–4: Sc in each st around. At end of last rnd, join with sl st in first sc. Fasten off.

Rnd 5: For **sleeve,** join white with sc in first st, sc in each st around.

Rnds 6–22: Sc in each st around. At end of last rnd, join. Leaving 8" for sewing, fasten off. Stuff.

Flatten last rnd, sew together. Sew at slight angle over rnds 26 and 27 on side of Body.

Ear (make 2)
Rnd 1: With tan, ch 2, 6 sc in second ch from hook. *(6 sc made)*

Rnd 2: 2 hdc in each of first 2 sts, sl st in next st leaving last 3 sts unworked. Fasten off.

Sew over rnds 12–14 on each side of Head about 4½" apart.

With brown, using satin stitch *(see Stitch Guide),* embroider eyes as shown in photo over rnds 11 and 12 on Head.

With red, using fly stitch *(see Stitch Guide),* embroider mouth over rnds 15 and 16.

Continued on page 106

Continued from page 105

Hair

For **each fringe,** cut 5" strand brown, fold in half, insert hook around st, pull fold through st, pull ends through fold, tighten.

Fringe in one st on each row around face and behind Ears forming hairline. Fringe in every other st alternately on each row covering back of Head completely. Trim ends.

Collar

Row 1: With white, ch 21, 2 sc in second ch from hook, 2 sc in each ch across, turn. *(40 sc made)*

Row 2: Ch 1, sc in each st across. Fasten off.

Placing ends of Collar on each side of three center front sts on rnd 25 of Body, sew top edge of Collar in place around rnd 25.

Vest

Row 1: With black, ch 37, sc in second ch from hook, sc in each ch across, turn. *(36 sc made)*

Rows 2–5: Ch 1, sc in each st across, turn.

Row 6: Ch 1, sc first 2 sts tog, sc in each st across to last 2 sts, sc last 2 sts tog, turn. *(34)*

Row 7: For **right front,** ch 1, sc first 2 sts tog, sc in next 4 sts, sc next 2 sts tog leaving last 26 sts unworked, turn. *(6)*

Row 8: Ch 1, sc in each st across, turn.

Row 9: Repeat row 6. *(4)*

Rows 10–13: Ch 1, sc in each st across, turn. At end of last row, **do not turn.** Fasten off.

Row 7: For **armhole,** skip next 2 unworked sts on row 6; for **back,** join with sl st in next st, ch 1, sc same st and next st tog, sc in next 10 sts, sc next 2 sts tog leaving last 10 sts unworked, turn. *(12)*

Row 8: Ch 1, sc in each st across, turn.

Row 9: Ch 1, sc first 2 sts tog, sc in next 8 sts, sc last 2 sts tog, turn. *(10)*

Rows 10–12: Ch 1, sc in each st across, turn.

Row 13: Ch 1, sc in first 4 sts, sl st in each of next 2 sts, sc in last 4 sts. Fasten off. *(8)*

Row 7: For **armhole,** skip next 2 unworked sts on row 6; for **left front,** join with sl st in next st, ch 1, sc first 2 sts tog, sc in next 4 sts, sc last 2 sts tog, turn. *(6)*

Rows 8–13: Repeat rows 8–13 of right front.

Match and sew shoulders together, forming seams.

Working around armhole, join black with sc in any st at bottom of armhole, sc in each st and in end of each row around, join with sl st in first sc. Fasten off. Repeat on other armhole.

Working around outer edge, join black with sc in any st, sc in each st and in end of each row around with 3 sc in each corner, join with sl st first sc. Fasten off.

Place Vest on Boy, sew rows 1–5 together. Sew buttons evenly spaced over rows 1–5 on left front.

Tie

Rnd 1: With red, ch 2, 6 sc in second ch from hook. *(6 sc made)*

Rnd 2: (Sc in next st, 2 sc in next st) around. *(9)*

Rnd 3: Sc in each st around.

Rnd 4: (Sc next 2 sts tog) 4 times, sc in last st. *(5)*

Rnd 5: Sl st in each st around.

Rnd 6: 2 sc in each of first 4 sts, sc in last st. *(9)*

Rnd 7: Sc in each st around.

Rnd 8: (Sc in next st, sc next 2 sts tog) around, join with sl st in first sc. Leaving 8" for sewing, fasten off. Sew opening closed.

Sew Tie to front of shirt between ends of Collar.

KNICKERS

Leg (make 2)

Rnd 1: Starting at **knee,** with green, ch 20, sl st in first ch to form ring, ch 1, sc in each ch around. *(20)*

Rnd 2: (Sc in next st, 2 sc in next st) around. *(30)*

Rnds 3–14: Sc in each st around. At end of last rnd, join with sl st in first sc. Fasten off.

For **crotch,** hold last rnd of Legs together, matching six sts of each edge; sew matched six sts together.

Body

Rnd 1: Join green with sc in first st after Crotch, sc in each st around each Leg leaving seam of Crotch unworked. *(48)*

Rnd 2: (Sc in next 6 sts, sc next 2 sts tog) around. *(42)*

Rnds 3–8: Sc in each st around.

Rnd 9: (Sc in next 5 sts, sc next 2 sts tog) around. *(36)*

Rnd 10: Sc in each st around, join with sl st in first sc. Fasten off.

Place knickers on Boy, tack last rnd to Body just under bottom edge of Vest.

HAT
Rnds 1–4: With gray, repeat rnds 1–4 of Boy's Head & Body on page 105.
Rnd 5: (Sc in each of next 3 sts, 2 sc in next st) around. *(30)*
Rnd 6: (Sc in next 4 sts, 2 sc in next st) around. *(36)*
Rnd 7: (Sc in next 5 sts, 2 sc in next st) around. *(42)*
Rnd 8: (Sc in next 6 sts, 2 sc in next st) around. *(48)*
Rnd 9: (Sc in each of next 3 sts, 2 sc in next st) around. *(60)*
Rnds 10–13: Sc in each st around.
Rnd 14: (Sc in next st, sc next 2 sts tog) around. *(40)*
Rnd 15: Sc in each st around.
Row 16: For **visor**, working in rows, sc in first 16 sts leaving last 24 sts unworked, turn. *(16)*
Rows 17–21: Ch 1, sc first 2 sts tog, sc in each st across to last 2 sts, sc last 2 sts tog, turn. At end of last row *(6)*.
Rnd 22: Working around outer edge, ch 1, sc in each st and in end of each row around, join with sl st in first sc. Fasten off.
Tack center of row 18 on visor to rnd 15 of Hat.

Button
Rnds 1–2: With gray, repeat rnds 1–2 of Boy's Head & Body.
Rnd 3: Sc in each st around.
Rnd 4: (Sc next 2 sts tog) around, join with sl st in first sc. Leaving 8" for sewing, fasten off. Sew opening closed.
Sew rnd 4 to rnd 1 on top of Hat. Place on Boy's Head with brim slightly to side *(see photo)*, tack in place.

BEAR
Head & Body
Rnds 1–6: With gold, repeat rnds 1–6 of Boy's Head & Body.
Rnds 7–11: Sc in each st around.
Rnd 12: (Sc next 2 sts tog) around. *(15)*
Rnd 13: Sc in each st around.
Rnd 14: 2 sc in each st around. *(30)*
Rnds 15–17: Sc in each st around.
Rnd 18: (Sc in next 4 sts, 2 sc in next st) around. *(36)*
Rnds 19–24: Sc in each st around.
Rnd 25: (Sc in next 4 sts, sc next 2 sts tog) around. *(30)*
Rnd 26: (Sc in each of next 3 sts, sc next 2 sts tog) around. *(24)*
Rnd 27: (Sc in each of next 2 sts, sc next 2 sts tog) around. Stuff. *(18)*
Rnd 28: (Sc in next st, sc next 2 sts tog) around. *(12)*
Rnd 29: (Sc next 2 sts tog) around. Leaving 8" for sewing, fasten off. Sew opening closed.

Muzzle
Rnd 1: With gold, ch 2, 6 sc in second ch from hook. *(6 sc made)*
Rnd 2: (Sc in next st, 2 sc in next st) around. *(9)*
Rnd 3: Sc in each st around.
Rnd 4: (Sc in each of next 2 sts, 2 sc in next st) around, join with sl st in first sc. Leaving 12" for sewing, fasten off. Stuff lightly.
Sew last rnd of Muzzle over rnds 8–11 of Head.
With black, using satin and straight stitches *(see Stitch Guide)*, embroider eyes over rnds 7 and 8 of Head as shown in photo.
With black, using satin and straight stitches, embroider nose and mouth over end of Muzzle as shown in photo.

Ear (make 2)
Rnds 1–3: Repeat rnds 1–3 of Muzzle.
Rnd 4: Sc in each st around.
Rnd 5: Sc in first st, (sc next 2 sts tog) around, join with sl st in first sc. Leaving 8" for sewing, fasten off.
Flatten last rnd, sew over rnds 5–7 on side of Head about 1" from eyes.

Arm (make 2)
Rnds 1–2: Repeat rnds 1–2 of Muzzle.
Rnds 3–9: Sc in each st around. At end of last rnd, join with sl st in first sc. Leaving 12" for sewing, fasten off. Stuff.
Flatten last rnd, sew opening closed.
Sew at slight angle over rnds 15–17 on side of Body.

Leg (make 2)
Rnd 1: With gold, ch 5, sc in second ch from hook, sc in each of next 2 chs, 3 sc in last ch; working in remaining lps of starting ch, sc in each of next 2 chs, 2 sc in last ch. *(10 sc made)*
Rnd 2: 2 sc in first st, sc in each of next 2 sts, 2 sc in each of next 3 sts, sc in each of next 2 sts, 2 sc in each of last 2 sts. *(16)*
Rnds 3–4: Sc in each st around.
Rnd 5: Sc in first 4 sts, (sc next 2 sts tog) 4 times, sc in last 4 sts. *(12)*
Rnds 6–12: Sc in each st around. At end of last rnd, join with sl st in first sc. Leaving 12" for sewing, fasten off. Stuff. Flatten last rnd, sew edges together.
Sew Legs side by side to bottom of Body. Place Bear in Boy's Arms, tack rnd 1 of hands together. ❧

Lisa Diane

Design by Pat Thom

Finished Size:
Approximately 25" tall.

Materials:
- Sport yarn:
  10 oz. blue
  7½ oz. white
  5¼ oz. fleshtone
  3 oz. rust
  Small amounts red,
  black, green
- Polyester fiberfill
- 4" × 7" piece plastic canvas
- 2 yds. each of white and blue ¼" satin ribbon
- 2 yds. of ½" white satin ribbon
- Nine white ½" buttons
- 2 yds. cord elastic
- Powdered blush
- Tapestry needle
- D hook or hook needed to obtain gauge

Gauge: 5 sc = 1", 5 sc rows = 1"; 5 dc = 1", 5 dc rows = 2".

Basic Stitches: Ch, sl st, sc, hdc, dc, tr.

Note: Work in continuous rnds, do not join rnds unless otherwise stated. Mark first st of each rnd.

HEAD & BODY

Rnd 1: With fleshtone, ch 2, 6 sc in second ch from hook. *(6 sc made)*

Rnd 2: 2 sc in each st around. *(12)*

Rnd 3: (Sc in next st, 2 sc in next st) around. *(18)*

Rnd 4: (Sc in each of next 2 sts, 2 sc in next st) around. *(24)*

Rnd 5: (Sc in each of next 3 sts, 2 sc in next st) around. *(30)*

Rnd 6: (Sc in next 4 sts, 2 sc in next st) around. *(36)*

Rnd 7: (Sc in next 5 sts, 2 sc in next st) around. *(42)*

Rnd 8: (Sc in next 6 sts, 2 sc in next st) around. *(48)*

Rnd 9: (Sc in next 7 sts, 2 sc in next st) around. *(54)*

Rnd 10: (Sc in next 8 sts, 2 sc in next st) around. *(60)*

Rnd 11: (Sc in next 9 sts, 2 sc in next st) around. *(66)*

Rnd 12: (Sc in next 10 sts, 2 sc in next st) around. *(72)*

Rnds 13–30: Sc in each st around.

Rnd 31: (Sc in next 10 sts, sc next 2 sts tog) around. *(66)*

Rnd 32: (Sc in next 9 sts, sc next 2 sts tog) around. *(60)*

Rnd 33: (Sc in next 8 sts, sc next 2 sts tog) around. *(54)*

Rnd 34: (Sc in next 7 sts, sc next 2 sts tog) around. *(48)*

Rnd 35: (Sc in next 6 sts, sc next 2 sts tog) around. *(42)*

Rnd 36: (Sc in next 5 sts, sc next 2 sts tog) around. *(36)*

Rnd 37: (Sc in next 4 sts, sc next 2 sts tog) around. *(30)*

Rnd 38: (Sc in each of next 3 sts, sc next 2 sts tog) around. *(24)*. Stuff half of Head. Sew long sides of plastic canvas together to form cylinder. Stuff. Push half of cylinder into Head. Stuff around cylinder.

Rnds 39–46: Sc in each st around.

Rnd 47: 2 sc in each st around. *(48)*

Rnd 48: (2 sc in next st, sc in next 23 sts) 2 times. *(50)*

Rnd 49: (2 sc in next st, sc in next 24 sts) 2 times. *(52)*

Rnd 50: (2 sc in next st, sc in next 25 sts) 2 times. *(54)*

Rnds 51–85: Sc in each st around. At end of last rnd, fasten off. Stuff. Sew opening closed.

LEG (make 2)

Rnd 1: With fleshtone, ch 32, sl st in first ch to form ring, ch 2, sc in each ch around. *(32 sc made)*

Rnds 2–31: Sc in each st around. At end of last rnd, change to white in last st made *(see Stitch Guide).*

Continued on page 110

Continued from page 109

Rnds 32–36: Hdc in each st around, join with sl st in first hdc.

Rnd 37: Working this rnd in **back lps** *(see Stitch Guide)*, ch 2, (hdc next 2 sts tog) around changing to black in last st, join with sl st in top of ch-2. *(16 hdc)*

Rnd 38: Ch 2, hdc in next 7 sts, 3 hdc in each of next 8 sts, join. *(32)*

Rnds 39–42: Ch 2, hdc in each st around, join.

Rnds 43–44: Ch 2, (hdc next 2 sts tog) around to last st, skip last st, join. At end of last rnd, fasten off. *(16, 8)*

Rnd 45: Working in **front lps** of rnd 36, join white with sl st in any st, ch 4, (sl st in next st, ch 4) around, join with sl st in same st as first sl st. Fasten off. Sew opening closed. Stuff.

Fold rnd 1 in half, sew to last rnd on Body. Cut ¼" white ribbon 16" long, tie to center top of foot on rnd 37.

ARM (make 2)

Rnd 1: With fleshtone, ch 20, sl st in first ch to form ring, ch 1, sc in each ch around. *(20 sc made)*

Rnds 2–30: Sc in each st around.

Rnd 31: Sc in each of first 2 sts, (sc next 2 sts tog, sc in next st) around. *(14)*

Rnd 32: (Sc in next st, 2 sc in next st) around. *(21)*

Rnds 33–35: Sc in each st around.

Rnd 36: Sc in next 10 sts; for **thumb**, ch 5, sc in second ch from hook, sc in each of next 3 chs; sc in last 11 sts on rnd 35.

Rnd 37: Sc in next 10 sts, skip thumb, sc in next 11 sts.

Rnd 38: Sc in each st around.

Rnd 39: (Sc in each of next 2 sts, sc next 2 sts tog) 5 times, sc in last st. *(16)*

Row 40: For **fingers**, sc in first st, ch 4, sc in second ch from hook, sc in each of next 2 chs; fold rnd 39 flat; working through both thicknesses, (sc in each of next 2 sts on rnd 39, ch 5, sc in second ch from hook, sc in each of next 3 chs), sc in each of next 2 sts on rnd 39, ch 6, sc in second ch from hook, sc in next 4 chs; repeat between ( ), sl st in last st. Fasten off. Stuff.

Sew rnd 1 to each side of Body with thumbs up.

HAIR

NOTE: Curls are worked in only one lp on ch.

Long Curl (make 18)

With rust, ch 50, 3 hdc in second ch from hook, 3 hdc in each ch across. Fasten off. Sew to back of Head along rnd 19.

Short Curl (make 52)

With rust, ch 15, 3 hdc in second ch from hook, 3 hdc in each ch across. Fasten off. Sew to top of Head forming bangs and overlapping long curls slightly.

FACE

With fleshtone, going from back of Head to front of Head, make indentions for eyes and mouth as shown in photo. Using satin and straight stitches *(see Stitch Guide)*, embroider nose with fleshtone, mouth with red, eyes with green and white, eyelashes with black. Brush cheeks lightly with powdered blush.

DRESS

Bodice Front

Row 1: With blue, ch 32, dc in fourth ch from hook, dc in each ch across, turn. *(30 dc made)*

Rows 2–13: Ch 3, dc in each st across, turn.

Row 14: Ch 3, dc in next 7 sts, ch 3, sl st in next 14 sts, ch 3, dc in next 8 sts. Fasten off. *(18 sts)*

Bodice Back (make 2)

Row 1: With blue, ch 20, dc in fourth ch from hook, dc in each ch across, turn. *(18 dc made)*

Rows 2–13: Ch 3, dc in each st across, turn.

Row 14: Ch 3, dc in next 7 sts, ch 3, sl st in next 10 sts. Fasten off.

Sew nine sts of row 14 on Front and Back together for shoulder seams. Sew ends of rows 1–6 on Front and Back together for side seams.

Skirt

Row 1: Working in remaining lps on opposite side of starting ch on Bodice, join blue with sl st in first ch on Bodice Back, ch 3, dc in same ch, 2 dc in each ch across, turn. *(132 dc made)*

Row 2: Ch 3, dc in same st, 2 dc in each st across, turn. *(264)*

Rnd 3: Working in rnds, ch 3, dc in each st around, join with sl st in top of ch-3.

Rnd 4: Ch 3, dc in each of next 2 sts, (2 dc in next st, dc in each of next 3 sts) around to last st, 2 dc in last st, join. *(330)*

Rnds 5–24: Ch 3, dc in each st around, join.

Rnd 25: Ch 3, dc in same st, 2 dc in each st around, join.

Rnd 26: Ch 3, dc in each st around, join. Fasten off.

Sleeves

Rnd 1: Join blue with sl st in side seam, ch 3, 2 dc in same st, 3 dc in end of each row around armhole, join with sl st in top of ch-3. *(51 dc made)*

Rnds 2–19: Ch 3, dc in each st around, join.

Rnd 20: Ch 3, dc in same st, 2 dc in each st around, join. Fasten off.

Weave 4½" piece elastic through rnd 19, sew ends together.

Repeat on other armhole.

Collar

Row 1: Join blue with sl st on right Bodice Back,

ch 3, dc in same st, 2 dc in each st across to left Bodice Back, turn. *(60 dc made)*

Row 2: Ch 3, dc in each st across. Fasten off.

Sew 4 buttons to right Bodice Back using sps between sts on left Bodice Back for buttonholes. Sew 2 buttons to top center front on Bodice.

APRON

Bodice Front

Row 1: With white, ch 32, dc in fourth ch from hook, dc in each ch across, turn. *(30 dc made)*

Rows 2–6: Ch 3, dc in each st across, turn.

Rows 7–10: Ch 3, dc next 2 sts tog, dc in each st across to last 2 sts, dc last 2 sts tog, turn. At end of last row, fasten off. *(28, 26, 24, 22)*

Bodice Back (make 2)

Row 1: With white, ch 20, dc in fourth ch from hook, dc in each ch across, turn. *(18 dc made)*

Rows 2–6: Ch 3, dc in each st across, turn.

Rows 7–10: Ch 3, dc in each st across to last 2 sts, dc last 2 sts tog, turn. At end of last row, fasten off. *(17, 16, 15, 14)*

Strap (make 2)

Row 1: With white, ch 8, dc in fourth ch from hook, dc in each ch across, turn. *(6 dc made)*

Rows 2–10: Ch 3, dc in each st across, turn. At end of last row, fasten off.

Sew row 1 of each Strap to row 10 on Bodice Front at outer edge. Sew row 10 to decrease end of row 10 on each Bodice Back. Sew ends of rows 1–4 together for side seams.

Skirt

Row 1: Working in remaining lps on opposite side of starting ch on Bodice, join white with sl st in first ch on Back, ch 3, dc in same ch, 2 dc in each ch across, turn. *(132 dc made)*

Rows 2–3: Ch 3, dc in same st, 2 dc in each st across, turn. *(264, 528)*

Rows 4–19: Ch 3, dc in each st across, turn.

Rows 20–21: Ch 3, dc in same st, 2 dc in each st across, turn.

Row 22: Ch 3, dc in each st across. Fasten off.

Neck Ruffle

Row 1: Join white with sl st in first st on right Bodice Back, ch 3, 2 dc in same st, 3 dc in each st and in end of each row around neck edge to left Bodice Back, turn.

Row 2: Ch 3, 2 dc in same st, 2 dc in each st across, turn.

Row 3: Ch 3, dc in each st across. Fasten off.

Sew 3 buttons to right Bodice Back using sps between sts on left Bodice Back for buttonholes. Tie 10" piece of ¼" blue ribbon in bow to center front of row 1 on Neck Ruffle. Cut six pieces from ½" ribbon each 10" long, tie each piece in a bow evenly spaced around rnd 19 of Skirt.

PANTIES SIDE (make 2)

Row 1: With white, ch 54, dc in fourth ch from hook, dc in each ch across, turn. *(52 dc made)*

Rows 2–15: Ch 3, dc in each st across, turn.

Row 16: Ch 3, 2 dc in same st, 3 dc in each st across. Fasten off.

Row 17: Join blue with sc in first st, sc in each st across. Fasten off. On each Panties Side, sew ends of rows 14–17 together to form leg opening.

Sew Sides together across ends of rows 1–13 for front and back seam. Weave 14" piece elastic through row 1, sew ends together for waistband. Weave 7" piece elastic through row 15 on each leg, sew ends together.

HAT

Row 1: With blue, ch 28, dc in fourth ch from hook, dc in each ch across, turn. *(26 dc made)*

Rnd 2: Working in rnds, ch 4, 3 tr in same st, 4 tr in each st across; working in remaining lps on opposite side of starting ch, 4 tr in each ch across, join with sl st in top of ch-4.

Rnd 3: Ch 4, 2 tr in same st, 3 tr in each st around, join.

Rnd 4: Ch 4, tr in each st around, join. Fasten off.

Rnd 5: Join white with sc in any st, ch 3, skip next st, (sc in next st, ch 3, skip next st) around, join with sl st in first sc. Fasten off.

Cut ½" white ribbon 60" long, weave through row 1, making ends of ribbon same length for ties. Sew ends of row 1 to ribbon. Place on Head, tie in bow under chin. ❧

Bitty Baby

Design by Pam McGhee

BABY

HEAD

NOTE: Piece will ruffle until stuffed.

Rnd 1: With lt. peach, ch 2, 10 sc in second ch from hook. *(10 sc made)*

Rnd 2: 2 sc in each st around. *(20)*

Rnd 3: (Sc in next st, 2 sc in next st) around. *(30)*

Rnd 4: (2 sc in next st, sc in each of next 2 sts) around. *(40)*

Rnd 5: (Sc in each of next 3 sts, 2 sc in next st) around. *(50)*

Rnd 6: (2 sc in next st, sc in next 4 sts) around. *(60)*

Rnd 7: (Sc in next 5 sts, 2 sc in next st) around. *(70)*

Rnds 8–28: Sc in each st around.

Rnd 29: (Sc in each of next 3 sts, sc next 2 sts tog) around. *(56)*

Rnd 30: (Sc in each of next 2 sts, sc next 2 sts tog) around. *(42)*

Rnd 31: (Sc next 2 sts tog) around, join with sl st in first sc. Fasten off. Stuff. *(21)*

Sculpting & Facial Features

With lt. peach, leaving 6" end, starting at bottom back of Head, coming out on odd numbers and going in on even numbers, sculpt face following numbers on diagram ending at bottom back. Tie and weave in ends to secure.

For **right cheek,** make small st at right corner of mouth then at outside corner of right eye, pull tight. Secure ends. Repeat for **left cheek.**

For **ears,** starting 1¼" from eye indentation, sculpt each ear following numbers on diagram, pulling sts tight. Secure ends.

For **eyes,** with two strands floss, using satin stitch *(see Stitch Guide),* embroider eyes on muslin according to diagram. For **sparkle in eye,** make two small white sts next to top of pupil on same side of each eye.

Trim muslin to ¼" from edge on each eye. Tack raw edge to wrong side of each eye. With two strands white floss, making small tight sts around outer edge, sew one eye to each eye indentation.

Brush cheeks with blush.

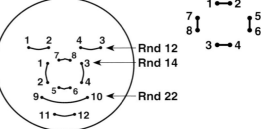

FACE DIAGRAM   **EAR DIAGRAM**

EYE DIAGRAM

BLACK   EYE COLOR   WHITE

Continued on page 114

Continued from page 113

For **girl,** tie ribbon in bow. Sew to rnd 3 on right side of Head.

BODY

Rnd 1: With lt. peach, ch 21, sl st in first ch to form ring, ch 1, 2 sc in each ch around. *(42 sc made)*

Rnd 2: (Sc in each of next 2 sts, 2 sc in next st) around. *(56)*

Rnds 3–32: Sc in each st around. At end of last rnd, join with sl st in first sc. Fasten off. Stuff.

Flatten rnd 32; matching sts, sew opening closed. Sew last rnd on Head to opposite side of starting ch on Body.

For **bellybutton and hips,** leaving 6" end, starting at back about 1" from bottom seam, insert needle through to center front 2" from bottom seam. Make small st going back to beginning, make long st to bottom seam, pull tight to form hips. Secure ends.

HAND & ARM (make 2)

Rnd 1: With lt. peach, ch 7, 2 sc in second ch from hook, sc in next 4 chs, 5 sc in last ch; working in remaining lps on opposite side of starting ch, sc in last 5 chs, join with sl st in first sc. *(16 sc made)*

Rnd 2: Ch 1, sc in each st around.

Rnds 3–4: Sc in each st around.

Rnd 5: Sc in first st, 2 sc in next st, sc in next 5 sts; for **thumb,** 2 sc in each of next 4 sts; sc in next 4 sts, 2 sc in last st. *(22)*

Rnds 6–32: Sc in each st around. At end of last rnd, join with sl st in first sc. Fasten off. Stuff.

Flatten rnd 32; matching sts, sew opening closed.

Sculpting

Leaving 6" end, insert needle at rnd 32; coming out on odd numbers and going in on even numbers, working over end of Hand for fingers, sculpt according to Arm diagram. Secure ends at rnd 32.

Sew one Arm to rnds 5–12 on each side of Body with thumbs up and top tilted slightly forward. Secure ends.

ARM DIAGRAM

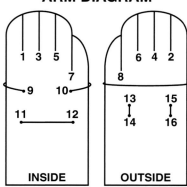

INSIDE   OUTSIDE

FOOT & LEG (make 2)

Rnds 1–2: Repeat rnds 1–2 of Hand & Arm.

Rnds 3–8: Sc in each st around.

Row 9: For **heel,** working in rows, sc in first 5 sts, 2 sc in each of next 3 sts, sc in each of next 2 sts leaving last 6 sts unworked, turn. *(13)*

Row 10: Ch 1, sc in first 8 sts, sl st in next st leaving last 4 sts unworked, turn. *(9 sts)*

Row 11: Ch 1, skip first sl st, sc in next 7 sts, sl st in last st, turn. *(8)*

Row 12: Ch 1, skip first sl st, sc in next 6 sts, sl st in last st, sl st in next unworked st on row 9, turn. *(8)*

Rnd 13: For **leg,** working in rnds, ch 1, skip each of first 2 sl sts, sc in each of next 2 sts, 2 sc in each of next 2 sts, sc in each of next 2 sts, sl st in end of row 11, sc in next 4 sts on rnd 8, 2 sc in each of next 2 sts, sc in each of last 3 sts, join with sl st in first sc. *(20)*

Rnd 14: Ch 1, sc in first 7 sts, 2 sc in next st, skip next sl st, 2 sc in each of next 2 sts, sc in next 7 sts, 2 sc in each of last 2 sts. *(24 sc)*

Rnd 15: Sc in each st around.

Rnd 16: (Sc in each of next 3 sts, 2 sc in next st) around. *(30)*

Rnds 17–40: Sc in each st around. At end of last rnd, join with sl st in first sc. Fasten off. Stuff.

Flatten rnd 40 with foot pointing up; matching sts, sew opening closed.

Sculpting

Insert needle at rnd 40, working same as Arm from bottom to top going over end of Foot for toes, sculpt according to Leg Diagram. Secure ends at rnd 40.

Sew Legs to bottom seam on Body with toes pointing forward.

LEG DIAGRAM

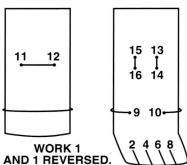

WORK 1
AND 1 REVERSED.

DIAPER SET

SHIRT

Back

Row 1: With MC, ch 29, hdc in third ch from hook, hdc in each ch across, turn. *(28 hdc made)*

Rows 2–10: Ch 2, hdc in each st across, turn.

Row 11: For **armhole,** sl st in each of first 3 sts,

ch 2, hdc in next 23 sts leaving last 2 sts unworked, turn. *(24)*

Rows 12–15: Ch 2, hdc in each st across, turn.

Row 16: For **left shoulder,** ch 1, sc in each of first 2 sts, hdc in each of next 2 sts, dc in next st, dc next 2 sts tog, dc in next st leaving last 16 sts unworked. Fasten off. *(7 sts)*

Row 16: For **right shoulder,** skip next 8 sts on row 15, join with sl st in next st, ch 3, dc next 2 sts tog, dc in next st, hdc in each of next 2 sts, sc in each of last 2 sts. Fasten off. *(7)*

Right Front

Row 1: With MC, ch 18, hdc in third ch from hook, hdc in each ch across, turn. *(17 hdc made)*

Rows 2–10: Ch 2, hdc in each st across, turn.

Row 11: Ch 2, hdc in next 14 sts leaving last 2 sts unworked for **armhole,** turn. *(15)*

Rows 12–13: Ch 2, hdc in each st across, turn.

Row 14: Ch 2, hdc in next 5 sts, hdc next 2 sts tog, hdc in next st leaving last 6 sts unworked for **neck,** turn. *(8)*

Row 15: For **shoulder,** ch 3, dc next 2 sts tog, dc in next st, hdc in each of next 2 sts, sc in each of last 2 sts. Fasten off. *(7 sts)*

Left Front

Rows 1–10: Repeat rows 1–10 of Right Front.

Row 11: For **armhole,** sl st in each of first 3 sts, ch 2, hdc in each st across, turn. *(15)*

Rows 12–13: Ch 2, hdc in each st across, turn.

Row 14: For **neck,** sl st in first 7 sts, ch 2, hdc next 2 sts tog, hdc in each st across, turn. *(8)*

Row 15: For **shoulder,** ch 1, sc in each of first 2 sts, hdc in each of next 2 sts, dc in next st, dc next 2 sts tog, dc in last st. Fasten off. *(7 sts)*

Sew shoulder and side seams.

Trim

Working around outer edge in ends of rows and in sts, join MC with sc in bottom corner on Left Front, sc in each st around with 2 sc in each row and 3 sc in each bottom corner, join with sl st in first sc. Fasten off.

Working around one armhole in sts and in ends of rows, join with sc in side seam, sc in each st around with 2 sc in each row, join with sl st in first sc. Fasten off. Repeat on other armhole.

Sew buttons evenly spaced to Left Front for girl and Right Front for boy using spaces on opposite Front for buttonholes.

DIAPER

Row 1: With white, ch 31, hdc in third ch from hook, hdc in each ch across, turn. *(30 hdc made)*

Rows 2–6: Ch 2, hdc in each st across, turn.

Rows 7–9: Ch 2, hdc next 2 sts tog, hdc in each st across to last 3 sts, hdc next 2 sts tog, hdc in last st, turn. At end of last row *(24)*.

Rows 10–19: Ch 2, hdc in each st across, turn.

Rows 20–22: Ch 2, 2 hdc in next st, hdc in each st across to last 2 sts, 2 hdc in next st, hdc in last st, turn. At end of last row *(30)*.

Rows 23–28: Ch 2, hdc in each st across, turn. At end of last row, fasten off.

Liner

Row 1: With white, ch 23, hdc in third ch from hook, hdc in each ch across, turn. *(22 hdc made)*

Rows 2–4: Ch 2, hdc in each st across, turn.

Rows 5–7: Repeat row 7 of Diaper. *(20, 18, 16)*

Rows 8–17: Ch 2, hdc in each st across, turn.

Rows 18–20: Repeat row 20 of Diaper. (18, 20, 22)

Rows 21–24: Ch 2, hdc in each st across, turn. At end of last row, fasten off.

Finishing

Using Liner as pattern, cut two pieces from batting same size. Center Liner on Diaper with batting between, sew Liner to Diaper.

Weave elastic thread through rows 6–23 on each side of Diaper ¼" from Liner. Gather slightly. Secure ends.

Cut loopy side of each Velcro® piece to 1". Sew one to each outside front corner ¼" from top edge and ¾" from side edge. Sew ¾" of fuzzy side of Velcro® pieces to outside back corner of Diaper ¼" from top edge.

SOCK (make 2)

NOTE: *Do not join rnds unless otherwise stated. Mark first st of each rnd.*

Rnd 1: With MC, ch 5, 3 sc in second ch from hook, sc in each of next 2 chs, 3 sc in last ch; working in remaining lps on opposite side of starting ch, sc in each of next 2 chs. *(10 sc made)*

Rnd 2: (2 sc in each of next 3 sts, sc in each of next 2 sts) around. *(16)*

Rnds 3–10: Sc in each st around.

Rnds 11–12: Sc in first 4 sts, hdc in each of next 2 sts, dc in each of next 3 sts, hdc in each of next 2 sts, sc in last 5 sts.

Continued on page 116

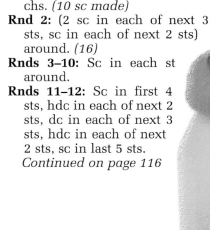

Continued from page 115

Rnd 13: Sc in first 5 sts, hdc in next 5 sts, sc in last 6 sts.

Rnds 14–15: Sc in each st around.

Rnd 16: (Sc in next st, 2 sc in next st) around. *(24)*

Rnds 17–24: Sc in each st around. At end of last rnd, join with sl st in first sc.

Rnd 25: Ch 1, sc in first st; for **puff st, yo, insert hook in next st, yo, pull lp through st to measure ⅜", (yo, insert hook in same st, yo, pull lp through st to measure ⅜") 3 times, yo, pull through all 9 lps on hook;** (sc in next st, puff st in next st) around. *(12 puff sts)*

Rnd 26: Sc in each st around, join with sl st in first sc. Fasten off.

Fold last rnds down for cuff.

BOTTLE

Rnd 1: With white, ch 2, 6 sc in second ch from hook. *(6 sc made)*

Rnd 2: 2 sc in each st around. *(12)*

Rnd 3: (Sc in next st, 2 sc in next st) around. *(18)*

Rnd 4: (Sc in each of next 2 sts, 2 sc in next st) around. *(24)*

Rnd 5: Working this rnd in **back lps** *(see Stitch Guide)*, sc in each st around.

Rnds 6–18: Sc in each st around. At end of last rnd, join with sl st in first sc. Fasten off.

Rnd 19: Working this rnd in **front lps,** join MC with sc in first st, sc in same st, 2 sc in each st around, join. *(48)*

Rnd 20: Working this rnd in **back lps,** ch 1, sc in each st around, join.

Rnd 21: Working this rnd in **back lps,** ch 1, sc first 2 sts tog, (sc next 2 sts tog) around, join. Fasten off. *(24)*

Rnd 22: Working this rnd in **back lps,** join lt. peach with sc in first st, sc in each st around. **Do not join.**

Rnds 23–24: Sc in each st around. Stuff.

Rnd 25: (Sc next 2 sts tog) around. *(12)*

Rnd 26: (Sc in next st, sc next 2 sts tog) around. *(8)*

Rnds 27–29: Sc in each st around.

Rnd 30: (Sc next 2 sts tog) around. Leaving 6" for sewing, fasten off. Stuff. Sew opening closed. ✤

Facing Up to Doll Features

One of the most challenging, and ultimately rewarding, aspects of doll making is creating a doll's personality through the perfect selection of facial features. Luckily, the possibilities here are almost endless.

To design an original face, cut a piece of tissue paper the same size and shape as the finished face after stuffing. Experiment drawing faces with a pencil until you draw one you really like, keeping it as simple as possible.

Then, simply pin the tissue pattern to the face and embroider right through the tissue, tearing it off when finished.

Using patterns also works well when designing felt features. Tape typing paper patterns to the felt and use very sharp scissors to cut the felt pieces one at a time.

Circles crocheted from yarn work well for eyes and cheeks. Try one or two rounds of single crochet, but if they seem too large or heavy, just separate 4-ply yarn into two strands and use a smaller hook.

Buttons and beads also work well for eyes. Try plastic shank buttons for eyes, adding a dab of white paint for "twinkle" or paint in black pupils on colored buttons.

Besides the large variety of humorous and realistic animal eyes available through craft suppliers, eyes from a taxidermist also work very well. These are usually attached easily with washers.

Don't forget novelty eyelashes, eyebrows or whiskers to add expression!

Embroidered features are safe and easy. Use embroidery floss, crewel yarn or the yarn used in the item. If you already have the color you need in a 3- or 4-ply yarn, separate the plys of the yarn into one or two plys and substitute them for floss.

Keep the features simple, using basic embroidery stitches. Try a satin stitch for nose, cheeks and mouth, and outline with black straight stitches or backstitches for the eyes. Don't forget to add white highlights to the eyes. And French knots make good freckles! Just scatter them randomly across doll's cheeks and nose.

And when it comes to finding flesh-colored yarn, simply work with a strand of white yarn and a strand of apricot sewing thread held together.

Let's face it! Making doll features come alive can be downright fun! ♣

Chapter
Six

Fashion Doll Fun

Playing dress-up is a fanciful urge we never seem to outgrow. Why should we? Crocheting stylish fashions for doll models fulfills haute couture fantasies without emptying pocketbooks!

Queen Elizabeth

Design by Linda Murray

Finished Size: Fits 11½" fashion doll.

Materials:

- Size 10 crochet cotton thread:
  - 900 yds. metallic gold
  - 15 yds. white
- 4 yds. metallic gold thread
- 16" of gold cord
- 10" of gold braid with loops
- ½ yd. gold rickrack
- ½ yd. white fake fur
- ¼ yd. yellow taffeta
- Matching sewing thread
- 3" of ⅛" elastic
- Horsehair braid
- Four size 4/0 snaps
- One package 2-mm. pearls
- One package each of red and green rhinestones
- Two teardrop-shaped pearls
- One pearlhead hat pin
- Sewing needle
- No. 1 and No. 0 steel hooks or hooks needed to obtain gauges

Gauges: No. 1 hook, 8 dc = 1"; 4 dc rows = 1". **No. 0 hook,** 11 dc = 2"; 7 dc rows = 2".

Basic Stitches: Ch, sl st, sc, hdc, dc.

DRESS
Bodice

Row 1: With No. 1 hook and gold, ch 44, dc in third ch from hook, dc in each ch across, turn. *(42 dc made)*

Rows 2–6: Ch 3, dc in each st across, turn.

Row 7: Ch 1, sc in each st across, turn.

Row 8: Ch 3, dc in each st across, turn.

Row 9: Ch 1, sc in first 8 sts; for **armhole**, ch 9, skip next 3 sts; (sc next 2 sts tog, sc in each of next 2 sts) 5 times; for **armhole**, ch 9, skip next 3 sts, sc in last 8 sts, turn. *(31)*

Row 10: Ch 1, sc in first 7 sts, skip next st, 7 sc in next ch-9 sp, sc in next 15 sts, 7 sc in next ch-9 sp, skip next st, sc in last 7 sts, turn. *(43)*

Row 11: Ch 1, sc in first 7 sts, (sc next 2 sts tog, sc in next st) 10 times, sc in last 6 sts, turn. *(33)*

Row 12: Ch 1, sc in first 7 sts, (sc next 2 sts tog, sc in next st, sc next 2 sts tog), sc in next 9 sts; repeat between ( ), sc in last 7 sts, turn. *(29)*

Row 13: Ch 1, sc in first 7 sts, sc next 2 sts tog, sc in next 11 sts, sc next 2 sts tog, sc in last 7 sts, turn. *(27)*

Row 14: Ch 1, sc in first 7 sts, (sc next 2 sts tog, sc in each of next 2 sts) 3 times, sc next 2 sts tog, sc in last 6 sts, turn. *(23)*

Row 15: Ch 1, sc in first 6 sts, sc next 2 sts tog, sc in next 7 sts, sc next 2 sts tog, sc in last 6 sts, turn. *(21)*

Row 16: Ch 1, sc in first st, (sc next 2 sts tog) across, turn. *(11)*

Row 17: Ch 1, sc in each st across. Fasten off.

Sleeves

Rnd 1: With No. 1 hook, join gold with sc in second skipped st of armhole on row 8 of Bodice, sc in next st, sc in side of next st on row 9; working around ch-9, (sc between next 2 sc of row 10, 2 sc between next 2 sc of row 10) 4 times, sc in side of next st on row 9, sc in next skipped st, join with sl st in first sc. *(17 sc made)*

Rnds 2–9: Ch 3, dc in each st around, join with sl st in top of ch-3.

Rnd 10: Ch 3, (dc next 2 sts tog) around, join. Fasten off. *(9)*

Rnd 11: With No. 1 hook, join white with sc in first st, (2 sc in next st, sc in next st) around, join. *(13)*

Rnd 12: Ch 2 *(counts as first hdc),* 4 hdc in same st, 5 hdc in each st around, join with sl st in top of ch 2 Fasten off. *(65 hdc).*

Rnd 13: With No. 1 hook, join metallic gold thread with sc in first st, sc in each st around, join. Fasten off.

Repeat on other armhole.

Front Skirt Panel

Row 1: Working in remaining lps on opposite side of starting ch on Bodice, with No. 0 hook, join gold with sl st in 17th ch, ch 3, skip next ch, dc in next 6 chs, skip next ch, dc in next ch leaving last 16 chs unworked, turn. *(8 dc made)*

Rows 2–3: Ch 3, skip next st, dc in each st across to last 2 sts, skip next st, dc in last st, turn. *(6, 4)*

Row 4: Ch 3, skip each of next 2 sts, dc in last st. Fasten off.

Skirt

Rnd 1: Working in remaining lps on opposite side of starting ch on Bodice and in ends of rows of Front Skirt Panel, with No. 0 hook, join gold with sc in first ch, sc in each ch, 2 sc in end of each row around with 3 sc in row 4 of Front Panel, join with sl st in first sc. *(47 sc made)*

Row 2: Working in rows, sl st in next 16 sts leaving last 30 sts unworked, turn.

Row 3: Working across to other side of Front Panel, (ch 3, sc in next st) 32 times, sl st in next st, turn. *(32 ch sps)*

Rows 4–8: Ch 3, (sc in next ch-3 sp, ch 3) across, sc in next unworked st of rnd 1, sl st in next st, turn.

Rnd 9: Working in rnds, (ch 3, sc in next ch-3 sp) across, ch 3, sc in next unworked st of rnd 1, (ch 3, sc in next st) 2 times, ch 3, join with sl st in first ch-3 sp, **turn.**

NOTE: Mark joining st of each rnd.

Rnd 10: Ch 3, (sc in next ch-3 sp, ch 3) around, join with sc in joining sl st of last rnd. *(41 sc, 41 ch sps).*

Rnd 11: (2 sc in next ch sp, sc in next st) around with last sc in joining sc of last rnd. *(123 sc)*

Rnd 12: Ch 3, (sc in next st, ch 3) around, join with sl st in first ch of first ch-3. *(123 ch sps)*

Rnds 13–18: Sl st in next ch, ch 3, (sc in next ch sp, ch 3) around, join.

Rnd 19: (2 sc in next ch sp, sc in next st) around, join with sl st in first sc. *(369 sc)*

Rnd 20: Repeat rnd 12. *(369 ch sps)*

Rnds 21–23: Repeat rnd 13.

Rnd 24: Sl st in next ch, ch 5, (sc in next ch sp, ch 5) around, join with sl st in first ch of first ch-5.

Rnds 25–28: Sl st in each of next 2 chs, ch 5, (sc in next ch sp, ch 5) around, join with sl st in first ch of first ch-5.

Rnd 29: (5 sc in next ch 5 sp, sc in next st) around, join with sl st in first sc. Fasten off.

Facing

Working in ends of rows on right back edge, with No. 1 hook, join gold with sc in row 17 of Bodice, sc in next 8 rows, 2 sc in next row, sc in next row, 2 sc in each of next 6 rows, 2 sl st in rnd 1 of Skirt; working on left back edge, 2 sc in each of next 6 rows, sc in next row, 2 sc in next row, sc in last 9 rows. Fasten off.

Sew snaps evenly spaced on facing.

Continued on page 120

Continued from page 119

Collar

Row 1: With No. 1 hook, join white with sl st in first st on row 17 of Bodice, ch 3, 4 dc in same st, 5 dc in each st across. Fasten off. *(55 dc made)*

Row 2: Join metallic gold thread with sc in first st, sc in each st across. Fasten off.

CAPE

Row 1: Starting at neck, with No. 0 hook and gold, ch 42, dc in third ch from hook, dc in each ch across, turn. *(40 dc made)*

Rows 2–3: Ch 3, dc in each st across, turn.

Row 4: Ch 3, dc in each of next 2 sts, 2 dc in next st, (dc in each of next 3 sts, 2 dc in next st) across, turn. *(50)*

Rows 5–7: Ch 3, dc in each st across, turn.

Row 8: Ch 3, dc in each of next 2 sts, 2 dc in next st, (dc in each of next 3 sts, 2 dc in next st) across to last 2 sts, dc in each of last 2 sts, turn. *(62)*

Rows 9–11: Ch 3, dc in each st across, turn.

Row 12: Repeat row 8. *(77)*

Rows 13–15: Ch 3, dc in each st across, turn.

Row 16: Ch 3, dc in next 4 sts, (dc in each of next 3 sts, 2 dc in next st) across, turn.

Rows 17–19: Ch 3, dc in each st across, turn.

Row 20: Ch 3, dc in each of next 2 sts, (2 dc in next st, dc in each of next 3 sts) across, turn. *(118)*

Rows 21–23: Ch 3, dc in each st across, turn.

Row 24: Repeat row 8. *(147)*

Rows 25–27: Ch 3, dc in each st across, turn.

Row 28: Repeat row 20. *(183)*

Rows 29–31: Ch 3, dc in each st across, turn.

Row 32: Repeat row 20. *(228)*

Rows 33–35: Ch 3, dc in each st across, turn. At end of last row, fasten off.

Assembly

Block Cape.

Using crocheted piece for pattern, cut Cape from fake fur allowing 1" along sides and bottom for trim. Place crocheted piece on wrong side of fur piece; matching neck edges, turn 1" allowance of fur over crochet edges and pin trim to secure.

Turn under ⅛" on raw edges of trim.

Cut fake fur Collar according to full-size pattern piece. Place wrong side of Collar on crochet side of Cape. Pin at neckline and sides with raw edges turned under ⅛"; sew along side and neckline.

Sew looped gold braid lengthwise across center of Collar, leaving 1" extending at each end. Turn under ½" on ends. Sew snap at ends of braid. Sew one green rhinestone, one teardrop pearl and one red bead on left side at end of braid.

Sew the following sequence (two pearls, one red rhinestone, two pearls, one green rhinestone) 5 times evenly spaced across braid.

SHOE (make 2)

Rnd 1: With No. 1 hook and white, ch 6, sc in second ch from hook, sc in each of next 3 chs, 3 sc in last ch; working on opposite side of ch, sc in each of next 3 chs, 2 sc in last ch, **do not join.** Mark first st of each rnd. *(12 sc made)*

Rnd 2: Working this rnd in **back lps** (see Stitch Guide), sc in first 5 sts, 3 sc in next st, sc in last 6 sts. *(14)*

Rnd 3: Sc in first 12 sts, sc last 2 sts tog. *(13)*

Rnd 4: Sc in first 4 sts, sc next 2 sts tog, sc in next 5 sts, sc last 2 sts tog, join with sl st in first sc. *(11)*

For **strap,** ch 6, sl st in next st. Fasten off.

SLIP

From fabric, cut 8¾" x 29" piece.

Allowing ¼" seams, sew short edges right sides together.

For **waist casing,** press under ⅛" on 1 raw edge, press under another ½". Topstitch close to both folds leaving ½" opening to insert elastic. Hem 1" at bottom edge of Slip. Sew 29" piece horsehair braid to inside of Slip over hem.

Run elastic through casing, secure ends. Sew opening closed.

CROWN

Cut 5¼" piece gold rickrack. Overlap ends ¼" forming circle; sew together. Cut two 3¼" pieces. Sew onto circle from front to back and from side to side. Sew one green rhinestone, one teardrop pearl and one small pearl at end of one 3¼" piece. Sew one pearl, one red rhinestone and one pearl between each 3¼" piece. Sew one green rhinestone to end of each 3¼" piece. Place on head, attach with hat pin in center top. ❖

Wedding Party

Bridal Gown
Instructions begin on page 122

Bridesmaid Dress
Instructions begin on page 123

Bridal Gown

Design by Frances Morse

Finished Size: Fits 11½" fashion doll.

Materials:
- 280 yds. white size 10 crochet cotton thread
- 3 yds. white ⅜" satin ribbon
- 80 white 3-mm. seed pearls
- 4" of ¼" elastic
- 8" × 10" piece netting
- Small bouquet artificial flowers
- Four size 4/0 snaps
- White sewing thread
- Sewing and tapestry needles
- No. 7 and No. 5 steel hooks or hooks needed to obtain gauge

Gauges: No. 7 hook, 8 sc = 1"; 9 sc rows = 1".
No. 5 hook, 9 dc and 5 ch sps = 2"; 7 dc rows = 2".

Basic Stitches: Ch, sl st, sc, hdc, dc.

Special Stitch: For **V st,** (dc, ch 2, dc) in next st.

DRESS
Row 1: For **bodice,** starting at neckline, with No. 7 hook, ch 53, sc in second ch from hook, sc in each ch across, turn. *(52 sc made)*

Row 2: Ch 1, sc in first 8 sts; (for **armhole,** ch 6, skip next 7 sts); sc in next 22 sts; repeat between ( ), sc in last 8 sts, turn. *(38 sc, 12 chs)*

Row 3: Working in sts and in chs, ch 1, sc first 2 sts tog, sc in each of next 2 sts, (sc next 2 sts tog, sc in next 8 sts) 4 times, sc next 2 sts tog, sc in each of next 2 sts, sc last 2 sts tog, turn. *(43)*

Rows 4–10: Ch 1, sc in each st across, turn.

Row 11: Ch 1, sc in first 4 sts, sc next 2 sts tog, (sc in next 5 sts, sc next 2 sts tog) 5 times, sc in last 2 sts, turn. *(37)*

Row 12: Ch 1, sc in each of first 3 sts, sc next 2 sts tog, (sc in next 4 sts, sc next 2 sts tog) 5 times, sc in last 2 sts, turn. *(31)*

Row 13: Repeat row 4.

Row 14: Ch 1, sc in each of first 3 sts, sc next 2 sts tog, (sc in next 6 sts, sc next 2 sts tog) 3 times, sc in last 2 sts, turn. *(27)*

Rows 15–18: Repeat row 4.

Rnd 19: For **skirt,** working in rnds, with No. 5 hook, ch 5, dc in same st; **V st** *(see Special Stitch)* in each st around, join with sl st in third ch of ch-5. *(27 V sts)*

Rnd 20: Skipping ch sps, ch 3, dc in next dc, ch 2, (dc in each of next 2 dc, ch 2) around, join with sl st in top of ch-3. *(54)*

NOTE: Skip ch sps unless otherwise stated.

Rnd 21: Ch 5, (dc in each of next 2 sts, ch 2) around to last st, dc in last st, join.

Rnd 22: Ch 3, dc in next st, ch 3, (dc in each of next 2 sts, ch 3) around, join.

Rnd 23: Ch 6, (dc in each of next 2 sts, ch 3) around to last st, dc in last st, join with sl st in third ch of ch-6.

Rnds 24–45: Repeat rnds 22 and 23 alternately. At end of last rnd, fasten off.

Row 46: For **train,** working in rows, skip first 45 sts, join with sl st in next st, ch 6, (dc in each of next 2 sts, ch 3) 12 times, dc in next st leaving remaining sts unworked, turn. *(26 dc)*

Row 47: Ch 3, dc in next st, ch 3, (dc in each of next 2 sts, ch 3) 11 times, dc in next st, dc in third ch of ch-6, turn.

Row 48: Ch 6, (dc in each of next 2 sts, ch 3) across, dc in top of ch-3, turn.

Rows 49–59: Repeat rows 47 and 48 alternately, ending with row 47.

Rows 60–70: Sl st in each of first 2 sts, ch 3, dc in next st, (ch 3, dc in each of next 2 sts) across leaving ch-3 unworked, turn. At end of last row *(4 dc)*.

Row 71: Sl st in each of first 2 sts, ch 3, dc in next st leaving ch-3 unworked, turn. *(2)*

Rnd 72: Working around outer edge in sts, in chs and in ends of rows, ch 1, *(3 sc in next row, 2 sc in next row) 13 times*, sc in next st, (sc in each of next 3 chs, sc in each of next 2 sts) 14 times, sc in each of next 3 chs, sc in next st; repeat between first and second *, sc in last st, join with sl st in first sc, **do not turn.**

Rnd 73: Ch 1, sc in each st around, join. Fasten off.

Sleeves
Rnd 1: Working in sts and in ends of rows around armhole, join with sc in center st at bottom, evenly space 15 more sc around, join with sl st in first sc. *(16 sc made)*

Rnd 2: Ch 5, dc in same st, skip next st, (V st in next st, skip next st) around, join with sl st in third ch of ch-5. *(8 V sts)*

Rnd 3: Ch 3, dc in next st, ch 2, (dc in each of next 2 sts, ch 2) around, join with sl st in top of ch-3. *(16 dc)*

Rnd 4: Ch 5, (dc in each of next 2 sts, ch 2) around to last st, dc in last st, join.

Rnds 5–8: Repeat rnds 3 and 4 alternately.

Rnd 9: Skipping ch sps, ch 1, sc in each st around, join. *(16 sc)*

Rnd 10: Ch 1, sc in first st, skip next st, (sc in next st, skip next st) around, join. *(8)*

Rnds 11–15: Ch 1, sc in each st around, join. At end of last rnd, fasten off.

Repeat on other armhole.

Neck Trim
Row 1: Working in remaining lps on opposite side of starting ch on bodice, with wrong side

Continued on page 132

Bridesmaid Dress

Design by Elsie Caddey

Finished Size: Fits 11½" fashion doll.

Materials:
- 270 yds. pink size 10 crochet cotton thread
- Three size 4/0 snaps
- Matching sewing thread
- Sewing and tapestry needles
- No. 5 steel hook or hook needed to obtain gauge

Gauge: 9 dc = 1"; 7 dc rows = 2". 9 hdc rows = 2". 8 slanted puff sts = 2"; 6 slanted puff st rows = 2".

Basic Stitches: Ch, sl st, sc, hdc, dc.

Special Stitch: For **slanted puff st (slanted ps)**, *(yo, insert hook around post of last hdc made, yo, pull up long lp) 3 times, yo, skip next st, insert hook in next st, yo, pull through st, yo, pull through 2 lps on hook *(hdc for next st made)*, yo, pull through all 8 lps on hook.

DRESS

Row 1: Starting at neck, ch 37 to measure 6⅛", sc in second ch from hook, sc in each ch across, turn. *(36 sc made)*

Row 2: Ch 2, hdc in same st, 2 hdc in each st across, turn. *(72 hdc)*

Row 3: Ch 2, hdc in next st; **slanted ps** *(see Special Stitch)*, (ch 1, slanted sp) across, turn. *(35 slanted ps)*

Row 4: Ch 1, sc in each st and in each ch across, turn. *(70 sc)*

Row 5: Ch 2, hdc in next 4 sts; (for **armhole**, ch 3, skip next 15 sts); hdc in next 30 sts; repeat between ( ), hdc in last 5 sts, turn. *(40 hdc, 6 chs)*

Row 6: Working in sts and in chs, ch 2, hdc in next 4 sts, hdc next 2 sts tog, (hdc in next st, hdc next 2 sts tog) 10 times, hdc in each of next 2 sts, hdc next 2 sts tog, hdc in last 5 sts, turn. *(34 hdc)*

Row 7: Ch 2, hdc in each of next 3 sts, (hdc next 2 sts tog) 2 times, (slanted ps, ch 1) 9 times, (hdc next 2 sts tog) 2 times, hdc in last 4 sts, turn. *(12 hdc, 9 slanted ps)*

Rows 8–9: Ch 3, dc in next 4 sts, hdc in next st, (slanted ps, ch 1) 9 times, dc in last 6 sts, turn.

At end of last row, *(11 dc, 1 hdc and 9 slanted ps)*.

Row 10: Working in sts and in chs, ch 1, 2 sc in each of first 2 sts, sc in each st across with 2 sc in each of last 2 sts, turn. *(34 sc)*

Row 11: For **skirt**, ch 2, hdc in same st, hdc in next st, (2 hdc in next st, hdc in next st) across, turn. *(51 hdc)*

Rnd 12: Working in rnds, ch 3, (dc in next st, 2 dc in next st) around, join with sl st in top of ch-3, **turn**. *(76 dc)*

Rnds 13–29: Ch 3, hdc in next st, (slanted ps, ch 1) around, join with sl st in top of ch-3, **turn**.

Rnd 30: Ch 1, sc in each st and in each ch around, join with sl st in first sc. Fasten off.

Sleeves

Rnd 1: Join with sc in center ch at bottom of armhole, evenly space 25 more sc around armhole, join with sl st in first sc. *(26 sc made)*

Rnd 2: Ch 3, dc in next st, hdc in next st, (slanted ps, ch 1) 10 times, dc in each of last 3 sts, join with sl st in top of ch-3.

Rnd 3: Ch 2, hdc in each st and in each ch around, join with sl st in top of ch-2. *(27 hdc)*

Rnd 4: Ch 3, hdc in next st, (slanted ps, ch 1) 12 times, dc in last st, join with sl st in top of ch-3.

Rnd 5: Ch 1, sc in each st and in each ch around, join with sl st in first sc. Fasten off.

Repeat on other armhole.

Sew snaps evenly spaced down back opening.

HAT

Rnd 1: Ch 4, sl st in first ch to form ring, ch 3, 17 dc in ring, join with sl st in top of ch-3. *(18 dc made)*

Rnd 2: Ch 1, 2 sc in each st around, join with sl st in first sc. *(36 sc)*

Rnd 3: Ch 3, dc in same st, dc in each of next 2 sts, (2 dc in next st, dc in each of next 2 sts) around, join. *(48)*

Rnds 4–6: Working these rnds in **back lps** *(see Stitch Guide)*, ch 1, sc in each st around, join.

Rnd 7: Ch 3, 2 dc in next st, (dc in next st, 2 dc in next st) around, join. *(72)*

Rnd 8: Ch 4, skip next st, (dc in each of next 2 sts, ch 1, skip next st) 23 times, dc in last st, join with sl st in third ch of ch-4.

Rnd 9: Ch 3, (2 dc in next ch-1 sp, dc in next 2 sts) 23 times, 2 dc in next ch-1 sp, dc in last st, join. *(96)*

Rnd 10: Ch 3, skip next st, (sc in next st, ch 3, skip next st) around, join with sl st in first ch of first ch-3. Fasten off. ❖

Sleepytime Sisters

Little Sister's Gown & Robe Set

Instructions begin on page 126

Little Sister's Gown & Robe Set

Design by Helen Blevins

Finished Size: Fits 9"–9½" fashion doll.

Materials:
- Size 10 crochet cotton thread:
    180 yds. blue
    160 yds. white
- 24" white ¼" satin ribbon
- Two size 4/0 snaps
- Cord elastic
- White and blue sewing thread
- Sewing and tapestry needles
- No. 7 steel hook or hook needed to obtain gauge

Gauge: 8 sc = 1"; 10 sc rows = 1". 8 hdc = 1"; 6 hdc rows = 1". 8 dc = 1"; 4 dc rows = 1".

Basic Stitches: Ch, sl st, sc, hdc, dc.

Special Stitches: For **V st,** (dc, ch 1, dc) in next ch sp.
For **picot,** ch 3, sl st in 3rd ch from hook.

GOWN

Row 1: Starting at top of yoke, with white, ch 41, sc in second ch from hook, sc in each ch across, turn. *(40 sc made)*

Rows 2–4: Ch 1, sc in each st across, turn. At end of last row, **do not turn.**

Rnd 5: For **skirt,** working in rnds, ch 1, sc in end of first 4 rows; working in opposite ends of rows, sc in row 1, sc in each of next 3 rows; for **armhole,** ch 5, skip first 14 sts on row 4; for **front,** sc in next 12 sts; for **armhole,** ch 5, skip last 14 sts, join with sl st in first sc. *(20 sc, 10 chs)*

Rnd 6: Sl st in first 4 sts, ch-4, (dc, ch 1) in each st and in each ch around, (dc, ch 1) in first 4 sl sts, join with sl st in third ch of ch-4. *(30 ch sps)*

Rnds 7–26: Sl st in first ch sp, ch 4, dc in same sp; **V st** *(see Special Stitches)* in each ch sp around, join.

Rnd 27: Ch 1, sc in each st and in each ch sp around, join with sl st in first sc. Fasten off.

Rnd 28: For **neck trim,** working in remaining lps on opposite side of starting ch, join white with sc in first ch, sc in each ch around, join with sl st in first sc. *(40)*

Rnd 29: Ch 1, sc in each of first 3 sts, (sc in each of next 3 sts, picot—*see Special Stitches)* around to last st, (sc, picot) in last st, join. Fasten off.

From elastic, cut 3" piece. Weave through sts of rnd 6 on Skirt. Sew ends together.

ROBE

Bodice

Row 1: Starting at bottom, with blue, ch 33, sc in second ch from hook, sc in each ch across, turn. *(32 sc made)*

Rows 2–3: Ch 2 *(counts as first hdc),* hdc in each st across. turn.

Row 4: For **right front,** ch 2, hdc in next 5 sts leaving last 26 sts unworked, turn. *(6 hdc)*

Rows 5–8: Ch 2, hdc in each st across, turn.

Row 9: For **shoulder,** ch 2, hdc in each of next 2 sts leaving last 3 sts unworked, turn. Fasten off.

Row 4: For **armhole,** skip next 4 sts on row 3; for **back,** join blue with sl st in next st, ch 2, hdc in next 11 sts leaving last 10 sts unworked, turn. *(12)*

Rows 5–8: Ch 2, hdc in each st across, turn.

Row 9: For **first shoulder,** ch 2, hdc in next st, ch 2, sl st in next 8 sts; for **second shoulder,** ch 2, hdc in each of last 2 sts, turn. Fasten off.

Row 4: For **armhole,** skip next 4 sts on row 3; for **left front,** join blue with sl st in next st, ch 2, hdc in each st across, turn. *(6)*

Rows 5–8: Ch 2, hdc in each st across, turn.

Row 9: For **shoulder,** sl st in first 4 sts, ch 2, hdc in each of last 2 sts. Fasten off.

Sew shoulders together.

Skirt

Row 1: With wrong side facing you, working in remaining lps on opposite of starting ch on Bodice, join blue with sl st in first ch, ch 2, hdc in each ch across, turn. *(32 hdc made)*

Row 2: Ch 3, dc in same st, 2 dc in each st across, turn. *(64 dc)*

Rows 3–32: Ch 2, sc in next st, (hdc in next st, sc in next st) across, turn. At end of last row, fasten off.

Row 33: Join white with sl st in first st, ch 2, sc in next st, (hdc in next st, sc in next st) across, turn.

Rows 34–36: Repeat row 3. At end of last row, fasten off.

Trim

With right side facing you, working in sts and ends of rows around outer edge, join blue with sc in top corner on right front, mark sc just made; evenly space 15 sc across neck edge, sc in each row and in each st around with 2 sc in each dc row and 3 sc in each corner changing colors *(see Stitch Guide)* as needed to match colors on Gown, join with sl st in first sc. Fasten off.

Lapping right over left, sew snap to ends of row 1 on Skirt.

From ribbon, cut 15" piece. Going over one st and under two sts, weave through sts of row 1 on Skirt. Tie end in bow at front.

Collar

Row 1: With right side facing you, join white with sl st in marked st on trim, ch 2, hdc in same st, 2 hdc in each of next 14 sts, turn. *(30 hdc made)*

Rows 2–4: Ch 2, sc in next st, (hdc in next st, sc in next st) across, turn. At end of last row, fasten off.

Sleeves

Rnd 1: Working in ends of rows and in sts around armhole, join blue with sc in last skipped st, evenly space 21 more sc around, join with sl st in first sc. *(22 sc made)*

Rnd 2: Ch 1, 2 sc in first st, hdc in next st, (sc in next st, hdc in next st) around, join. *(23)*

Rnd 3: Ch 1, 2 sc in first st, (hdc in next st, sc in next st) around, join. *(24)*

Rnds 4–11: Repeat rnds 2 and 3 alternately. At end of last rnd, fasten off. *(32)*

Rnd 12: Join white with sc in first st, sc in same st, hdc in next st, (sc in next st, hdc in next st) around, join. *(33)*

Rnds 13–14: Repeat rnds 3 and 2. At end of last rnd, fasten off. *(35)*

Repeat on other armhole.

CAP

Rnd 1: With blue, ch 3, sl st in first ch to form ring, ch 3, 15 dc in ring, join with sl st in top of ch-3. *(16 dc made)*

Rnd 2: Ch 3, dc in same st, 2 dc in each st around, join. *(32)*

Rnds 3–5: Ch 3, 2 dc in next st, (dc in next st, 2 dc in next st) around, join. At end of last rnd, fasten off. *(108)*

Rnd 6: Join white with sl st in first st, ch 3, dc in each st around, join.

Rnd 7: Ch 1, (sc, ch 1) in each st around, join with sl st in first sc. Fasten off.

From ribbon, cut 9" piece. Weave through sts of rnd 5. Tie ends in knot adjusting to fit head. Trim ends to ½" from knot. ♣

Big Sister's Gown & Robe Set

Design by Elsie Caddey

Finished Size: Fits 11½" fashion doll.

Materials:
- Size 10 crochet cotton thread:
    - 220 yds. white
    - 170 yds. blue
- 45" white ¼" satin ribbon
- Two size 4/0 snaps
- White and blue sewing thread
- Sewing and tapestry needles
- No. 7 steel hook or hook needed for gauge

Gauge: 8 sc =1"; 10 sc rows = 1". 8 hdc = 1"; 6 hdc rows = 1". 8 dc = 1"; 4 dc rows = 1".

Basic Stitches: Ch, sl st, sc, hdc, dc.

Special Stitch: For **star st,** insert hook in eye, yo, pull through eye, insert hook in same st as last lp of last star st, yo, pull through st, (insert hook in next st, yo, pull through st) 2 times, yo, pull through all 5 lps on hook; for **eye,** ch 1.

GOWN

Row 1: Starting at neckline, with white, ch 69, sc in second ch from hook, sc in each ch across, turn. *(68 sc made)*

Row 2: Ch 3, dc in each st across, turn.

Row 3: Ch 3, dc in next 7 sts; (for **armhole,** ch 6, skip next 17 sts); for **front,** dc in next 18 sts; repeat between ( ), dc in last 8 sts, turn. *(34 dc, 12 chs)*

Row 4: Ch 3, dc in each st and in each ch across, turn. *(46 dc)*

Row 5: Repeat row 2.

Rnd 6: Working in rnds, ch 3, dc in each st around, join with sl st in top of ch-3.

Rnd 7: Ch 5, skip next st, (dc in next st, ch 2, skip next st) around, join with sl st in third ch of ch-5.

Rnd 8: For **skirt,** ch 1, sc in each st around with 3 sc in each ch sp, join with sl st in first sc. *(92)*

Rnd 9: Ch 2, insert hook in second ch from hook, yo, pull through ch, insert hook in same st as ch-2, yo, pull through st, (insert hook in next st, yo, pull through st) 2 times, yo, pull through all 5 lps on hook; for **eye,** ch 1 *(first star st made);* **star st** *(see Special Stitch)* around to last st, hdc in last st, join with sl st in top of ch-2. *(45 star sts)*

Rnd 10: Ch 2, 2 hdc in each eye around to last st, hdc in last st, join.

Rnd 11: Ch 3, dc in each st around, join with sl st in top of ch-3.

Rnds 12–41: Repeat rnds 9–11 consecutively.

Rnd 42: Ch 1, sc in each st around, join with sl st in first sc.

Rnd 43: Ch 1, sc in first st, ch 2, skip next st, (sc in each of next 2 sts, ch 2, skip next st) around, join. Fasten off.

Neck Trim

Row 1: With wrong side facing you, working in remaining lps on opposite side of starting ch, join white with sl st in first ch, ch 1, sc first 2 sts tog, (sc next 2 sts tog) across, turn. *(34 sc made)*

Row 2: Ch 1, sc in first st, (ch 2, skip next st, sc

Continued on page 128

Continued from page 127

in each of next 2 sts) across. Fasten off.
Sew snap to top of back opening.

Armhole Trim

Rnd 1: Join white with sc in first ch at bottom of armhole, sc in each ch and in each st around, join with sl st in first sc. *(23 sc made)*

Rnd 2: Ch 1, sc in first st, ch 2, skip next st, (sc in each of next 2 sts, ch 2, skip next st) around, join. Fasten off.

Repeat on other armhole.

From ribbon, cut 18" piece. Weave through sts of rnd 7 on Gown. Tie ends in bow at center front.

ROBE

Bodice

Row 1: Starting at bottom, with blue, ch 33, sc in second ch from hook, sc in each ch across, turn. *(32 sc made)*

Row 2: Ch 2, 2 hdc in next st, (hdc in next st, 2 hdc in next st) across, turn. *(48)*

Rows 3–4: Ch 2, hdc in each st across, turn.

Row 5: For **right front,** ch 2, hdc in next 9 sts leaving last 38 sts unworked, turn. *(10)*

Rows 6–9: Repeat row 3.

Row 10: For **shoulder,** ch 2, hdc in next 4 sts leaving last 5 sts unworked, turn. Fasten off.

Row 5: For **armhole,** skip next 4 unworked sts on row 4; for **back,** join with sl st in next st, ch 2, hdc in next 19 sts leaving last 14 sts unworked, turn. *(20)*

Rows 6–9: Repeat row 3.

Row 10: For **first shoulder,** ch 2, hdc in next 4 sts, ch 2, sl st in next 10 sts; for **second shoulder,** ch 2, hdc in last 5 sts, turn. Fasten off.

Row 5: For **armhole,** skip next 4 unworked sts on row 4; for **left front,** join with sl st in next st, ch 2, hdc in each st across, turn. *(10)*

Rows 6–9: Repeat row 3.

Row 10: For **shoulder,** sl st in first 6 sts, ch 2, hdc in last 4 sts. Fasten off.

Sew shoulders together.

Skirt

Row 1: With wrong side facing you, working in remaining lps on opposite side of starting ch on Bodice, join blue with sl st in first ch, ch 2, hdc in each st across, turn. *(32 hdc made)*

Row 2: Ch 3, dc in same st, 2 dc in each st across, turn. *(64 dc)*

Rows 3–40: Ch 2, sc in next st, (hdc in next st, sc in next st) across, turn. At end of last row, fasten off.

Row 41: Join white with sl st in first st, ch 2, sc in next st, (hdc in next st, sc in next st) across, turn.

Rows 42–48: Repeat row 3. At end of last row, fasten off.

Trim

With right side facing you, working in sts and in ends of rows around outer edge, join blue with sc in top corner on right front of Bodice, mark sc just made; evenly space 21 sc across neck edge, sc in each sc row and in each st around with 2 sc in each hdc row, 2 sc in each dc row and 3 sc in each corner changing colors *(see Stitch Guide)* as colors change on Robe, join with sl st in first sc. Fasten off.

Lapping right over left, sew snap to ends of row 1 on Skirt.

From ribbon, cut 18" piece. Going under one st and over two sts, weave through sts of row 1 on Skirt. Tie ends in bow at front.

Collar

Row 1: With right side facing you, join white with sl st in marked st on Trim, ch 2, hdc in same st, 2 hdc in each of next 21 sts, turn. *(44 hdc made)*

Rows 2–4: Ch 2, sc in next st, (hdc in next st, sc in next st) across, turn. At end of last row, fasten off.

Sleeves

Rnd 1: Working in ends of rows and in sts around armhole, join blue with sc in first skipped st, evenly space 21 sc around, join with sl st in first sc. *(22 sc made)*

Rnd 2: Ch 1, 2 sc in first st, hdc in next st, (sc in next st, hdc in next st) around, join. *(23)*

Rnd 3: Ch 1, 2 sc in first st, (hdc in next st, sc in next st) around, join. *(24)*

Rnds 4–13: Repeat rnds 2 and 3 alternately. At end of last rnd, fasten off. *(34)*

Rnd 14: Join white with sc in first st, sc in same st, hdc in next st, (sc in next st, hdc in next st) around, join. *(35)*

Rnds 15–16: Repeat rnds 3 and 2. At end of last rnd, fasten off. *(37)*

Repeat on other armhole.

CAP

Rnd 1: With blue, ch 3, sl st in first ch to form ring, ch 3, 15 dc in ring, join with sl st in top of ch-3. *(16 dc made)*

Rnd 2: Ch 3, dc in same st, 2 dc in each st around, join. *(32)*

Rnds 3–5: Ch 3, 2 dc in next st, (dc in next st, 2 dc in next st) around, join. At end of last rnd, fasten off. *(108)*

Rnd 6: Join white with sl st in first st, ch 3, dc in each st around, join.

Rnd 7: Ch 1, (sc, ch 1) in each st around, join with sl st in first sc. Fasten off.

From ribbon, cut 9" piece. Weave through sts of rnd 5. Tie ends in knots, adjusting to fit head. Trim ends to ½" from knot. ❖

Arabian Nights

Designs by Linda Murray

Arabian Princess
Instructions begin on page 130

Genie
Instructions begin on page 131

Arabian Princess

Finished Size: Fits 11½" fashion doll.

Materials:
- Size 10 crochet cotton thread:
    - 32 yds. white with gold metallic
    - 126 yds. gold metallic thread
- 107 gold sequins
- Rocaille beads:
    - 57 green
    - 107 gold
- One 5-mm. green rhinestone
- Elastic thread
- Gold sewing thread
- Two size 4/0 snaps
- 6" × 12" piece netting
- Sewing and tapestry needles
- No. 11 and No. 7 steel hooks or hooks needed to obtain gauges

Gauges: No. 11 hook, 10 sc = 1"; 12 sc rows = 1". **No. 7 hook,** 8 sc = 1"; 10 sc rows = 1".

Basic Stitches: Ch, sl st, sc, hdc, dc.

TOP

Cup (make 2)
Rnd 1: With No. 11 hook and gold thread, ch 2, 5 sc in second ch from hook, join with sl st in first sc. *(5 sc made)*

Rnd 2: Ch 1, 2 sc in each st around, join. *(10)*

Rnd 3: Ch 1, sc in first 4 sts, 2 sc in next st, sc in next 4 sts, 2 sc in next st, join. *(12)*

Rnd 4: Ch 1, 2 sc in first st, sc in each of next 3 sts, (2 sc in next st, sc in each of next 3 sts) around, join. *(15)*

Rnd 5: Ch 1, sc in first 4 sts, 2 sc in next st, (sc in next 4 sts, 2 sc in next st) around, join. *(18)*

Rnd 6: Ch 1, 2 sc in first st, sc in next 5 sts, (2 sc in next st, sc in next 5 sts) around, join. *(21)*

Rnd 7: Ch 1, sc in first 6 sts, 2 sc in next st, (sc in next 6 sts, 2 sc in next st) around, join. Fasten off. *(24)*

Matching two sts on each Cup, sew together. Sew rhinestone over seam.

For **back strap,** join gold thread with sl st in side of one Cup, ch 30, sl st in side of other Cup. Fasten off. Weave 2" piece of elastic thread through ch 30. Secure ends.

PANTS
Row 1: Starting at waist, with No. 7 hook and white, ch 21, sc in each ch across, turn. *(20 sc made)*

Rows 2–5: Ch 1, sc in each st across, turn.

Row 6: Ch 1, 2 sc in each st across, turn. *(40)*

Rows 7–13: Ch 1, sc in each st across, turn.

Rnds 14–20: Working in rnds, ch 1, sc in each st around, join with sl st in first sc. At end of last rnd, ch 5, skip first 20 sts, sl st in next st. Fasten off.

Rnd 21: For **first leg,** with No. 11 hook, join gold thread with sc in first st, sc in same st, 2 sc in each st and in each ch around, join with sl st in first sc. *(50)*

Rnd 22: (Ch 5, skip next st, sc in next st) around to last st, ch 3, skip last st, join with dc in first ch of first ch-5. *(25 ch sps)*

Rnds 23–46: (Ch 5, sc in next ch sp) around, ch 3, join with dc in first ch of first ch-5.

Rnd 47: Sc in each ch sp around, join with sl st in first sc. *(25)*

Rnd 48: Ch 1, sc first 2 sts tog, (sc next 2 sts tog) around to last st, sc in last st, join. Fasten off.

Rnd 21: For **second leg,** with No. 11 hook, join gold thread with sc in first unworked st on rnd 20, sc in same st, 2 sc in each st and in each ch around, join with sl st in first sc. *(50)*

Rnds 22–48: Repeat rnds 22–48 of first leg.

Facing
Row 1: Working in ends of rows on left back opening, with No. 7 hook, join white with sc in row 13, sc in next 12 rows, turn. *(13 sc made)*

Rows 2–5: Ch 1, sc in each st across, turn. At end of last row, fasten off.

Sew snaps evenly spaced down back opening. Sew three rows of sequins with beads to top of Pants. With beads and sequins, sew a "V" shape to front and back with bottom of "V" at center bottom of front and back *(see photo).*

HEAD VEIL
From netting, cut 4½" × 9" piece.

With No. 11 hook, join gold thread with sl st in any corner hole on netting, sl st in same hole, sl st in each hole around with 2 sl sts in each corner, join with sl st in first sl st. Fasten off.

FACE VEIL
From netting, cut 1½" × 3" piece.

With No. 11 hook, join gold thread with sc in any corner hole on netting, sc in same hole, sc in each hole around with 2 sc in each corner, join with sl st in first sc. Fasten off.

Gather one long edge to measure 1½". Cut 1½" piece elastic thread. Tie ends of elastic to ends of gathered edge. Sew green bead to each end of gathered edge.

ARM BAND (make 2)
String 20 green beads on elastic thread. Tie ends together.

ANKLE BAND
String 15 green beads on elastic thread. Tie ends together. ✤

Genie

Finished Size: Fits 12" fashion doll.

Materials:
- Size 10 crochet cotton thread:
    - 240 yds. blue
    - 33 yds. white
    - 30 yds. red
- White sewing thread
- Gold metallic thread
- One 5-mm. green rhinestone
- 50 green rocaille beads
- Elastic thread
- Sewing and tapestry needles
- No. 1 steel hook or hook needed to obtain gauge

Gauge: 6 sc = 1"; 8 sc rows = 1". 6 dc = 1"; 3 dc rows = 1".

Basic Stitches: Ch, sl st, sc, dc.

VEST
Back
Row 1: With red, ch 21, sc in second ch from hook sc in each ch across, turn. *(20 sc made)*
Rows 2–8: Ch 1, sc in each st across, turn.
Row 9: Sl st in each of first 3 sts, ch 1, sc in next 14 sts leaving last 3 sts unworked, turn. *(14)*
Rows 10–17: Ch 1, sc in each st across. turn. At end of last row, fasten off.

Front (make 2)
Row 1: With red, ch 11, sc in second ch from hook, sc in each ch across, turn. *(10 sc made)*
Rows 2–8: Ch 1, sc in each st across, turn.
Row 9: Ch 1, sc in first 7 sts leaving last 3 sts unworked, turn. *(7)*
Rows 10–17: Ch 1, sc in each st across, turn. At end of last row, fasten off.
Sew ends of rows 1–8 of fronts and back together. Sew outer four sts of shoulders together, leaving inside sts unsewn for neck opening.

Trim
Working around outer edge in sts and in ends of rows, join two strands gold held together with sc in bottom left corner, 2 sc in same st, sc in each st and in each row around with 3 sc in each corner, join with sl st in first sc. Fasten off.

PANTS
Row 1: With two strands blue held tog, ch 42, dc in fourth ch from hook, dc in each ch across, turn. *(40 dc made)*
Rows 2–15: Working these rows in **back lps** *(see Stitch Guide)*, ch 3, dc in each st across, turn.
Row 16: For **first leg**, fold piece in half lengthwise, matching sts of row 15 and opposite side of starting ch; working through both thicknesses, ch 1, sc in first 25 sts, sc in **back lps** of last 15 sts on row 15, turn.
Row 17: Working this row in **back lps**, ch 1, sc in first 15 sts leaving last 25 sts unworked, ch 27, turn. *(15 sc, 27 chs)*
Row 18: Dc in fourth ch from hook, dc in next 23 chs; working in **back lps**, dc in each st across, turn. *(40 dc)*
Rows 19–32: Working these rows in **back lps**, ch 3, dc in each st across, turn.
Row 33: Ch 1, sc in **back lps** of first 15 sts; for **second leg**, fold rows 17–32 in half lengthwise, matching sts of row 32 and opposite side of ch on row 17; working through both thicknesses, ch 1, sc in last 25 sts. Fasten off.
Sew 15 sts of rows 1 and 33 together.

Waistband
Rnd 1: Working in ends of rows, join two strands gold held tog with sc in row 1 of Pants, sc in same row, 2 sc in each row around, join with sl st in first sc. *(62)*
Row 2: Ch 3, dc in each st around, join with sl st in top of ch-3.
Row 3: Ch 1, sc in each st around, join. Fasten off.

Cuffs
Rnd 1: Join two strands gold held tog with sc in end of first row on one leg, sc in end of each row around, join with sl st in first sc. *(16 sc made)*
Rnd 2: Ch 3, dc in each st around, join with sl st in top of ch-3.
Rnd 3: Ch 1, sc in each st around, join with sl st in first sc. Fasten off.
Repeat on other leg.

Tie
With two strands gold held together, ch 151, sl st in second ch from hook, sl st in each ch across. Fasten off.
Starting at center front, weave through sts of rnd 2 on Waistband. Tie ends in bow.

TURBAN
*NOTE: Entire piece is worked in **back lps**.*
Rnd 1: With two strands white held tog, ch 28, sl st in first ch to form ring, ch 1, sc in each ch around, join with sl st in first sc. *(28 sc made)*
Rnds 2–3: Ch 1, sc in each st around, join.
Rnd 4: Ch 1, sl st in each of first 3 sts, sc in next 22 sts, sl st in each of last 3 sts, join with sl st in first sl st. *(28 sts)*
Rnd 5: Ch 1, sl st in first 5 sts, sc next 2 sts tog, sc in next 14 sts, sc next 2 sts tog, sl st in last 5 sts, join. *(26)*
Rnd 6: Ch 1, sl st in first 5 sts, sc next 2 sts tog, sc in next 12 sts, sc next 2 sts tog, sl st in last 5 sts, join. *(24)*

Continued on page 132

Continued from page 131

Rnd 7: Ch 1, sl st in first 5 sts, sc next 2 sts tog, sc in next 10 sts, sc next 2 sts tog, sl st in last 5 sts, join. *(22)*

Rnd 8: Ch 1, sl st in first 5 sts, sc next 2 sts tog, sc in next 8 sts, sc next 2 sts tog, sl st in last 5 sts, join. *(20)*

Rnd 9: Ch 1, sl st in first 5 sts, sc next 2 sts tog, sc in next 6 sts, sc next 2 sts tog, sl st in last 5 sts, join. Fasten off. *(18)*

Flatten rnd 9, sew together. Fold rnd 1 under at

joining, tack. Sew rhinestone to rnd 3 at joining.

For **gold chains,** join single strand gold with sl st in **front lp** of rnd 3 next to rhinestone, ch 10, sl st in fifth **front lp** of rnd 2, (ch 15, skip next 8 sts, sl st in next **front lp** of rnd 2) 2 times, ch 10, skip next 4 sts, sl st in last **front lp** of rnd 3. Fasten off.

ARM BAND

String 25 beads on elastic thread. Tie ends together. Place on upper arm. ✣

Bridal Gown

Continued from page 122

facing you, join with sl st in first ch, ch 1, sc first ch and next ch tog, *(sc in each of next 2 chs, sc next 2 chs tog) 2 times*, (sc next 2 chs tog) 2 times, sc in next 11 chs, sc next 2 chs tog, sc in next 11 chs, (sc next 2 chs tog) 3 times; repeat between first and second *, turn. *(41 sc made)*

Row 2: Ch 3, dc in each of next 2 sts, skip next 2 sts, (V st in next st, skip next 2 sts) 11 times, dc in each of last 3 sts, turn. *(11 V sts)*

Row 3: Ch 1, sc in each st across, turn. *(28 sc)*

Row 4: Ch 1, sc in first st, sc next 2 sts tog, (sc in each of next 2 sts, sc next 2 sts tog) across to last st, sc in last st. Fasten off. *(21)*

Sew snaps evenly spaced down back opening.

Sew 33 pearls evenly spaced across row 1 of Neck Trim. Sew 20 pearls evenly spaced across row 4 of bodice.

ROSETTE (make 27)

From ribbon, cut 3" piece. Sew ends together, run gathering thread along inside edge, pull tightly to form Rosette. Sew 1 pearl to center.

Sew 11 Rosettes evenly spaced across bottom front of Dress. Sew 10 Rosettes evenly spaced down center front of Dress.

CROWN & VEIL

Rnd 1: For **Crown,** ch 28, sl st in first ch to form ring, ch 1, sc in each ch around, join with sl st in first sc. *(28 sc made)*

Rnd 2: Ch 1, sc in each of first 2 sts, 2 sc in next st, (sc in each of next 2 sts, 2 sc in next st) around to last st, sc in last st, join. Fasten off.

Folding netting in half lengthwise, trim corners at one end to curve edges. With sewing thread, run gathering thread across top next to fold, gather to 2" in width; sew to wrong side of Crown. Sew six Rosettes evenly spaced around Crown.

BOUQUET

Rnd 1: Ch 6, sl st in first ch to form ring, ch 1, 14 sc in ring, join with sl st in first sc. *(14 sc made)*

Rnd 2: Ch 5, dc in same st, (skip next st, V st in next st) around, join with sl st in third ch of ch-5. *(7 V sts)*

Rnd 3: Ch 3, dc in next st, ch 3, (dc in each of next 2 sts, ch 3) around, join with sl st in top of ch-3. *(14 dc)*

Rnd 4: Ch 1, (sc in each of next 2 sts, 2 sc in next ch sp) around, join with sl st in first sc. Fasten off.

Place bouquet of flowers in center of crochet piece. Tie 12" piece ribbon in bow around stem of flowers.

PANTIES

NOTE: Sew ends of 4" piece of elastic together.

Rnd 1: Working around elastic *(see illustration),* evenly space 39 sc around, join with sl st in first sc. *(39 sc made)*

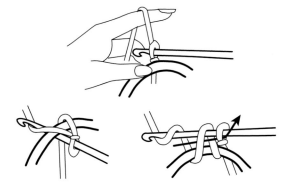

Rnds 2–7: Ch 3, dc in each st around, join with sl st in top of ch-3. At end of last rnd, fasten off.

Sew center two sts together to form crotch. ✣

Chapter
Seven

Special Occasion Dolls

Special days simply radiate the need for sentimental
celebration. Fill them with lavish
blessings: dolls to cherish from
crochet made one loving
stitch at a
time.

Bridal Belles

Designs by Pamela Sullivan

Finished Size:
Approximately 8" tall.

Materials For One:
- Size 10 crochet cotton:
  - 174 yds. dress color
  - 35 yds. brown small amount each lt. peach and pink
- 28" of ¼" ribbon
- Artificial flowers
- Sewing thread to match ribbon
- Spray starch
- Fabric stiffener
- 2½"-square cardboard
- Toothpick
- 3½" × 5½" Styrofoam® egg
- Craft glue
- Polyester fiberfill
- Sewing needle
- No. 7 steel hook or hook needed to obtain gauge

Gauge: 6 V st rows = 2".

Basic Stitches: Ch, sl st, sc, hdc, dc, tr.
Continued on page 136

Bridal Belles

Continued from page 135

HEAD & BODICE

NOTES: *Work in continuous rnds; do not join rnds unless otherwise stated. Mark first st of each rnd.*

For Head and Arms, wrong side of sts is right side of work.

Rnd 1: Starting at **Head,** with lt. peach, ch 2, 8 sc in second ch from hook. *(8 sc made)*

Rnds 2–3: 2 sc in each st around. *(16, 32)*

Rnd 4: Sc in each st around.

Rnd 5: Sc in each of first 2 sts, (sc next 2 sts tog, sc in each of next 3 sts) around. *(26)*

Rnds 6–8: Sc in each st around.

Rnd 9: Sc in first 5 sts, (sc next 2 sts tog, sc in next 5 sts) around. *(23)*

Rnds 10–11: Sc in each st around.

Rnd 12: Sc in each of first 3 sts, sc next 2 sts tog, (sc in next 4 sts, sc next 2 sts tog) around. *(19)* Stuff. Continue stuffing Head as you work.

Rnd 13: Sc in each of first 2 sts, sc next 2 sts tog, (sc in each of next 3 sts, sc next 2 sts tog) around. *(15)*

Rnd 14: Sc in first st, sc next 2 sts tog, (sc in each of next 2 sts, sc next 2 sts tog) around. *(11)*

Rnds 15–16: Sc in each st around. At end of last rnd, join with sl st in first sc.

Rnd 17: Ch 3, dc in same st, 2 dc in each st around, join with sl st in top of ch-3. *(22 dc)*

Rnd 18: Ch 3, 2 dc in each st around to last st, dc in last st, join. Fasten off. *(42)*

Rnd 19: For **bodice,** with wrong side of sts facing you, join dress color with sc in first st, sc in each st around, join.

Rnd 20: Ch 4, tr in same st, 2 tr in each st around, join with sl st in top of ch-4. *(84 tr)*

Rnd 21: Ch 6, skip next st, (dc in next st, ch 3, skip next st) around, join with sl st in third ch of ch-6. *(42 dc, 42 ch sps)*

Rnd 22: Ch 1, (sc, hdc, dc, hdc, sc) in each ch-3 sp around, join. Fasten off.

Skirt

Rnd 1: With dress color, ch 20, sl st in first ch to form ring, ch 1, sc in each ch around, join with sl st in first sc. *(20 sc made)*

Rnds 2–3: Ch 3, dc in each st around, join with sl st in top of ch-3.

Rnd 4: Ch 4, dc in same st; *for **V st, (dc, ch 1, dc)** in next st; repeat from * around, join with sl st in third ch of ch-4. *(20 V sts)*

Rnd 5: For **beginning V st (beg V st), sl st in next ch sp, ch 4, dc in same ch sp;** ch 1, (V st in ch sp of next V st, ch 1) around, join.

Rnd 6: Beg V st, ch 2, (V st in next V st, ch 2) around, join.

Rnd 7: Beg V st, ch 3, (V st in next V st, ch 3) around, join.

Rnds 8–18: Beg V st, ch 4, (V st in next V st, ch 4) around, join.

Rnd 19: Sl st in next ch sp, ch 8, (dc in next V st, ch 5) around, join with sl st in third ch of ch-8.

Rnd 20: Ch 1, (sc, hdc, dc, tr, dc, hdc, sc) in each ch sp around, join with sl st in first sc.

Rnd 21: Ch 1, sc in first st, ch 8, skip next 6 sts, (sc in next st, ch 8, skip next 6 sts) around, join.

Rnd 22: Ch 1, 8 sc in each ch-8 lp around, join. Fasten off.

Fold Bodice in half. Tack each end of 10 center front sts on rnd 20 of Bodice to each end of 10 center back sts on same row *(remaining sts form sleeve ruffles).* Sew rnd 1 of Skirt to center sts on front and back.

Arm (make 2)

Rnd 1: With dress color, ch 4, 11 dc in fourth ch from hook, join with sl st in top of ch 3. *(12 dc made)*

Rnds 2–3: Ch 4, tr in each st around, join with sl st in top of ch 4. Stuff. Continue stuffing as you work.

Rnd 4: Ch 1, sc in each st around, **do not join.** *(12 sc)*

Rnds 5–12: Sc in each st around.

Rnds 13–14: Sc first 2 sts tog, sc in each st around. *(11, 10)*

Rnd 15: Working this rnd in **back lps** *(see Stitch Guide),* 3 hdc in each st around, join with sl st in first hdc. Fasten off.

Rnd 16: Working this rnd in **front lps** of rnd 14, for **hand,** join lt. peach with sc in first st, sc in each st around.

Rnd 17: Sc in first 4 sts, sc next 2 sts tog, sc in last 4 sts. *(9)*

Rnd 18: Sc in first st, (sc next 2 sts tog, sc in each of next 2 sts) around. *(7)*

Rnd 19: Sc in first st, (sc next 2 sts tog, sc in next st) around, join with sl st in first sc. Fasten off. *(5)*

Sew rnd 1 of each Arm to rnd 18 of Bodice under sleeve ruffles.

Stuff Bodice.

VEIL (for bride doll only)

Row 1: With dress color, ch 11, sc in second ch from hook, sc in each ch across, turn. *(10 sc made)*

Row 2: Ch 4, dc in same st, V st in each st across, turn.

Row 3: Beg V st, (ch 1, V st in next V st) across, turn.

Row 4: Beg V st, (ch 2, V st in next V st) across, turn.

Row 5: Beg V st, (ch 3, V st in next V st) across, turn.

Continued on page 151

New Year's Gala

Design by Mary Layfield

Instructions begin on page 138

New Year's Gala

Finished Size: Fits 15" fashion doll.

Materials:
- Worsted yarn:
  - 14½ oz. white
  - 13 oz. med. red
  - 4 oz. dk. red
- Small amount white baby yarn
- 7" silver strung sequins
- One each of red, white and black marabou feathers
- 3½" square black felt
- 12½" white marabou boa
- 1¼ yds. white ⅛" ribbon
- Nine ½" ribbon roses
- 6½" of ⅛" wooden dowel
- Black marker
- Red and white sewing thread
- Craft glue
- 4 size 2/0 snaps
- Sewing and tapestry needles
- No. 2 steel and F hooks or hook needed to obtain gauge

Gauge: F hook and worsted yarn, 9 sc = 2"; 5 sc rows = 1"; 2 shell rows = 1".

Basic Stitches: Ch, sl st, sc, hdc, dc, tr.

Note: Use F hook unless otherwise stated.

DRESS
Bodice
Row 1: With dk. red, ch 25, sc in second ch from hook, sc in each ch across, turn. *(24 sc made)*

Row 2: Ch 1, sc in first 5 sts, 2 sc in next st, sc in next 12 sts, 2 sc in next st, sc in last 5 sts, turn. *(26)*

Row 3: Ch 1, sc in first 5 sts, 2 sc in next st, sc in next 14 sts, 2 sc in next st, sc in last 5 sts, turn. *(28)*

Rows 4–5: Ch 1, sc in each st across, turn.

Row 6: (Ch 3, dc) in first st, dc in next 10 sts, 3 dc in next st, dc in next 4 sts, 3 dc in next st, dc in next 10 sts, 2 dc in last st, turn. Fasten off. *(34 dc—First ch 3 counts as first dc.)*

Row 7: Skip first 8 sts, join dk. red with sc in next st, sc in each of next 2 sts, hdc in next 5 sts, sc in each of next 2 sts, hdc in next 5 sts, sc in each of next 3 sts leaving remaining sts unworked, turn. *(18)*

Row 8: Sl st in first st, sc in each of next 2 sts, hdc in next 5 sts, sc in each of next 2 sts, hdc in next 5 sts, sc in each of next 2 sts, sl st in last st, turn. Fasten off.

Row 9: Working in skipped sts of row 6, join dk. red with sc in first st, sc in next 7 sts, sc in each st across row 8, sc in next 8 unworked sts on row 6. Fasten off.

Collar
Row 1: With med. red, ch 43, 2 sc in second ch from hook, (sc in next 4 chs, 2 sc in next ch) 4 times, 2 sc in next ch; repeat between ( ) 4 times, turn. *(52 sc made)*

Row 2: Ch 1, 2 sc in first st, sc in each st across, turn. *(53)*

Row 3: Ch 1, sc in first st, (ch 3, sc in next st) across, turn.

Row 4: Ch 1, sc in first ch sp, (ch 4, sc in next ch sp) across. Fasten off.

Row 5: Join med. red with sc in first st of row 9 on Bodice, sc in next 3 sts; working in remaining lps on opposite side of starting ch on row 1 of Collar, sc in each ch across; being careful not to twist Collar, sc in last 4 sts on row 9 of Bodice, turn. *(50)*

Row 6: Ch 1, sc in each st across, **do not turn.** Fasten off.

Row 7: For **ruffle,** with No. 2 hook and white baby yarn, join with sc in first st, (ch 4, sc in next st) across. Fasten off.

Mark first and last st of center 8 sts on row 9 of Bodice. Match first and last st of center 14 sts on row 6 of Collar to marked sts; tack matched sts together, forming shoulder straps. Place center 14 sts on row 6 of Collar down below row 8 of Bodice and tack in place *(see photo)*.

Pull center front st of row 4 on Collar up and tack in place below Ruffle. Cut a piece of ribbon 5" long. Tie in bow, glue to tacked stitch. Glue ribbon rose to center of bow.

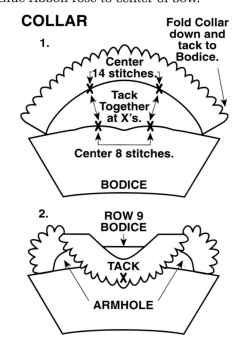

COLLAR

1.

Fold Collar down and tack to Bodice.

Center 14 stitches.

Tack Together at X's.

Center 8 stitches.

BODICE

2.

ROW 9 BODICE

TACK X

ARMHOLE

Overskirt
Row 1: Working in remaining lps of starting ch on row 1 of Bodice, join med. red with sl st in

first ch, (ch 3, dc) in same ch, 2 dc in each ch across, turn. *(48 dc made)*

Row 2: Ch 3, dc in each st across, turn.

Row 3: Ch 1, sc in each of first 3 sts changing to dk. red *(see Stitch Guide)* in last st made, (sc in each of next 3 sts changing to med. red in last st made, sc in each of next 3 sts changing to dk. red in last st made) across to last 3 sts, sc in each of last 3 sts changing to med. red in last st made, turn.

Rnd 4: Working in rnds, ch 3, dc in each st around, join with sl st in top of ch-3, **turn.**

Rnd 5: (Ch 3, dc) in first st, (2 dc in next st, dc in each of next 2 sts) around to last 2 sts, 2 dc in each of last 2 sts, join, **do not turn.** *(66)*

Rnd 6: Ch 1, sc in each of first 3 sts changing to dk. red in last st, (sc in each of next 3 sts changing to med. red in last st made, sc in each of next 3 sts changing to dk. red in last st made) around to last 3 sts, sc in each of last 3 sts changing to med. red in last st made, join with sl st in first sc.

Rnd 7: Ch 3, 2 dc in next st, (dc in next st, 2 dc in next st) around, join with sl st in top of ch-3. *(99)*

Rnd 8: Ch 3, dc in next st, ch 2, skip next st, (dc in each of next 2 sts, ch 2, skip next st) around, join.

Rnds 9–11: Sl st in next st, (sl st, ch 3, dc, ch 1, 2 dc) in next ch sp, ch 1, *(2 dc, ch 1, 2 dc) in next ch-2 sp, ch 1; repeat from * around, join.

Rnds 12–15: Sl st in next st, (sl st, ch 3, dc, ch 2, 2 dc) in next ch sp, ch 1, *(2 dc, ch 2, 2 dc) in next ch-2 sp, ch 1; repeat from * around, join.

Rnd 16: Sl st in next st, (sl st, ch 3, dc, ch 2, 2 dc) in next ch sp, ch 2, *(2 dc, ch 2, 2 dc) in next ch-2 sp, ch 2; repeat from * around, join.

Rnd 17: Sl st in next st, (sl st, ch 3, dc, ch 2, 2 dc) in next ch sp, sc in next ch sp, *(2 dc, ch 2, 2 dc) in next ch sp, sc in next ch sp; repeat from * around, join.

Rnd 18: Sl st in next st, (sl st, ch 3, dc, ch 2, 2 dc, ch 2, 2 dc) in next ch sp, ch 3, sc in next sc, ch 3, *(2 dc, ch 2, 2 dc, ch 2, 2 dc) in next ch sp, ch 3, sc in next sc, ch 3; repeat from * around, join.

Rnd 19: Ch 4, (sc in next st or ch sp, ch 4) around, join with sl st in first ch of first ch-4. Fasten off.

Underskirt

Rnd 1: With wrong side of Overskirt facing you, working in skipped sts of rnd 7 on Overskirt, join med. red with sc in any st, ch 1, sc in same st, ch 1, *(sc, ch 1, sc) in next st, ch 1; repeat from * around, join with sl st in first sc, **turn.** Fasten off. *(66 sc, 66 ch sps made)*

Rnd 2: Join dk. red with sl st in any st, ch 4, tr in each st and in each ch around, join with sl st in top of ch-4. *(132 tr)*

Rnd 3: Ch 4, (tr in next 8 sts, 2 tr in next st) 14 times, tr in last 5 sts, join. *(146)*

Rnds 4–6: Ch 4, tr in each st around, join. Fasten off.

Rnd 7: Join white worsted with sl st in any st, ch 4, (dc, ch 1) in each st around, join with sl st in third ch of ch-4.

Rnd 8: Sl st in next ch sp, ch 6, skip next ch sp, (sl st in next ch sp, ch 4, skip next ch sp) around, join with sl st in first ch of ch-6.

Rnd 9: (Sl st, ch 4, tr) in first ch sp, 2 tr in each ch sp around, join with sl st in top of ch-4. *(146)*

Rnd 10: Ch 5, (tr in next st, ch 1) 6 times, (tr, ch 1) 2 times in next st, *(tr in next st, ch 1) 7 times, (tr, ch 1) 2 times in next st; repeat from * around to last 2 sts, tr in each of last 2 sts, join with sl st in fourth ch of ch-5. *(164)*

Rnd 11: Skipping chs, ch 4, (tr in next 5 tr, 2 tr in next tr) 26 times, tr in last 7 tr, join with sl st in top of ch-4. *(190)*

Rnd 12: Ch 4, (tr in next 5 sts, 2 tr in next st) 14 times, (tr in next 4 sts, 2 tr in next st) around, join. *(225)*

Rnd 13: Ch 1, sc in first st, ch 6, skip next 2 sts, (sc in next st, ch 6, skip next 2 sts) around, join.

Rnd 14: Sl st in each of first 2 chs, ch 1, (sc, ch 6) 2 times in same ch sp, (sc, ch 6) 2 times in each ch sp around, join.

Rnd 15: Sl st in each of first 2 chs, ch 1, (sc, ch 6) 3 times in same ch sp, (sc, ch 6) 3 times in each ch sp around, join.

Rnd 16: Sl st in each of next 2 chs, ch 1, sc in same ch sp, ch 6, (sc in next ch sp, ch 6) around, join. Fasten off.

Rnd 17: For **Ruffle,** working in skipped ch sps of rnd 7, join white worsted with sc in any ch sp, ch 6, (sc in next skipped ch sp, ch 6) around, join with sl st in first sc.

Rnds 18–20: Repeat rnds 14–16.

Rnd 21: For **Ruffle,** working in skipped ch sps of rnd 10, join white worsted with sc in any ch sp, ch 6, (sc in next ch sp, ch 6) around, join with sl st in first sc. Fasten off.

Rnd 22: Join med. red with sc in any ch sp, (ch 6, sc, ch 6) in same ch sp, (sc, ch 6) 2 times in each ch sp around, join with sl st in first sc.

Rnds 23–24: Repeat rnds 15 and 16.

Cut eight pieces of ribbon each 5" long. Tie each in bow and glue evenly spaced around Overskirt on rnd 11. Glue one ribbon rose to center of each bow.

Sew snaps evenly spaced down back opening of Dress.

Tack rnd 16 of Overskirt to rnd 6 of Underskirt.

HAT

Rnd 1: With med. red, ch 5, sl st in first ch to form ring, ch 3, 17 dc in ring, join with sl st in top of ch-3. *(18 dc made)*

Rnd 2: (Ch 3, 2 dc) in first st, (dc in next st, 2 dc in next st) 8 times, 2 dc in last st, join. *(29)*

Continued on page 154

Prom Night Pair

Tuxedo

Instructions begin on page 142

Prom Dress

Design by Joyce Bishop

Finished Size: Fits 11½" fashion doll.

Materials:
- Pompadour baby yarn:
  - 3 oz. red
  - 3 oz. white
- Four size 3/0 snaps
- Nine white ⅜" ribbon roses
- Thread elastic
- Matching sewing thread and needle
- E hook or hook needed to obtain gauge

Gauge: 5 dc = 1"; 5 dc rows = 2".

Basic Stitches: Ch, sl st, sc, hdc, dc, tr.

DRESS

Overskirt

Row 1: With red, ch 17, sc in second ch from hook, sc in each ch across, turn. *(16 sc made)*

Row 2: Ch 1, sc in first st, 2 sc in each st across, turn. *(31)*

Row 3: Ch 3, dc in same st, 2 dc in each of next 12 sts, dc in next st, 2 dc in each st across, turn. *(61 dc)*

NOTE: *Work in continuous rnds, do not join or turn unless otherwise stated. Mark first st of each rnd.*

Rnd 4: Working in rnds, ch 1, sc in first st; for **love knot (lk), pull up long lp on hook to measure ⅜", yo, pull through lp, sc in back strand of long lp (see illustration 1), pull up ⅜" lp, yo, pull through lp, sc in back strand of long lp (see illustration 2), skip next st, sc in next st;** (lk, skip next st, sc in next st) around; for **joining,** pull up ⅜" lp, yo, pull through lp, sc in back strand of long lp, sc in center of first lk *(see illustration 3).* *(30 lk)*

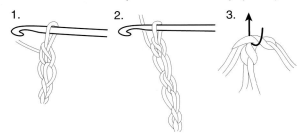

Rnds 5–16: (Lk, sc in center of next lk) around. At end of last rnd, fasten off.

Underskirt

Row 1: With white, ch 17, sc in second ch from hook, sc in each ch across, turn. *(16 sc made)*

Row 2: Ch 3, dc in same st, 2 dc in each st across, turn. *(32 dc)*

Row 3: Ch 3, dc in same st, (2 dc in each of next 2 sts, dc in next st) across to last st, dc in last st, turn. *(53)*

Rnd 4: Working in rnds, ch 3, dc in each st around, join with sl st in top of ch-3.

Rnd 5: Ch 3, (2 dc in next st, dc in each of next 3 sts) around, join. *(66)*

Rnd 6: Ch 3, (dc in next 4 sts, 2 dc in next st) around, join. *(79)*

Rnd 7: Ch 3, (2 dc in next st, dc in next 5 sts) around, join. *(92)*

Rnd 8: Ch 3, (dc in next 6 sts, 2 dc in next st) around, join. *(105)*

Rnd 9: Ch 3, (2 dc in next st, dc in next 7 sts) around, join. *(118)*

Rnd 10: Ch 3, dc in next 5 sts, (2 dc in next st, dc in next 6 sts) around, join. *(134)*

Rnd 11: Ch 3, dc in next 6 sts, 2 dc in next st, (dc in next 7 sts, 2 dc in next st) 15 times, dc in last 6 sts, join. *(150)*

Rnd 12: Ch 3, dc in each st around, join.

Rnd 13: Ch 3, dc in same st, dc in next 9 sts, (2 dc in next st, dc in next 9 sts) around, join. *(165)*

Rnds 14–15: Ch 3, dc in each st around, join.

Rnd 16: For **ruffle,** ch 3, 2 dc in next st, 3 dc in each st around, join. *(492)*

Rnds 17–18: Ch 3, dc in each st around, join. At end of last rnd, fasten off.

Rnd 19: Join red with sc in first st, ch 3, skip next st, (sc in next st, ch 3, skip next st) around, join with sl st in first sc. Fasten off.

Bodice

Row 1: With Overskirt over top of Underskirt, working in remaining lps on opposite side of starting ch through both thicknesses, join white with sc in first ch, sc in each ch across, turn. *(16 sc made)*

Row 2: Ch 3, dc in each of next 3 sts, (2 dc in next st, dc in each of next 3 sts) across, turn. *(19)*

Row 3: Ch 3, dc in next 6 sts, 2 dc in each of next 2 sts, dc in each of next 2 sts, 2 dc in each of next 2 sts, dc in last 6 sts, turn. *(23 dc)*

Row 4: Ch 3, dc in next 7 sts, 2 dc in each of next 3 sts, dc in each of next 2 sts, 2 dc in each of next 3 sts, dc in last 7 sts, turn. *(29)*

Row 5: Ch 2, hdc in next 8 sts, (hdc next 2 sts tog) 6 times, hdc in last 8 sts, turn. *(23 hdc)*

Row 6: Ch 1, sc in each st across. Fasten off.

Weave thread elastic through back of row 1 on Bodice. Secure ends.

Sew three snaps evenly spaced down Bodice back.

Sew eight roses evenly spaced through both thicknesses of last rnd on Overskirt and rnd 15 on Underskirt.

Bodice Ruffle

Row 1: With red, ch 32; working in **back bar of ch** *(see Stitch Guide),* sc in second ch from

Continued on page 142

Continued from page 141

hook, sc in each of next 3 chs, (3 sc in next ch, sc in next 10 chs) 2 times, 3 sc in next ch, sc in last 4 chs, turn. *(37 sc made)*

Row 2: Ch 1, sc in first st, (lk, skip next 2 sts, sc in next st) across, turn. *(12 lk)*

Row 3: (Lk, sc in center of next lk) across, lk, sc in last sc on row 2. Fasten off.

Sew one snap at ends of row 1. Tack center of Ruffle to center front of Bodice on rnd 5.

Sew rose to center front of ruffle *(see photo)*. ❖

Tuxedo

Design by Mary Layfield

Finished Size: Fits 12" male fashion doll.

Materials:
- Sport yarn:
  2 oz. black
  Small amount each white and red
- Six size 3/0 snaps
- Four small black beads
- Thread elastic
- Matching sewing thread
- Tapestry and sewing needles
- B and E hooks or hooks needed to obtain gauges

Gauges: **B hook,** 7 sts = 1"; 7 sc rows = 1"; 7 dc rows = 2". **E hook,** 5 sts = 1"; 5 sc rows = 1".

Basic Stitches: Ch, sl st, sc, hdc, dc.

Note: Use B hook unless otherwise stated.

PANT SIDE (make 2)

Row 1: Starting at **Waist**, with black, ch 23, sc in second ch from hook, sc in each ch across, turn. *(22 sc made)*

Rows 2–8: Ch 1, sc in each st across, turn.

Row 9: For **crotch**, ch 1, 2 sc in first st, sc in each st across, turn. *(23)*

Row 10: Ch 1, sc in each st across, turn.

Rows 11–12: Ch 1, 2 sc in first st, sc in each st across, turn. At end of last row *(25)*.

Rows 13–26: Ch 1, sc in each st across, turn.

Row 27: Ch 1, sc first 2 sts tog, sc in each st across to last 2 sts, sc last 2 sts tog, turn. *(23)*

Row 28: Ch 1, sc in each st across, turn.

Rows 29–30: Repeat rows 27–28. *(21)*

Rows 31–44: Ch 1, sc in each st across, turn. At end of last row, fasten off.

Hold both pieces together, matching ends of rows; for **front**, sew rows 1–12 together. For **back**, sew rows 5–12 together. Sew inseams.

For **front pleats**, working on each side of front seam on row 1, match sixth and ninth sts from

seam, fold to inside toward seam. Tack in place.

CUMMERBUND

Row 1: With right side facing you, working in remaining lps on opposite side of starting ch through both thicknesses of pleats, join red with sc in first st on back, sc in each st across, turn. *(36 sc made)*

Rows 2–6: Ch 1, sc in each st across, turn. At end of last row, fasten off.

Weave thread elastic through back of sts on row 6. Secure ends.

Sew 2 snaps evenly spaced on ends of Cummerbund.

DICKIE

Row 1: For **first side**, with white, ch 19, sc in second ch from hook, sc in each ch across, turn. Fasten off. *(18 sc made—Front of row 1 is right side of work.)*

Row 2: For **shoulder**, ch 9, dc in first st on row 1, dc in each st across, **do not turn.** Fasten off. *(18 dc, 9 chs)*

Row 3: Join white with sc in first ch, sc in each ch and in each st across, turn. *(27 sc)*

Row 4: Ch 3, dc in next 21 sts, (2 dc in next st, dc in next st) 2 times, dc in last st, turn. *(29 dc)*

Row 5: Ch 1, sc in each st across, turn.

Row 6: Ch 3, dc in next 9 sts leaving remaining sts unworked, turn. *(10)*

Row 7: Sl st in each of first 2 sts, ch 3, dc in each st across, turn. *(9)*

Row 8: Ch 3, dc in next 6 sts leaving last 2 sts unworked, turn. *(7)*

Rows 9–11: Ch 3, dc in each st across, turn. At end of last row, fasten off.

Row 2: For **second side**, with wrong side of row 1 facing you, working in remaining lps on opposite side of starting ch, join white with sl st in first st, ch 3, dc in each st across; for **shoulder,** ch 10, turn. *(18 dc, 10 chs)*

Row 3: Sc in second ch from hook, sc in each ch and in each st across, turn. *(27 sc)*

Rows 4–11: Repeat rows 4–11 of first side.

Neck Band

Row 1: With right side facing you, working around neck edge on Dickie, join white with sl st in first st, ch 3, dc in next 8 sts, 3 dc in end of next row, dc in next row, 3 dc in next row, (dc in each of next 2 sts, 2 dc in next st) 2 times, dc in next st leaving last 2 sts unworked, turn. *(25 dc made)*

Row 2: For **ruffle**, ch 1, sc in first st, (ch 3, sc in next st) across. Fasten off.

For **front ruffles**, working in worked sts on row 3 of Dickie, for **first ruffle,** join white with sc at waist, (ch 3, sc in next st) across to Neck Band. Fasten off.

For **second ruffle,** join white with sc in first st at bottom of Neck Band, (ch 3, sc in next st) across to waist. Fasten off.

For **bow tie,** with red, ch 4, (hdc, ch 3, hdc) in first ch of ch-4. Fasten off.

Sew bow tie to Dickie centered on row 1 of Neck Band.

Sew beads evenly spaced down center front of Dickie ⅜" apart.

Sew 2 snaps evenly spaced on center back neck edge.

Sew 2 snaps evenly spaced on center back waist edge.

JACKET

Back

Row 1: Starting at **neck,** with black, ch 8, 2 sc in second ch from hook, sc in each ch across with 2 sc in last ch, turn. *(9 sc made)*

Rows 2–4: Ch 1, 2 sc in each of first 2 sts, sc in each st across to last 2 sts, 2 sc in each of last 2 sts, turn. At end of last row *(21).*

Row 5: Sl st in each of first 2 sts, ch 1, sc in each st across leaving last 2 sts unworked, turn. *(17)*

Row 6: Ch 2, hdc in next st, sc in next 13 sts, hdc in each of last 2 sts, turn.

Rows 7–9: Ch 1, sc in each st across, turn.

Rows 10–11: Ch 1, 2 sc in first st, sc in each st across to last st, 3 sc in last st, turn. At end of last row *(23).*

Rows 12–13: Ch 1, sc in each st across, turn.

Row 14: Ch 1, sc first 2 sts tog, sc in each st across to last 2 sts, sc last 2 sts tog, turn. *(21)*

Rows 15–24: Ch 1, sc in each st across, turn.

Row 25: For **first tail,** ch 1, sc in first 9 sts, 2 sc in next st leaving remaining sts unworked, turn. *(11)*

Rows 26–33: Repeat rows 14 and 15 alternately. At end of last row *(3).*

Row 34: Ch 1, sc in each st across, turn.

Row 35: Ch 1, sc 3 sts tog, **do not turn.** Fasten off.

Row 25: For **second tail,** skip next unworked st on row 24, join black with sc in next st, sc in same st, sc in each st across, turn. *(11 sc)*

Rows 26–35: Repeat rows 26–35 of first tail.

Front (make 2)

Row 1: Starting at **neck,** with black, ch 6, sc in second ch from hook, sc in each ch across with 2 sc in last ch, turn. *(6 sc made)*

Row 2: Ch 1, 2 sc in first st, sc in each st across, turn. *(7)*

Rows 3–4: Ch 1, sc in each st across, turn.

Row 5: Ch 2, hdc in each of next 2 sts, sc in each st across, turn. *(7 sts)*

Row 6: Ch 1, sc in first 4 sts, hdc in each of last 3 sts, turn.

Rows 7–10: Ch 1, sc in each st across, turn.

Row 11: Ch 1, sc in each st across to last st, 3 sc in last st, turn. *(9 sc)*

Row 12: Repeat row 2. *(10)*

Rows 13–14: Ch 1, sc in each st across, turn.

Row 15: Ch 1, sc in first 8 sts, sc last 2 sts tog, turn. *(9)*

Rows 16–23: Ch 1, sc in each st across, turn.

Row 24: Ch 1, sc in first 5 sts, ch 1, hdc in last 4 sts, turn. *(9 sts, 1 ch)*

Row 25: Ch 3, dc in each of next 3 sts, ch 1, skip next ch-1 sp, sc in each st across. Fasten off.

For **shoulder,** sew starting ch of each Front to ends of rows 1–4 on each side of Back.

Sleeve (make 2)

Row 1: Starting at **wrist,** with black, ch 21, sc in second ch from hook, sc in each ch across, turn. *(20 sc made)*

Rows 2–9: Ch 1, sc in each st across, turn.

Row 10: Ch 1, 2 sc in first st, sc in each st across to last st 2 sc in last st, turn. *(22)*

Rows 11–20: Ch 1, sc in each st across, turn.

Rows 21–27: Sl st in first st, ch 1, sc in each st across leaving last st unworked, turn. At end of last row *(8).*

Row 28: Sl st in first st, sc in next 6 sts, sl st in last st. Fasten off.

Matching center of row 28 to shoulder seam, sew Sleeves to armholes. Sew side and Sleeve seams.

Lapels

Working around outer edge of Jacket, with right side facing you, for **first lapel,** join black with sl st in shoulder seam, ch 4, tr in next 4 rows, 2 tr in each of next 2 rows, tr in next 8 rows, dc in next 9 rows, 2 dc in next row, 3 dc in last row; sc in each st, in each ch-1 sp and end of each row around bottom of Jacket with 3 sc in end of each tail; for **second lapel,** 3 dc in next row, 2 dc in next row, dc in next 9 rows, tr in next 8 rows, 2 tr in each of next 2 rows, tr in next 4 rows, tr in seam leaving sts across Back unworked. Fasten off.

Fold lapels to outside of Jacket. Tack top and bottom of lapel in place.

For **flower,** with white, ch 3, sl st in first st to form ring, (ch 3, sc in ring) 5 times. Fasten off.

Sew to left Front over rows 3–4.

DRESS SHOE (make 2)

Rnd 1: With E hook and black, ch 7, sc in second ch from hook, sc in each of next 3 chs, hdc in next ch, 5 dc in last ch; working remaining lps on opposite side of starting ch, hdc in next ch, sc in each of next 3 chs, 2 sc in last ch, join with sl st in first sc. *(16 sts made)*

Rnd 2: Working this rnd in **back lps** *(see Stitch Guide),* ch 1, sc in each st around, join.

Rnd 3: Ch 1, sc in each st around, join.

Rnd 4: Ch 1, sc in first 4 sts, hdc in each of next 2 sts, (dc next 2 sts tog) 2 times, hdc in each of next 2 sts, sc in next 4 sts, join. *(14 sts)*

Rnd 5: Ch 1, sc in first 4 sts, (sc next 2 sts tog) 3 times, sc in last 4 sts, join. *(11)*

Rnds 6–7: Ch 1, sc in each st around, join. At end of last rnd, fasten off. ❖

Cookie Cutter Witch

Design by Michelle Crean

Finished Size: Approximately 5½" tall.

Materials:
- Size 10 crochet cotton thread:
    100 yds. black/silver metallic
    75 yds. orange
    25 yds. green
- 8 yds. orange worsted yarn
- 5" gingerbread man cookie cutter
- Green satin ribbon:
    1 yd. of ¼"-wide
    7" of ⅛"-wide
- Small bunch autumn-colored silk flowers
- Craft glue
- Sewing thread
- Sewing and tapestry needles
- No. 5 steel hook or hook needed to obtain gauge

Gauge: 9 dc = 1"; 5 dc rows = 1¼".

Basic Stitches: Ch, dc, sc, sl st and tr.

Special Stitches: For **treble front post (tr fp)**, yo 2 times, insert hook from front to back to front around post of next st, yo, pull through, (yo, pull through 2 lps on hook) 3 times.

For **treble back post (tr bp)**, yo 2 times, insert hook from back to front to back around post of next st, yo, pull through, (yo, pull through 2 lps on hook) 3 times.

For **shell,** (dc, ch 2, dc, ch 2, dc) in next st.

UNDERSKIRT

Row 1: With black/silver, ch 37, sc in second ch from hook and in each ch across, **turn.** Fasten off. *(36 sc made)*

Row 2: Working in **front lps** *(see Stitch Guide)*, join orange thread with sl st in first sc, ch 1, 2 sc in same st, sc in next st, (2 sc in next st, sc in next st) across, turn. *(54)*

Row 3: Ch 3, dc in each of next 2 sts, **tr fp** *(see Special Stitches)* around same st last dc was made in, (dc in next 6 sts, tr fp around same st last dc was made in) 7 times, dc in each of last 3 sts, turn. *(63 sts)*

Row 4: Ch 3, dc in next st, 2 dc in next st, **tr bp** *(see Special Stitches)* around first tr fp, (2 dc in next st, dc in next 4 sts, 2 dc in next st, tr bp around next tr fp) 7 times, 2 dc in next dc, dc in each of last 2 dc, turn. *(72)*

Rnd 5: Working in rnds, ch 3, dc in each of next 3 sts, tr fp around first tr bp, (dc in next 8 sts, tr fp around next tr bp) 7 times, dc in last 4 sts, join with sl st in top of ch-3.

Rnd 6: Ch 3, dc in each of next 2 sts, 2 dc in next st, tr fp around first tr fp, (2 dc in next st, dc in next 6 sts, 2 dc in next st, tr fp around next tr fp) 7 times, 2 dc in next st, dc in each of last 3 sts, join. *(88)*

Rnd 7: Ch 3, dc in each of next 4 sts, tr fp around first tr fp, (dc in next 10 sts, tr fp around next tr fp) 7 times, dc in last 5 sts, join.

Rnd 8: Ch 3, dc in each of next 2 sts, dc next 2 sts tog, tr fp around first tr fp, (dc next 2 sts tog, dc in next 6 sts, dc next 2 sts tog, tr fp around next tr fp) 7 times, dc next 2 sts tog, dc in each of last 3 sts, join. *(72)*

Rnd 9: Ch 3, dc in each of next 3 sts, tr fp around first tr fp, (dc in next 8 sts, tr fp around next tr fp) 7 times, dc in last 4 sts, join.

Rnd 10: Ch 3, dc in next st, dc next 2 sts tog, tr fp around first tr fp, (dc next 2 sts tog, dc in next 4 sts, dc next 2 sts tog, tr fp around next tr fp) 7 times, dc next 2 sts tog, dc in each of last 2 sts, join. *(56)*

Rnd 11: Ch 3, dc in each of next 2 sts, tr fp around first tr fp, (dc in next 6 sts, tr fp around next tr fp) 7 times, dc in remaining 3 sts, join.

Rnd 12: Ch 1, sc in each of first 3 sts, skip first tr fp, (sc in next 6 sts, skip next tr fp) 7 times, sc in each of last 3 sts, join with sl st in first sc. Fasten off. *(46)*

Rnd 13: Join green with sc in same st as joining, sc in each st around, join.

Rnd 14: Ch 5, (dc, ch 2, dc) in same st, *skip next 2 sc, **shell** *(see Special Stitches)* in next sc; repeat from * around to last 2 sc, skip last 2 sc, join with sl st in third ch of ch-5.

Rnd 15: Ch 1, *sc in first ch-2 sp of shell, ch 3, (sc ch 3, sc) in center dc of shell *(picot made)*, ch 3, sc in next ch-2 sp; repeat from * around, join. Fasten off.

OVERSKIRT

Row 1: For **First Half,** with waist of Underskirt facing you, working in remaining lps on opposite side of starting ch, join black/silver with sl st in first st, ch 4, (dc, ch 1) in next 15 sts leaving remaining 20 sts unworked, turn. *(16 dc and 16 chs made)*

Row 2: Ch 5, dc in same dc *(beginning half shell made),* (dc in next dc, shell in next dc) 7 times, dc in third ch of ch-4 at end of row. Fasten off.

Rows 1–2: For **Second Half,** skip next 4 sts of Row 1 on Underskirt and join black with sl st in next st, repeat rows 1 and 2 of First Half. At end of row 2, turn, **do not fasten off.**

Row 3: Ch 5, dc in same st, (skip next dc and ch-2 sp, dc in center dc of next shell, skip next ch-2 sp and dc, shell in next dc) 7 times, dc in third ch of ch-5 at end of row; working across First Half, (shell in next dc, dc in center dc of next shell) 7 times, shell in next dc, dc in third ch of ch-5 at end of row, turn.

Rows 4–7: Ch 5, dc in same st, (dc in center dc of shell, shell in next dc) across, ending with dc in third ch of ch-5 at end of row, turn.

Row 8: Ch 3, 2 dc in same st, (sc in center dc of next shell, 5 dc in next dc) across with sc in third ch of ch-5 at end of row, turn.

Row 9: Ch 1, skip first sc, *(sc in next dc, ch 2) 4

Continued on page 154

Pilgrim Pillow Dolls

Designs by Michele Wilcox

Finished Sizes:
Mrs. Pilgrim is 12½" tall. Mr. Pilgrim is 14" tall.

Materials:
- Worsted yarn:
  4 oz. gray
  4 oz. black
  4 oz. white
  1½ oz. beige
  Small amount each lt. gold, red, green and rust
- Polyester fiber-fill
- Tapestry needle
- F hook or hook needed to obtain gauge

Gauge: 9 sc = 2"; 9 sc rows = 2".

Basic Stitches: Ch, sl st, sc, hdc, dc.

MRS. PILGRIM

FRONT

Row 1: Starting at dress, with gray, ch 29, sc in second ch from hook, sc in each ch across, turn. *(28 sc made)*

Rows 2–4: Ch 1, sc in each st across, turn. At end of last row, fasten off.

Row 5: Join white with sc in first st, sc in each st across, turn.

Rows 6–13: Repeat row 2.

Row 14: Ch 1, sc first 2 sts tog, sc in each st across to last 2 sts, sc last 2 sts tog, turn. *(26)*

Row 15: Repeat row 2.

Rows 16–21: Repeat rows 14 and 2 alternately. At end of last row, fasten off. *(20)*

Row 22: With gray, repeat row 5.

Row 23: Repeat row 2.

Rows 24–26: Repeat row 14. At end of last row *(14)*.

Row 27: Repeat row 2. Fasten off.

Row 28: For **head,** join beige with sc in first st, sc in each st across, turn.

Rows 29–30: Ch 1, 2 sc in first st, sc in each st across with 2 sc in last st, turn. *(16, 18)*

Rows 31–37: Repeat row 2.

Rows 38–42: Repeat row 14. At end of last row, fasten off. *(8)*

BACK

Rows 1–26: With gray, repeat rows 1–26 of Front. **Do not change colors. Do not fasten off.**

Row 27: Ch 1, sc in each st across, turn. Fasten off.

Row 28: Repeat row 5 of Front.

Rows 29–42: Repeat rows 29–42 of Front.

SHOE SIDE (make 2)

Row 1: With black, ch 21, sc in second ch from hook, sc in each ch across, turn. *(20 sc made)*

Rows 2–3: Repeat row 2 of Front.

Rows 4–7: Repeat row 14 of Front. At end of last row, fasten off. *(12)*

Sew row 7 of one Shoe Side to center 12 sts of row 1 on Front.

Repeat with other Shoe Side and Back.

EDGING

Rnd 1: For **front,** working around outer edge, changing colors *(see Stitch Guide)* as needed to match piece, join with sc in any st, sc in each st and in end of each row around with 3 sc in each end of row 1 on dress and shoes, join with sl st in first sc. Fasten off.

Repeat for back.

Rnd 2: Hold Front and Back wrong sides together, matching sts; working in **back lps** *(see Stitch Guide),* sew together with colors needed to match piece, stuffing before closing.

ARM SIDE (make 4)

Row 1: Starting at hand, with beige, ch 2, 3 sc in second ch from hook, turn. *(3 sc made)*

Row 2: Ch 1, 2 sc in each st across, turn. *(6)*

Rows 3–4: Repeat row 2 of Front. At end of last

row, fasten off.

Row 5: Join gray with sc in first st, sc in each st across, turn.

Rows 6–14: Repeat row 2 of Front.

Row 15: Ch 1, sc first 2 sts tog, (sc next 2 sts tog) across, turn. *(3)*

Rnd 16: Working around outer edge, changing colors as needed to match piece, ch 1, sc in each st and in end of each row around, join with sl st in first sc. Fasten off.

For **each Arm,** hold 2 Arm Sides wrong sides together, matching sts; working in **back lps,** sew together with colors needed to match piece, stuffing before closing.

Sew each Arm over rows 20–25 on each side of Front.

BRAID (make 2)

Cut 18 strands lt. gold each 12" long. Fold in half. Holding all strands together, tie separate 12" strand lt. gold around center of folded strands. Separate ends of strands into 3 groups. Braid. Secure ends.

Sew over rows 30–34 on each side of head front.

BANGS

For **each fringe,** cut 2 strands lt. gold each 3" long; with both strands held together, fold in half, insert hook in st, pull fold through st, pull ends through fold and tighten.

Fringe in **front lps** of center 4 sts on top edge of Front.

HAT BRIM

Row 1: With white, ch 37, sc in second ch from hook, sc in each ch across, turn. *(36 sc made)*

Rows 2–4: Ch 1, sc in each st across, turn.

Row 5: Ch 1, sc in first 5 sts, 2 sc in next st, (sc in next 5 sts, 2 sc in next st) across. Fasten off. *(42)*

Sew to seam around head.

TIE (make 2)

With white, ch 30, sl st in second ch from hook, sl st in each ch across. Fasten off.

Sew to each side of head below Hat Brim. Tie in bow.

PUMPKIN SIDE (make 2)

Row 1: With rust, ch 2, 3 sc in second ch from hook, turn. *(3 sc made)*

Rows 2–3: Ch 1, 2 sc in each st across, turn. *(6, 12)*

Rows 4–8: Ch 1, sc in each st across, turn.

Row 9: Ch 1, sc first 2 sts tog, (sc next 2 sts tog) across, turn. *(6)*

Rnd 10: Working around outer edge, ch 1, sc in each st and in end of each row around, join with sl st in first sc. Fasten off.

Hold Pumpkin Sides wrong side together, matching sts; working in **back lps,** sew together, stuffing before closing.

Continued on page 148

Pilgrim Pillow Dolls

Continued from page 147

To **sculpt Pumpkin,** with rust, leaving 6" end, insert needle in center top of Pumpkin coming out at center bottom, pull yarn to top, pull tight. Tie and weave in ends to secure. Repeat on three other sides of Pumpkin.

STEM
With green, ch 5, sc in second ch from hook, (ch 2, sl st in second ch from hook, sc in next ch on first ch 5) 2 times, sc in last ch, ch 6, sl st in second ch from hook, sl st in each ch across, join with sl st in last sc made. Fasten off.

Sew to top of Pumpkin.

Tack Pumpkin between hands.

FINISHING
With black, using satin stitch *(see Stitch Guide),* embroider eyes centered on row 35 of head 1" apart.

With red, using fly stitch *(see Stitch Guide),* embroider mouth centered on row 32 below eyes.

MR. PILGRIM

BODY SIDE (make 2)
Row 1: Starting at shoes, with black, ch 35, sc in second ch from hook, sc in each ch across, turn. *(34 sc)*

Rows 2–3: Ch 1, sc in each st across, turn.

Rows 4–7: Ch 1, sc first 2 sts tog, sc in each st across to last 2 sts, sc last 2 sts tog, turn. At end of last row, fasten off. *(26 sc)*

Row 8: Join white with sc in first st, sc in each st across, turn.

Rows 9–13: Repeat row 2. At end of last row, fasten off.

Row 14: With black, repeat row 8.

Rows 15–22: Repeat row 2. At end of last row, fasten off.

Row 23: With gray, repeat row 8.

Row 24: Repeat row 2. Fasten off.

Row 25: With black, repeat row 8.

Rows 26–30: Repeat rows 4 and 2 alternately, ending with row 4 and 20 sc.

Rows 31–32: Repeat row 4. At end of last row, Fasten off. *(16)*

Row 33: For **head,** with beige, repeat row 8.

Rows 34–35: Ch 1, 2 sc in first st, sc in each st across with 2 sc in last st, turn. *(18, 20)*

Rows 36–43: Repeat row 2. At end of last row, fasten off.

HAT SIDE (make 2)
Row 1: With black, ch 27, sc in second ch from hook, sc in each ch across, turn. *(26 sc made)*

Row 2: Ch 1, sc in each st across, turn. Fasten off.

Row 3: Skip first 3 sts, join gray with sc in next st, sc in next 19 sts leaving last 3 sts unworked, turn. *(20)*

Row 4: Repeat row 2.

Row 5: Join black with sc in first st, sc in each st across, turn.

Row 6: Repeat row 4 of Body Side on this page. *(18)*

Rows 7–14: Repeat rows 2 and 4 of Body Side alternately. At end of last row *(10).*

Row 15: Repeat row 2 of Hat Side.

Sew center 20 sts of row 1 on one Hat Side to row 43 of one Body Side. Repeat with remaining Hat Side and Body Side.

EDGING
Rnd 1: For **one Body Side,** working around outer edge, changing colors as needed to match piece, join with sc in any st, sc in each st and in end of each row around with 3 sc in each corner on Hat and in each end of row 1 on Shoes, join with sl st in first sc. Fasten off.

Repeat for other Body Side.

Rnd 2: Repeat rnd 2 of Mrs. Pilgrim's Edging on page 147.

ARM SIDE (make 4)
With beige and black, work same as Mrs. Pilgrim's Arm Side on page 147.

Sew to each side of Body over rows 27–30.

COLLAR
Row 1: With white, ch 37, sc in second ch from hook, sc in each ch across, turn. *(36 sc made)*

Row 2: Ch 3, dc in next 4 sts, hdc in next 5 sts, sc in next 16 sts, hdc in next 5 sts, dc in last 5 sts, turn.

Row 3: Repeat row 34 of Body Side. Fasten off. *(38)*

Sew row 1 of Collar around row 32 of Body Sides with ends of Collar at center front *(see photo).* Tack front corners to Body.

FINISHING
With lt. gold, using straight stitch *(see Stitch Guide),* for **buckle,** embroider rectangle around 3 center sts of rows 3–4 on front of Hat, rows 23–24 of front Body Side and over each side seam of Body Sides at rows 6–7.

With black, using satin stitch, embroider eyes centered on row 40 of front Body Side 1½" apart.

With red, using fly stitch, embroider mouth centered on row 37 below eyes.

To **shape legs,** working through both thicknesses of Body Sides, with matching colors, using running stitch, sew up center of rows 1–13.

EAR (make 2)
Rows 1–2: Repeat rows 1–2 of Mrs. Pilgrim's Arm Side. At end of last row, fasten off.

Sew to seam on each side of head even with eyes and mouth. ❖

Clothespin Christmas

Design by Carol Tessier

Finished Size:
Approximately 5¼" tall without hanger.

Materials:
- Size 10 crochet cotton thread:
  - 35 yds. white
  - 30 yds. red
  - 10 yds. green
- 22" red ⅛" satin ribbon
- Two tiny white ribbon roses with leaves
- 5" of 3-mm. white strung pearl beads
- 22" red ⅛" satin ribbon
- Six red double-end stamens
- Two gold 6-mm. jingle bells
- Wooden doll pin with stand
- 1¼" wooden ball knob
- Black, white and pale pink acrylic paint
- Tiny paint brush
- Spanish moss for hair
- 14" piece of gold or silver metallic cord for hanger *(optional)*
- Craft glue
- No. 7 steel hook or hook needed to obtain gauge

Gauge: 8 sts or chs = 1".

Basic Stitches: Ch, sl st, sc, hdc, dc, tr.
Continued on page 150

Clothespin Christmas

Continued from page 149

DRESS

Rnd 1: For **Bodice,** with red, leaving a 20" length at beginning, ch 14 loosely; being careful not to twist ch, sl st in first ch to form ring, (ch-3—*counts as first dc,* dc) in first ch, 2 dc in each of next 2 chs, (ch 1, dc, ch 1, dc) in each of next 2 chs, ch 1, 2 dc in each of next 5 chs, (ch 1, dc, ch 1, dc) in each of next 2 chs, ch 1, 2 dc in each of last 2 chs, join with sl st in top of ch-3. Fasten off. *(28 dc, 10 ch-1 sps made)*

Rnd 2: Working in **back lps** *(see Stitch Guide),* join white with sl st in first st, ch 3, dc in next 4 dc; for **armhole,** ch 1, skip next 11 dc and chs; dc in next 8 dc; for **armhole,** ch 1, skip next 11 dc and chs; dc in last 3 dc, join. *(16 dc, 2 ch-1 sps)*

Rnd 3: For **Skirt,** ch 1, sc in first dc, ch 3, sc in next dc, *ch 3, (sc, ch 3, sc) in next dc, ch 3, sc in next dc, ch 3, (sc, ch 3, sc) in next dc*, ch 3, sc in ch 1 at underarm; repeat between first and second *, (ch 3, sc in next dc) 2 times; repeat between first and second *, ch 3, sc in ch 1 at underarm; repeat between first and second *, ch 1, join with dc in first sc. *(Ch 1 and dc form joining sp—26 ch sps.)*

Rnds 4–6: Ch 1, sc in joining ch sp, (ch 3, sc in next ch sp) around, ch 1, join with dc in first sc.

Rnd 7: Ch 1, sc in joining ch sp, (ch 4, sc in next ch sp) around, ch 1, join with tr in first sc.

Rnd 8: (Sl st, ch 3, 2 dc) in joining ch sp, ch 2, (3 dc in next ch sp, ch 2) around, join with sl st in top of ch-3.

Rnd 9: Ch 1, sc in each of first 3 dc, ch 3, skip next ch sp, (sc in each of next 3 dc, ch 3, skip next ch sp) around, join with sl st in first sc.

Rnd 10: Ch 1, sc in next sc, ch 2, 3 dc in next ch sp, ch 2, (sc in second sc of next 3-sc group, ch 2, 3 dc in next ch sp, ch 2) around, join.

Rnd 11: Sl st in each of next 2 chs, ch 1, sc in each of first 3 dc, ch 5, skip next 2 ch sps, (sc in each of next 3 dc, ch 5, skip next 2 ch sps) around, join.

Rnd 12: (Sl st, ch 1, sc) in next st, ch 4, sc in next ch sp, ch 4, (sc in second dc of next 3-dc group, ch 4, sc in next ch sp, ch 4) around, join. Fasten off.

NECK TRIM

Working in remaining lps on opposite side of starting ch on rnd 1 of Dress, using the 20" length, insert hook in first ch, yo, pull through ch, ch 1, (sl st, ch 1) in each ch around, join with sl st in first sl st. Fasten off.

RUFFLE

Rnd 1: With Neck Trim toward you, working in remaining **front lps** of rnd 1, join red with sc in first st, sc in each st and in each ch around, join with sl st in first sc, **turn.** *(38 sc)*

Rnd 2: Ch 1; working in **back lps,** sc in first st, ch 3, (sc in next st, ch 3) around, join. Fasten off.

SLEEVES

Rnd 1: Working around one armhole, join red with sc in ch 1 at underarm, ch 3, sc in top of next dc on rnd 2, ch 3; working in remaining lps on rnd 1, sc in next dc, (ch 3, skip next ch, sc in next dc) 5 times, ch 3, sc in top of next dc on rnd 2, ch 1, join with dc in first sc. *(9 sps made)*

Rnds 2–6: Sc in joining sp, (ch 3, sc in next sp) around, ch 1, join with dc in first sc.

Rnd 7: Ch 1, sc in each ch sp around, join with sl st in first sc. *(9 sc)*

Rnds 8–11: Ch 1, sc in each st around, join. At end of last rnd, fasten off.

Repeat on other armhole.

WREATH

With green, ch 50, 3 dc in third ch from hook, 3 dc in each ch across forming a spiral. Fasten off.

Glue ends of spiral together.

Cut a 5" piece of ribbon and tie in a 1"-wide bow, glue bow over ends of spiral.

Fold each double-end stamen in half; place tiny drops of glue on folded ends and insert through spiral at random to resemble holly berries.

ASSEMBLY

Using pale pink for blush on cheeks, black for eyes and eyelashes and white for pupils of eyes, paint face on ball knob *(see illustration).* Let dry.

Place Dress on doll pin with neck at top edge of doll pin; glue flat side of ball knob to top of doll pin.

For **stand** *(optional),* paint doll pin stand with white. Glue bottom of doll pin in stand.

Cut a piece of strung beads to fit around neck, glue in place with ends at back.

Cut two 3-bead-long pieces of strung beads; glue one piece to outside of rnds 8–10 on each Sleeve.

For **hair,** glue a small amount of Spanish moss to ball knob framing face.

For **hanger** *(optional),* run metallic cord under first stitch on rnd 1 of Bodice at center back, tie ends together forming a 3" hanging loop, tie ends in a bow.

Tie remaining ribbon in a 2"-wide multi-loop

bow leaving 2½" ends, glue one ribbon rose over knot of bow. Glue one jingle bell to each end of ribbon.
Glue bow to crown of head.

Glue other ribbon rose to center front of Bodice just above the Ruffle.
Glue sides of Wreath to last rnds on Sleeves at front of Skirt. ❖

Bridal Belles

Continued from page 136

Rows 6–10: Beg V st, (ch 4, V st in next V st) across, turn.

Row 11: Sl st in next ch sp, ch 8, dc in next V st, (ch 5, dc in next V st) across, turn.

Row 12: Ch 1, sc in first st, (sc, hdc, dc, tr, dc, hdc, sc) in each ch sp across, turn.

Row 13: Ch 1, sc in first st, (ch 8, skip next 6 sts, sc in next st) across, turn.

Row 14: Ch 1, 8 sc in each ch-8 lp across. Fasten off.

Row 15: Working in remaining lps on opposite side of starting ch, join dress color with sc in first ch, sc in each ch across, turn.

Row 16: Working this row in **back lps,** ch 1, sc in each st across, turn.

Row 17: Ch 1, sc in first st; for **picot, ch 3, sl st in third ch from hook;** (sc in each of next 3 sts, picot) 2 times, sc in each of next 2 sts, picot, sc in last st. Fasten off.

HAIR

Wrap brown around cardboard 150 times, backstitch *(see Stitch Guide)* over one edge of loops to secure. Remove from cardboard. Sew secured loops around hairline from top of rnd 5 in front to rnd 11 in back. Tie separate strand brown around strands at top of head. Tuck loops down in back to form bun, tack in place.

CURL (make 2)

Wrap brown around toothpick, covering completely; secure ends. Spray with starch. Let dry completely. Gently slide Curl off toothpick. Fold Curl and glue to top of Head in front of bun *(see photo)*.

FINISHING

With fabric stiffener, starch Skirt. Place over large end of egg. Let dry.

With brown floss, using French knot *(see Stitch Guide)*, embroider eyes on rnd 9 of head three sts apart. With pink, using fly stitch, embroider mouth between rnds 11 and 12.

From ribbon, cut 9" piece. Tie in bow and sew to back of head below bun, or for bride, tack to center top of Veil. Beginning at left front, weave remaining ribbon through rnd 18 of Skirt, overlap ends with flower in center, tack in place.

Tack hands together in front of Skirt. Tack flowers to hands. ❖

Giving Lasting Shape to Your Dolls

The special appeal of some delicate crocheted dolls requires that the skirt or body of the doll be stiffened.

For long-lasting success in stiffening or starching crocheted dolls, first start with colorfast thread and a quality fabric stiffener. There are several excellent brands available through most craft outlets. To guard against yellowing, use only distilled water to dilute your liquid fabric stiffener.

If you use glue to stiffen your doll items, be sure you use craft glue only. Use half glue and half distilled water for an extra-stiff finish or two parts water and one part glue for less stiffness.

Shape on a padded surface, bowl or suitably shaped styrofoam object covered with finely woven cotton fabric such as an old sheet. If pinning is necessary, use stainless steel pins. Let dry completely and remove carefully, as stiffener may initially stick to the fabric.

And, for an old-fashioned look, there's always sugar starch. Mix ½ cup sugar with ¼ cup water in a pan over very low heat, stirring until it comes clear; do not let it boil. Remove from heat; let cool slightly to use. ❖

Potpourri Angel

Design by Beth Mueller

Finished Size: Approximately 5" tall.

Materials:
- Worsted yarn:
    - 1½ oz. white
    - ½ oz. burgundy
- 24" of ¹⁄₁₆" gold cord
- 1½" wooden flat-bottomed ball with ³⁄₁₆" hole
- 3¼" wooden ³⁄₁₆" dowel to fit in hole
- Two 12-mm. ½" round wooden beads
- 1½ cups potpourri
- 10½"-diameter circle of netting
- Dk. green ⅛"-wide satin ribbon:
    - One 18" piece
    - Two 10" pieces
- Two ⅜" gold jingle bells
- Small amount blonde curly doll hair
- Craft glue
- Black and red permanent markers
- Clear acrylic spray
- Pink powder blush
- White sewing thread and needle
- Tapestry needle
- H hook or hook needed to obtain gauge

Gauge: Rnds 1–2 = 2¼" across.

Basic Stitches: Ch, sl st, sc, hdc, dc, tr.

BODY

Rnd 1: With white, ch 5, sl st in first ch to form ring, ch 2 *(counts as first hdc)*, 12 hdc in ring, join with sl st in top of ch-2. *(13 hdc made)*

Rnd 2: (Ch 2, hdc) in first st, 2 hdc in each st around, join. *(26)*

Rnd 3: (Ch 2, hdc) in first st, hdc in next st, (2 hdc in next st, hdc in next st) around, join. *(39)*

Rnds 4–6: Ch 2, hdc in each st around, join.

Rnd 7: Working in **back lps** *(see Stitch Guide)*, ch 2, hdc in each st around, join.

Rnd 8: Working in **both lps,** ch 2, hdc in each st around, join.

Rnd 9: Ch 2, hdc next 2 sts tog, (hdc in next st, hdc next 2 sts tog) around, join. *(26)*

Rnds 10–11: Ch 2, hdc in each st around, join.

Rnd 12: For **beading,** ch 3, skip next st, (hdc in next st, ch 1, skip next st) around, join with sl st in second ch of beginning ch-3. Fasten off. *(13 ch sps)*

Rnd 13: For **neck ruffle,** join burgundy with sc in joining sl st, ch 3, sc in first ch sp, ch 3, (sc in next st, ch 3, sc in next ch sp, ch 3) around, join with sl st in first sc. Fasten off. *(26 ch sps)*

Rnd 14: With top of Body facing you, working in **front lps** of rnd 6, join burgundy with sl st in any st, ch 3, (sl st in next st, ch 3) around, join. Fasten off.

Arm (make 2)

Rnd 1: With white, ch 3, 5 hdc in third ch from hook, join with sl st in top of ch-3. *(6 hdc made)*

Rnd 2: (Ch 2, hdc) in first st, 2 hdc in each st around, join. *(12)*

Rnd 3: For **beading,** ch 1, sc in first st, ch 3, (sc in next st, ch 3) around, join with sl st in first sc. Fasten off.

Rnd 4: Join burgundy with sl st in first ch sp, ch 3, (sl st in next ch sp, ch 3) around, join. Fasten off.

WING (make 2)

Row 1: With white, ch 4, sl st in first ch to form ring, ch 3 *(counts as first dc)*, 5 dc in ring, turn. *(6 dc made)*

Row 2: Ch 4, dc in next st, (ch 1, dc in next st) across, turn. *(5 ch sps)*

Row 3: Ch 3, sc in next st, (ch 1, sc in next st) across, turn. Fasten off.

Row 4: Join burgundy with sl st in first ch sp, (ch 3, sl st) in same ch sp, (sl st, ch 3, sl st) in each ch sp across. Fasten off.

HALO

With gold cord, ch 11. Fasten off. Tie ends together and secure with glue at back of Halo.

FINISHING

For **Head,** on center front of wooden ball knob, make two dots with black marker ¼" apart for eyes. Draw mouth with red marker ¼" below eyes. Brush powered blush on cheeks. Spray with clear acrylic. Let dry.

Glue small amount of curly doll hair to top and sides of Head. Applying a little glue, insert dowel into hole at bottom of Head. Set aside.

Gather netting ½" from edge with sewing needle and thread. Place potpourri in center and pull thread to gather netting closed. Secure thread by tying in knot at top of potpourri ball.

Starting and ending at front, weave 18" ribbon through beading rnd on Body. Insert potpourri ball into Body. Insert end of stick through top of potpourri ball. Pull ribbon tightly and tie end in bow. Tie jingle bell to each end of ribbon.

For **each Arm,** weave 10" ribbon through beading rnd, pull to tighten and tie ends in bow. With matching yarn and tapestry needle, tack each Arm slightly toward the front over rnds 10–11 of Body just below neckline. Glue wooden bead to end of each Arm for hand.

Glue Halo to back of Head.

Tack center of Wings 1" apart to back of Body below neck ruffle. ♣

New Year's Gala

Continued from page 139

Rnd 3: (Ch 3, dc) in first st, (2 dc in next st, dc in next st) around, join. *(44)*

Rnd 4: Ch 3, (2 dc in next st, dc in next st) 2 times, sc in each st around, join with sl st in top of ch-3.

Rnd 5: For **Point**, ch 1, sc in first st, hdc in next st, dc in each of next 3 sts, hdc in next st, sc in next st leaving remaining sts unworked. Fasten off.

Sew white marabou boa around outer edge of Hat.

MASK

Cut two Mask pieces from felt according to pattern piece. Glue Mask pieces together with feather ends between at center top.

Glue sequins to front of Mask.

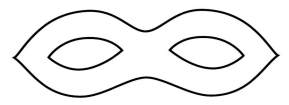

Color dowel with black marker. Let dry. Glue top end to right edge of Mask. ❧

Cookie Cutter Witch

Continued from page 145

times, sc in last dc of shell, skip next sc; repeat from * across ending with sc in first dc of half shell, ch 2, sc in next dc leaving ch-3 unworked, **do not turn.**

Row 10: Ch 1, 2 sc in end each row to waist, sl st in 4 unworked lps of row 1 on Underskirt, 2 sc in end of each row down opposite side of front, join with sl st in first sc.

Row 11: Sl st in next ch-2 sp, (ch 2, sc) in each ch-2 sp across. Fasten off.

Bodice

Row 1: With black/silver, ch 44, sc in second ch from hook, sc in next 20 chs, 3 sc in next ch, sc in last 21 chs, turn.

Row 2: Ch 3, (skip next sc, hdc in next sc, ch 1) 10 times, skip next sc, (hdc, ch 1, hdc, ch 1, hdc) in center sc, (ch 1, skip next sc, hdc in next sc) across, turn.

Row 3: Ch 1, sc in next 24 sts; working in hdc and ch-1 sps, 3 sc in center hdc, sc in each st and ch-1 sp across with last sc in second ch of ch-3 at end of row, turn.

Row 4: Ch 1, sc in first sc, (skip next sc, 5 dc in next sc, skip next sc, sc in next sc) 6 times, 5 dc in center sc, sc in next sc, (skip next sc, 5 dc in next sc, skip next sc, sc in next sc) 6 times, turn.

Row 5: Ch 1, *sc in next dc, (ch 2, sc in next dc) 4 times, skip next sc; repeat from * across, sl st in last sc, turn.

Row 6: Ch 2, *(sc in next ch-2 sp, ch 2) 3 times, sc in next ch-2 sp; repeat from * across, ch 2, sl st in last sc. Fasten off.

HAT

Rnd 1: With black, ch 3, sl st in first ch to form ring, ch 1, 6 sc in ring, join with sl st in first sc. *(6 sc made)*

Rnd 2: Ch 3, dc in each st around, join with sl st in top of ch-3.

Rnd 3: Ch 3, dc in same dc, 2 dc in each st around, join. *(12)*

Rnd 4: Ch 3, dc in same st, dc in next st, (2 dc in next st, dc in next st) around, join. *(18)*

Rnd 5: Ch 3, dc in each st around, join.

Rnd 6: Ch 3, dc in next st, 2 dc in next st, (dc in each of next 2 sts, 2 dc in next st) around, join.

Rnd 7: Ch 3, dc in each of next 2 sts, 2 dc in next st, (dc in each of next 3 sts, 2 dc in next st) around, join.

Rnd 8: Ch 1, sc in each st around, join.

Rnd 9: Ch 4, tr in same st, 3 tr in next st, (2 tr in next st, 3 tr in next st) around, join.

Rnd 10: Ch 1, sc in each st around, join. Fasten off.

FINISHING

From orange yarn, for **hair,** cut forty 6" lengths; for **bangs,** cut four 1" lengths. With all 6" lengths held together, tie separate strand of orange yarn around the middle for center part; pull 1" lengths through tie with ½" on each side of center part for bangs. Glue center part across head of cookie cutter with bangs in front; let dry. For pigtails, tie hair on each side of cookie cutter with separate strand of orange yarn. Glue in place on cookie cutter head.

Place Skirt on waist of cookie cutter; stitch in place with sewing needle and thread.

Weave ⅛"-wide ribbon through row 2 of Bodice.

Place Bodice around neck; sew back closed. Tack Bodice to center front and back of Skirt.

Tie ¼"-wide ribbon around pigtails and glue around Hat for hatband. Glue Hat over hair.

Glue flowers to pigtails, Hat and waist as shown in photo. Fold back each bottom end of Overskirt and glue flower to each side. ❧

Stitch Guide

CHAIN—ch:
Yo, pull though lp on hook.

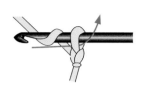

SLIP STITCH—sl st:
Insert hook in st, yo, pull through st and lp on hook.

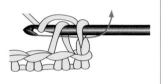

DOUBLE CROCHET—dc:
Yo, insert hook in st, yo, pull through st, (yo, pull through 2 lps) 2 times.

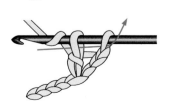

SINGLE CROCHET—sc:
Insert hook in st, yo, pull through st, yo, pull through both lps on hook.

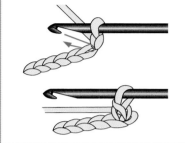

TREBLE CROCHET—tr:
Yo 2 times, insert hook in st, yo, pull through st, (yo, pull through 2 lps) 3 times.

HALF DOUBLE CROCHET— hdc:
Yo, insert hook in st, yo, pull through st, yo, pull through all 3 lps on hook.

DOUBLE TREBLE CROCHET—dtr:
Yo 3 times, insert hook in st, yo, pull through st, (yo, pull through 2 lps) 4 times.

TRIPLE TREBLE CROCHET—ttr:
Yo 4 times, insert hook in st, yo, pull through st, (yo, pull through 2 lps) 5 times.

Continued on page 156

Stitch Guide

OUNCES TO GRAMS		GRAMS TO OUNCES	
1 =	28.4	25 =	⅞
2 =	56.7	40 =	1⅖
3 =	85.0	50 =	1¾
4 =	113.4	100 =	3½

HOOK AND NEEDLE SIZES

U.S.		METRIC	U.K.
	14	.60 mm.	
	12	.75 mm.	
	10	1.00 mm.	
	6	1.50 mm.	
0	5	1.75 mm.	
1	B	2.00 mm.	14
2	C	2.50 mm.	12
3	D	3.00 mm.	10
4	E	3.50 mm.	9
5	F	4.00 mm.	8
6	G	4.50 mm.	7
		4.75 mm.	
8	H	5.00 mm.	6
9	I	5.50 mm.	5
10	J	6.00 mm.	4
		6.50 mm.	3
10½	K	7.00 mm.	2
		8.00 mm.	
		9.00 mm.	
	P	10.00 mm.	
	Q	16.00 mm.	

FRONT POST STITCH—fp; BACK POST STITCH—bp:
When working post st, insert hook from right to left around post of st on previous row specified.

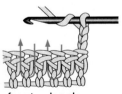

front   back

REVERSE SC
Working from left to right, insert hook in next st to the right, complete as sc.

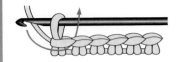

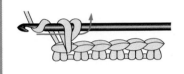

COLOR CHANGE
Drop first color; with second color, pull through last 2 lps of st.

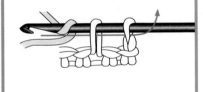

FRONT LOOP/BACK LOOP

front   back

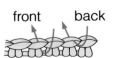

STANDARD ABBREVIATIONS

beg ....beginning
ch, chs ....chain, chains
dc ....double crochet
dec ....decrease
hdc ....half double crochet
inc ....increase
lp, lps ....loop, loops
rnd, rnds ....round, rounds
sc ....single crochet
sc next 2 sts tog.......(insert hook in next st, yo, pull through st) 2 times, yo, pull through all 3 lps on hook
hdc next 2 sts tog.....(yo, insert hook in next st, yo, pull through st) 2 times, yo, pull through all 5 lps on hook.
dc next 2 sts tog......(yo, insert hook in next st, yo, pull through st, yo, pull through 2 lps on hook) 2 times, yo, pull through all 3 lps on hook.
sl st ....slip stitch
sp, sp ....space, spaces
st, sts..................stitch, stitches
tog ....together
tr ....treble crochet
yo ....yarn over

HALF DOUBLE CROCHET COLOR CHANGE

BACK BAR OF CHAIN

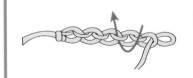

Embroidery Stitches

FRENCH KNOT
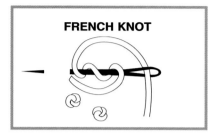

STRAIGHT STITCH
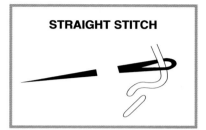

SATIN STITCH
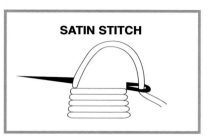

FLY STITCH
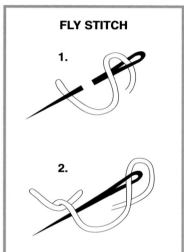

RUNNING STITCH
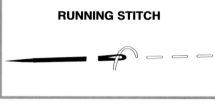

OUTLINE STITCH

FEATHER STITCH
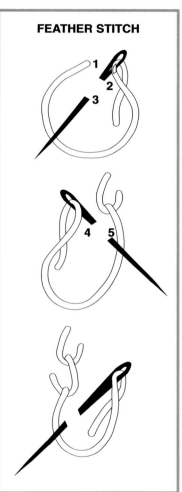

LAZY-DAISY STITCH
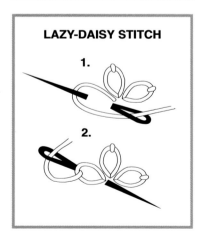

BACKSTITCH
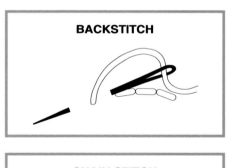

CHAIN STITCH

Index

Gift-Giving Diary

Gift Given to _____
Gift _____
Date & Occasion _____

Gift Given to _____
Gift _____
Date & Occasion _____

Gift Given to _____
Gift _____
Date & Occasion _____

Gift Given to _____
Gift _____
Date & Occasion _____

Gift Given to _____
Gift _____
Date & Occasion _____

Gift Given to _____
Gift _____
Date & Occasion _____

Gift Given to _____
Gift _____
Date & Occasion _____

Gift Given to _____
Gift _____
Date & Occasion _____

Gift Given to _____
Gift _____
Date & Occasion _____

Gift Given to _____
Gift _____
Date & Occasion _____